Amy Sillman
Faux Pas.

Selected Writings and Drawings

EXPANDED EDITION

Afterall Books

Faux Pas. Selected Writings and Drawings of Amy Sillman
EXPANDED EDITION

Editors: Charlotte Houette, François Lancien-Guilberteau, and Benjamin Thorel
Design: Marco Caroti
Copy editing: Janine Armin, Lou Ellingson
Administration: Antonia Carrara

Published by After 8 Books, Paris

Distributed in Asia and the Americas by ARTBOOK | D.A.P.
www.artbook.com

Distributed in the UK by Art Data
www.artdata.co.uk

Distributed in France and Belgium by Interart
www.interart.fr

Printed by Standart Impressa (Lithuania)
Second printing, 2024

After 8 Books
7 rue Jarry, F-75010 Paris
www.after8books.com

ISBN 978-2-492650-04-8
Dépôt légal: Octobre 2022

Amy Sillman
Faux Pas.

Selected Writings and Drawings

EXPANDED EDITION

Foreword by
Lynne Tillman

Edited by
Charlotte Houette
François Lancien-Guilberteau
Benjamin Thorel

After 8 Books

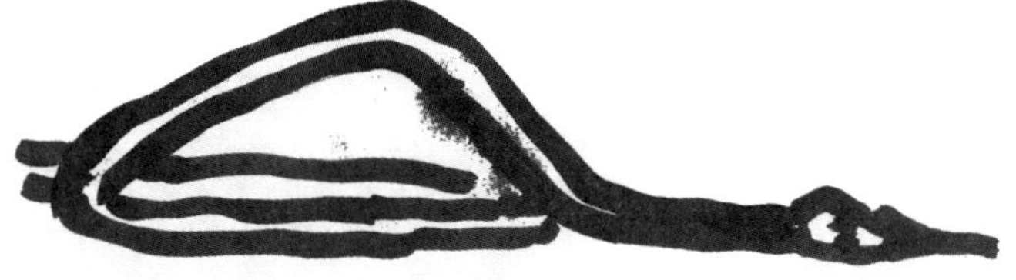

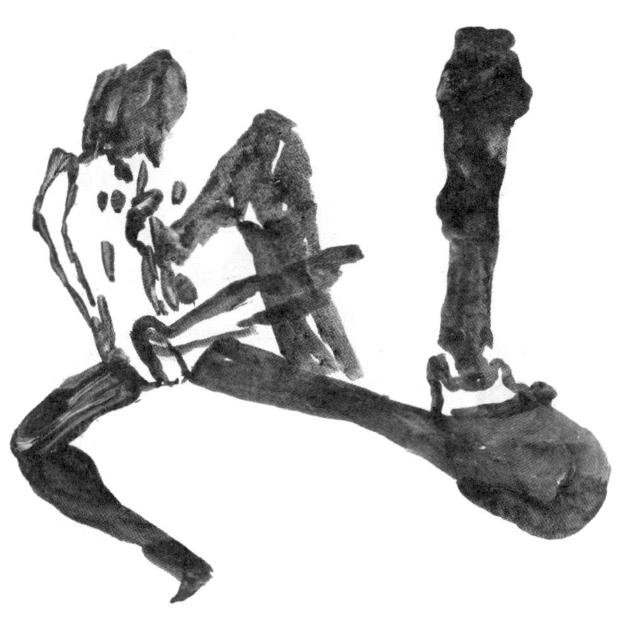

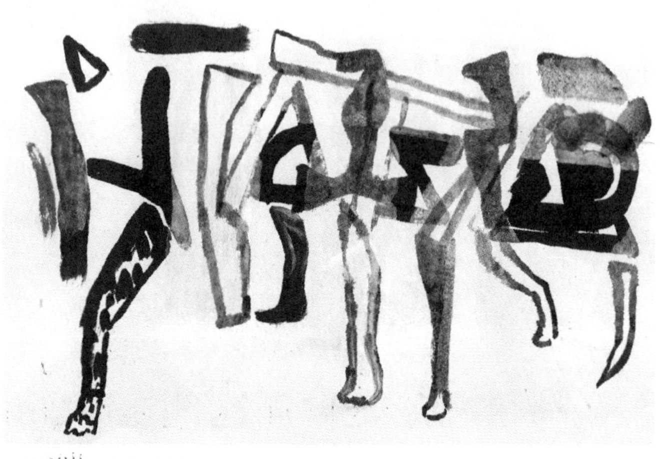

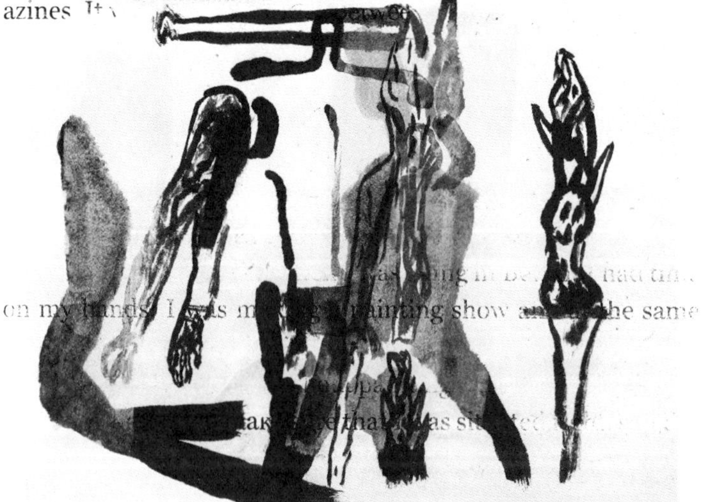

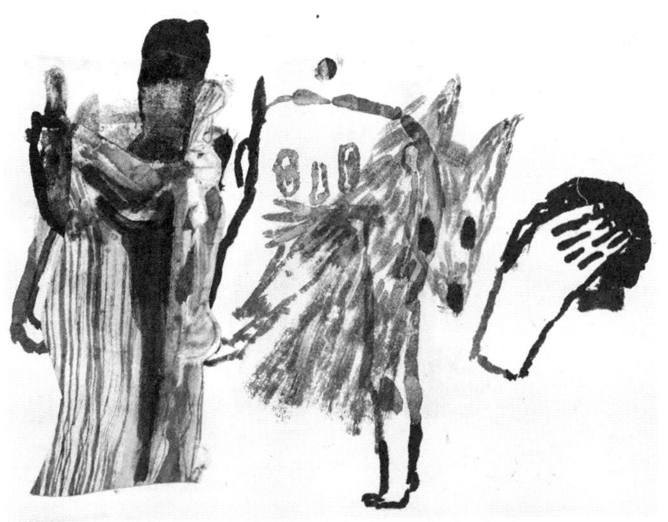

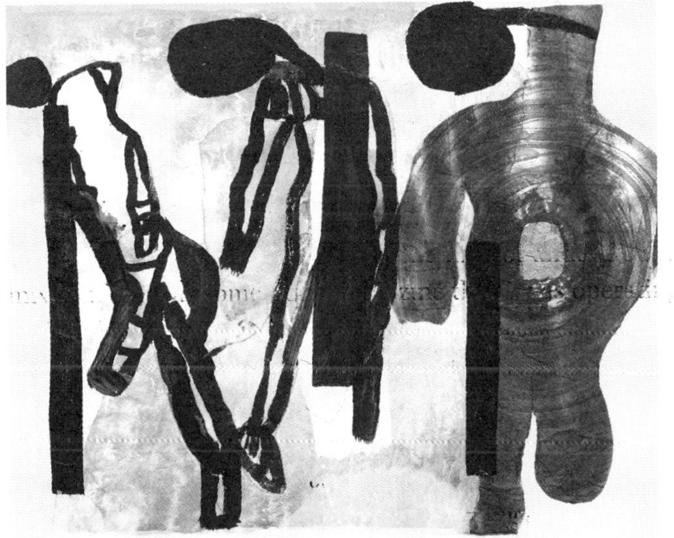

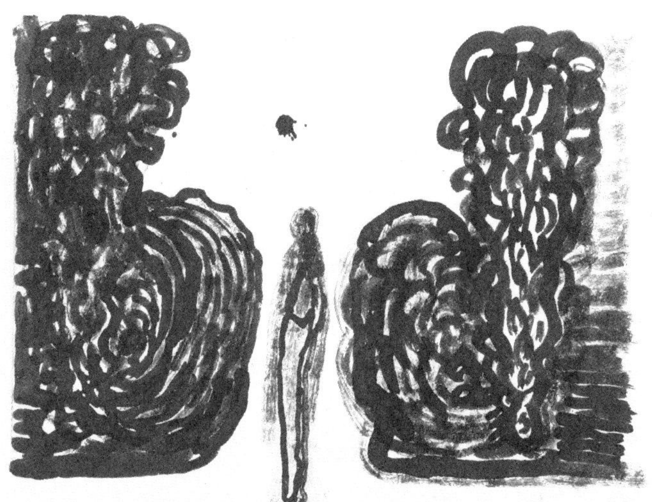

TABLE OF CONTENTS

TABLE OF CONTENTS

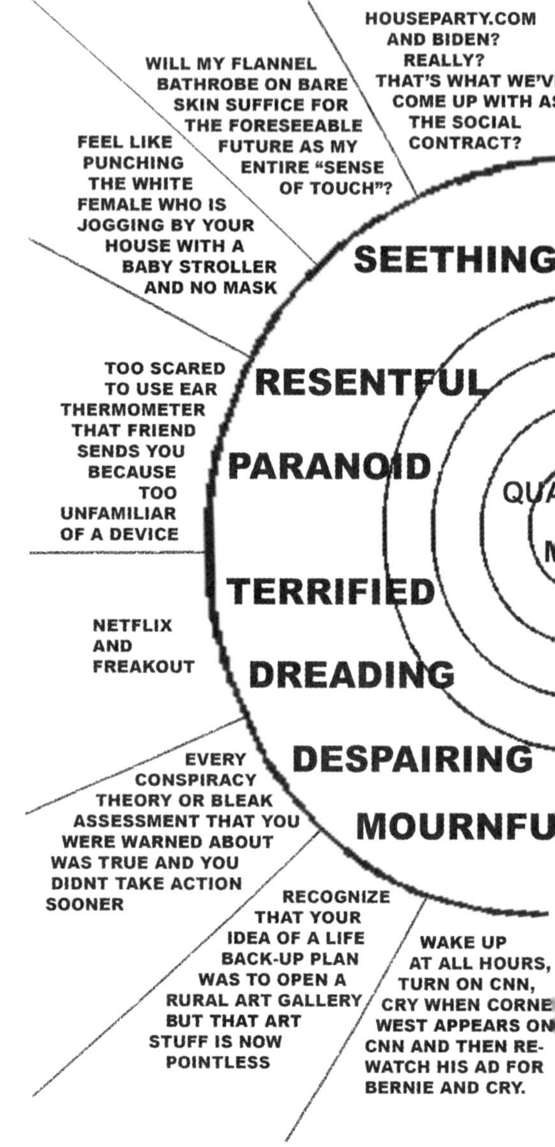

HOUSEPARTY.COM AND BIDEN? REALLY? THAT'S WHAT WE'V
COME UP WITH AS
THE SOCIAL CONTRACT?
WILL MY FLANNEL BATHROBE ON BARE SKIN SUFFICE FOR THE FORESEEABLE FUTURE AS MY ENTIRE "SENSE OF TOUCH"?
FEEL LIKE PUNCHING THE WHITE FEMALE WHO IS JOGGING BY YOUR HOUSE WITH A BABY STROLLER AND NO MASK
SEETHING
TOO SCARED TO USE EAR THERMOMETER THAT FRIEND SENDS YOU BECAUSE TOO UNFAMILIAR OF A DEVICE
RESENTFUL
PARANOID
TERRIFIED
NETFLIX AND FREAKOUT
DREADING
EVERY CONSPIRACY THEORY OR BLEAK ASSESSMENT THAT YOU WERE WARNED ABOUT WAS TRUE AND YOU DIDNT TAKE ACTION SOONER
DESPAIRING
MOURNFU
RECOGNIZE THAT YOUR IDEA OF A LIFE BACK-UP PLAN WAS TO OPEN A RURAL ART GALLERY BUT THAT ART STUFF IS NOW POINTLESS
WAKE UP AT ALL HOURS, TURN ON CNN, CRY WHEN CORNE
WEST APPEARS ON
CNN AND THEN RE-WATCH HIS AD FOR BERNIE AND CRY.

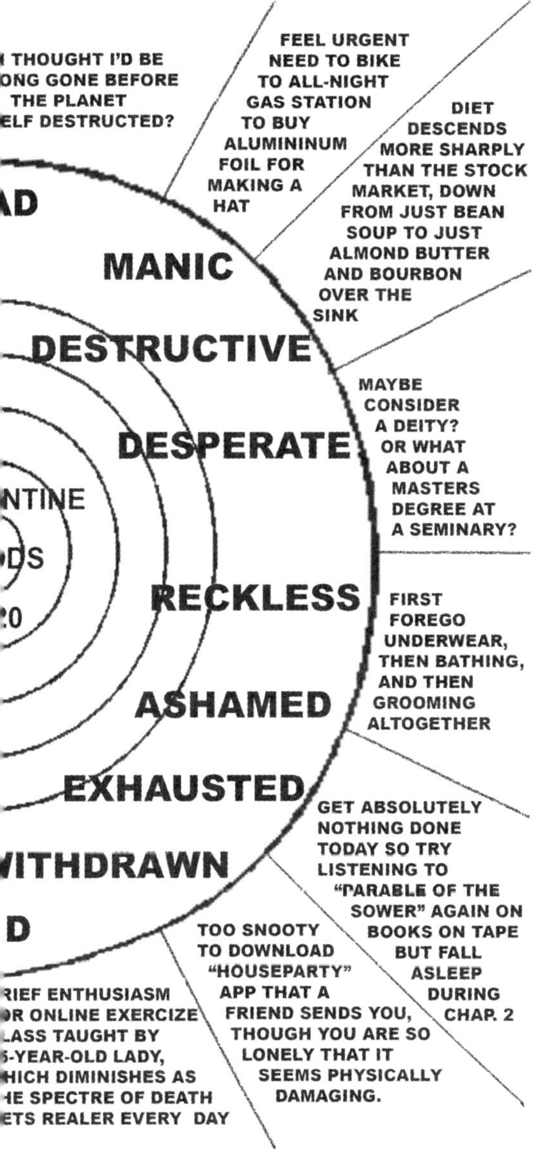
THOUGHT I'D BE
ONG GONE BEFORE
THE PLANET
ELF DESTRUCTED?
FEEL URGENT NEED TO BIKE TO ALL-NIGHT GAS STATION TO BUY ALUMINUM FOIL FOR MAKING A HAT
DIET DESCENDS MORE SHARPLY THAN THE STOCK MARKET, DOWN FROM JUST BEAN SOUP TO JUST ALMOND BUTTER AND BOURBON OVER THE SINK
AD
MANIC
DESTRUCTIVE
DESPERATE
NTINE
DS
20
RECKLESS
ASHAMED
EXHAUSTED
ITHDRAWN
D
MAYBE CONSIDER A DEITY? OR WHAT ABOUT A MASTERS DEGREE AT A SEMINARY?
FIRST FOREGO UNDERWEAR, THEN BATHING, AND THEN GROOMING ALTOGETHER
GET ABSOLUTELY NOTHING DONE TODAY SO TRY LISTENING TO "PARABLE OF THE SOWER" AGAIN ON BOOKS ON TAPE BUT FALL ASLEEP DURING CHAP. 2
TOO SNOOTY TO DOWNLOAD "HOUSEPARTY" APP THAT A FRIEND SENDS YOU, THOUGH YOU ARE SO LONELY THAT IT SEEMS PHYSICALLY DAMAGING.
RIEF ENTHUSIASM
OR ONLINE EXERCIZE
LASS TAUGHT BY
-YEAR-OLD LADY,
HICH DIMINISHES AS
HE SPECTRE OF DEATH
ETS REALER EVERY DAY

Even my usual look
could be described as
"building management."
But now I'm back to
Pleistocene Epoch.

There are no cosmetics.
There is no conditioner.
There is only bean soup.

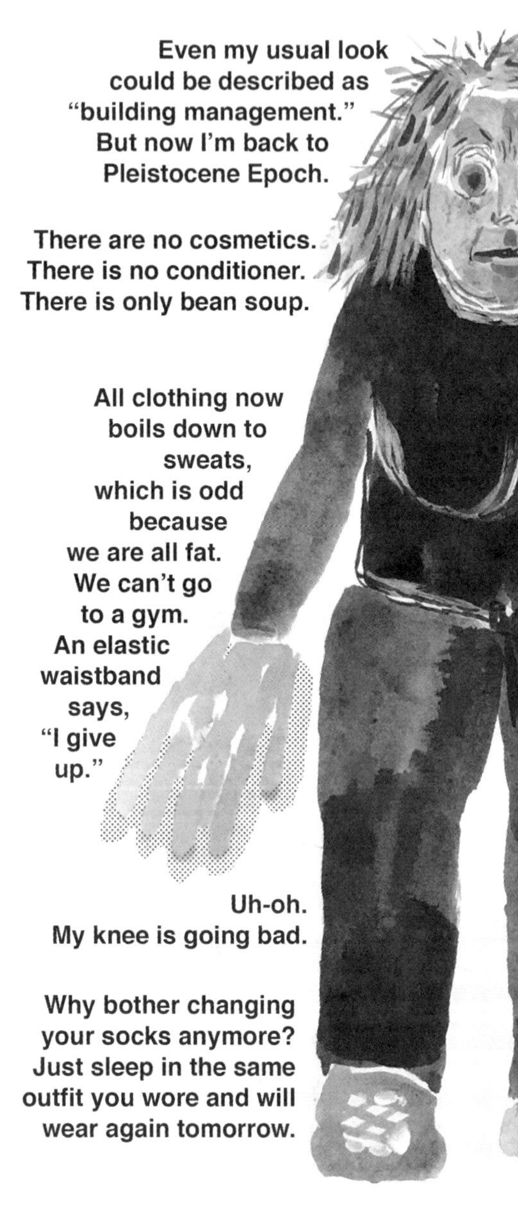

All clothing now
boils down to
sweats,
which is odd
because
we are all fat.
We can't go
to a gym.
An elastic
waistband
says,
"I give
up."

Uh-oh.
My knee is going bad.

Why bother changing
your socks anymore?
Just sleep in the same
outfit you wore and will
wear again tomorrow.

All days are bad hair days.
All hair is sort of like goat hair
at a petting zoo, though wouldn't
a petting zoo be great now.
Everyone knows what color
everyone else's hair REALLY
is now, though.

(That dental work I put off
last fall? Big mistake.)

The only reason to bother
with a bra now is to make
a pair of homemade masks
with it.

We don't have "hands"
anymore: we have toxic
petri dishes of dread
hanging at the end of
our arms.
We don't have skin:
we are upholstered with
a kind of hide, made of
"craquelure" texture
and topped with
eczema.

When I left my apartment last
week I forgot to bring more than
one pair of shoes: so now I only
have one pair of pink diabetics'
sneakers, missing the laces on the
left side. Forever.

This introduction was written in 2020,
for the first edition of Faux Pas.

Lines, Gaps, Shapes, Strokes, Jokes, Colors, Holes . . .

by Lynne Tillman

To writers, words are material, their matter, their only stuff. Words have value in themselves, tricky beasts, relished, debated, hated. Amy Sillman values words. Her essays are literary incitements, they're exciting, and felt. Sillman confers untested, non-consensual, verbal experiments on art, to visual ideas and compositions, to locate newer meanings. Let's say, Sillman seeks to describe the indescribable, which is all the more strange because she is primarily responding to visual forms and matters, there, supposedly, in plain sight. But they aren't, not without examination and engagement. That is, with a desire to apprehend more.

In a Sillman essay, words have their own weight, which is inestimable.

Her remarks on color weigh color on several scales, from the actual weight of pigments, to her consideration of how color weighs in the imagination and sensibility of painters. "Color is a material," she writes, and comes from other matter whose origins remain invisible, but not to her. One might say, the way labor is invisible in a commodity. Color, Sillman explains, is regularly separated from form as if it were negligible. But to her, for instance, pigments become "characters," a personification that creates more weight in a composition. So, viewers can now weigh paintings with an awareness of these elements.

It's exceptionally hard to articulate what color is, because the signified is incommensurate with its signifier. Like tongues to sex to bodies. Handling color affects an artist, substances encourage variations in practices and the sensibilities of artists. As they do in her paintings, Sillman's written descriptions of color pulse.

"The nomenclature of paint is all beautiful adjectives. You don't say 'pink,' you say *dianthus* pink, *hematite* purple, *flake* white . . . consider the esoteric feeling when working with stuff like the color carmine . . ."

An ambivalent disposition to conventional wisdoms, with pro and con attitudes to aesthetic theories, animates Sillman's mind. She tests and retests ideas. Rationality, explanation, and logic about art, the many theories about it, go so far, but will be confounded and troubled by the making of it—by artists' experience, subjectivity, knowledge of its history, sensibilities, repressions, sensuality, gender, psychology et al. There are inevitable contradictions.

Sillman's emphasis lies in the importance of process, and how making creates meanings. There is a refusal—Sillman is a joyful refusenik—of false antinomies, distinctions, categories, binaries. She professes, here, that art is a coalition of materials, visual thinking, objects, theories, bodies, physical and psychical activity, of dailiness, and, urgently, of lived lives. No to privileging theory over making.

(Painting communicates, it is information, and it is also a form of knowledge. I once wrote, in defense of stories, or narrative, against those who said they were dead: "Stories are a way to think." Sillman might accept this premise.)

Gertrude Stein famously wrote, "I am I because my little dog knows me."[1] Let's say that little dog is art. What if art doesn't know you; the artist doesn't, and the work changes, maybe radically—Philip Guston is usually cited here (about whom Sillman has also written). What happens to ideas about art, is a fixed idea fixing you? Change disarms armed positions.

In psychoanalytic theory, "working through" means that, through the process of analysis, neuroses are addressed; and, worked through sufficiently, emotions and intellect fuse. "Neurotic unhappiness" will be released or experienced differently with understanding. It will be, to some extent, disenabled, so that the analysand achieves "ordinary unhappiness." (I'm bemused by scholars who disdain the practice of psychoanalysis and use the theory in their work.)

There is no cure, only understanding.

Doing their work, artists experience the necessity of change, and work through ideas, visual and cerebral, while they work. There is no one solution, Sillman shows. That is, there is no cure for art, it's not neurotic, rather it proceeds with and without direction and intention as it goes along. "What urge makes

1. Gertrude Stein, "And now," *Vanity Fair*, September 1934, 35.

you want to do something that pushes further, on toward contingency, clumsiness, strangeness, or even brutality?" Different responses may be required, since stasis is no answer to a predicament.

Sillman's emphasis on process promotes the exposure of difficulties in art-making, the demands it makes, as the artist herself evolves, always in relationship to the world outside. The personal is political, yes, but the political is also personal, to Sillman. These evolutions, everywhere, make art evolve.

In "Some Thoughts on John Chamberlain," Sillman analyzes Chamberlain's car crash sculptures, insisting on the significance of his use of color. "Palpable material that you mold and crush. . . . The colors in Chamberlains ooze and spread across parts, and do all the things that color does in painting." She reveals syntheses in his body of work that have been overlooked.

Reading this essay, I remembered an exhibition of Chamberlain's sculptures, curated by Donald Judd, I saw not long ago at the Chinati Foundation in Marfa, Texas. I had seen his "car crashes" years before, perceived shapes, thought about destruction, and Warhol's car crash images. But Judd's curation opened up these sculptures. The work hadn't changed, I had, in time and with time. Time in all senses conditions perception, and is inalienably part of it, along with subjectivity.

Sillman's desire to contend with Chamberlain's under-seen, under-acknowledged, checkered career derives from two realizations: that he was "hidden in plain sight" and that "an artist could become a cliché *and* remain simultaneously under-known." Her insights on Chamberlain sparkle with her motivation: to grapple with his uneven, partial reputation, one that many good artists suffer—for instance, Meret Oppenheim, so famous for her fur teacup and saucer (*Object*, 1936), was known for little else, a great frustration to her. Oppenheim once satirized her place in art history by making a tourist version of the teacup and saucer.

In "Some Thoughts . . ." Sillman scopes Chamberlain's career thoroughly, and registers the reasons for this paradox. Doing it underscores her compassion for an artist's shifts and departures over time. Or, in their truths. She delineates Chamberlain's variances, his approaches to high/low, his choice of materials, junk, and, finally, through him, she shows an appreciation for vulgarity, which aligns with others of her favorites: awkwardness, jokes, cartoons, and more.

Pictures of body parts, filth, sex acts, excrement, all that stuff, will be called vulgar. It's revelatory how meanings change. The Vulgate was the fourth-century Bible, written in Latin; *vulgata* also means common language, while *vulgaris* means "of the common people." "Vulgar" should be descriptive, not a value judgment.[2]

But oh how words can't be held down. Words "live in the mind"; words "are democratic . . . uneducated words are as good as educated words, uncultivated words as good as cultivated words," as Virginia Woolf reminds readers.[3]

Sillman has declared her own dedicated class war in which high-minded-ness, "cultivated" art, has nothing to do with art.

2. Warhol wanted Pop Art to be called Common Art. A religious Catholic, he certainly knew that vulgar meant common. His art enraged the class that wanted art to show their good taste and distinguish them from common people.

3. Virginia Woolf, "Craftsmanship," BBC radio broadcast, *Words Fail Me*, April 29, 1937; reproduced in *The Essays of Virginia Woolf, Volume VI*, ed. Stuart N. Clarke (London: Hogarth Press, 2011).

There's a carnival of things in the carnival of life. Her aesthetics (pace Whitman) contain multitudes.

"I mix paint more than anyone I know," she writes. "My work is partly determined by the colors I buy." Those colors, pigments, I now know, are extremely expensive. Sillman's statements about her process strike me the way her paintings do—frank, disarming, open, bold, working through and embodying ideas and practices that have a necessity to her. All of her essays are highly informed, grounded in knowledge of her subjects, in art history, etc. They are cerebral, philosophical, and they are personal. The artists she discusses, the art, theories: all are close to her. But her revelations are not confessions, she is not whispering secrets, exposing what should not be known. In fact, it is what should be known about her practice, ideas, and what is at stake to her, what has profound meaning for her.

Sillman has skin in this game.

In "Why Amelie von Wulffen is Funny" Sillman wonders, after writing that comic strips are printed in newspapers, "what 'news' does vW's work bring?" Which also comments, I think, on the province of, and degradation of, fiction—painting, novels, poems, movies. In her aquarelles, Von Wulffen's characters "endur[e] the same tedium, tribulations, and triumphs that we occasionally do." Her work "links image to narrative, it is wed not to a saga or epic, but to a cheap novella. And to a critique of bourgeois subjectivity, these cartoons would answer: *What else is there?*"

Von Wulffen's scenarios "mirror our lives." Sillman doesn't make much use of the mirror metaphor; in my reading of her essays, its appearance is unusual. So with it, I infer Sillman's appreciation of certain kinds of representation, the love-side of her ambivalence toward representation. And there's her ambivalence toward abstraction. She does both and neither. She wills herself to, and does, defy categories, and so admires the inclusiveness and combinations in Von Wulffen's art, which uses stuff most artists don't.

Holding a mirror up to life, when it reflects its broken-ness, absurdity, comedy, and sadness, is not to make idealizations. The mirror is art that must be cracked and show the fissures of so-called reality. Her essay on Rachel Harrison's complex work, in "A Few Remarks on Rachel Harrison's Use of Color," shares a few of the qualities Sillman ascribes to Von Wulffen. She refers to Harrison's "farcical situations": "Absurdity generally prevails over gravitas . . . she throws in merchandise, manufactures surfaces, and jokes to further scrapple with the proceedings." Von Wulffen's work confronts painting: "She hobbles linearity with collage, overlay, interruption, fragmentation, glitch and omission . . . Within this painterly fracture, drawing appears as if it were glue, a form of recuperation, a way to hold things together."

"Drawing as a form of recuperation" is a fascinating concept. Drawing things in, drawing us and it together. Sillman is devoted to drawing, to the line. Drawing is a first cousin to writing—that mark-making on cave walls. Maybe the two married. Sillman's involvement in the line would relate to her intense investment in words, their value, their weight. And vice versa.

In cartoons, lines are both visual and textual.

Sillman's essay, "Further Notes on Shape," expands on and explicates her thinking toward curating the exhibition *The Shape of Shape* at the Museum of Modern Art, New York in fall 2019. This essay is "round," a roundup of her concerns and their intersections, augmented primarily and significantly by a realization: "I barely knew anything about shape." Sillman takes us along, as she delves into the "holes" and "gaps" in art history, and digs at them. She points to absences and dismissals and rhetorical positions that still mark and impress themselves upon contemporary art and theory.

So, composition vs. construction: Sillman traces the schism to the Russian Constructivists who saw composing as "reinscrib[ing] the values of a privileged bourgeois class, whereas to construct was the way to make a new society." Here, set historically in the crosshairs of this binary, Sillman's consideration of drawing returns, "an activity not founded on logic but made up of contingencies."

The dictum against composition, from the early twentieth century, maintains its grip, she argues, though "a singular position is precisely what radicals would have argued against." Her research into the complexity of these theoretical positions takes her to sculptor Phillip Pavia, editor of *It Is*, a 1950s artist-run magazine. He believed only through "'drawing, drawing, and more drawing' could an artist perform a vanguard inquiry."

Like her essay on Chamberlain, "Further Notes on Shape" is thorough and concise, building a different narrative for complex issues in art history and art-making. Considering shapes, I wondered: is a shape empty or full? Half-empty, half-full. Shapes shape patterns of thought, and ways of seeing. Which led to my recollecting the tools of childhood, its plethora of coloring books and jigsaw puzzles. These instruct with a particular logic—to color inside the lines; make objects fit neatly into spaces, and form alignments. But what if that wasn't how children learned; then, uncertainties, sketchiness, and impulses might not be contained or controlled easily. What if overflow was encouraged.

Compositions and drawings, Sillman postulates, and "artists fussing over shapes," have their own means of "register[ing] protest"; for one, "they make gestures of care and repair." The sense and suppositions of Sillman's proposals, in this essay and others, register her own protest against, say, the renunciation of bodies, hands, gestures, experience, materials, craft, and more, with an immense sensitivity to possibilities and to roads not taken.

In these scintillating essays—and each deserves its own essay—Amy Sillman excites, provokes ideas, plunders and aggravates language, detonates words with innovation, the way she does paint, pencil, color, line, stroke, mark, etc. She uniquely renders words to foreground pictures and picture-making, and builds avenues, pathways to lead to other ways of apprehending art.

So, she appreciates Laura Owens' paintings, because of, and not only, their "rejection of the rejection" of painting. The rhetorical dismissal "painting is dead" annoys the hell out of Sillman, and with good reason, because painters are not zombies. She begins her review of painter Carroll Dunham's *Into Words: The Selected Writing of Carroll Dunham* focusing on his most frequently used word "weird," followed by "perverse." "Takes one to know one," she writes, and employs a blizzard of adjectives to describe his texts. She says, "No one writes about art like this." And, when Sillman grapples with and interprets his texts, she writes: "Reading this book, one also senses a drive to a psychic singularity, a mysterious black hole located at the center of his thinking . . . and the sheer tactile craving to wrap the mesh of language around the mystery of art-making, to respond to art's forms with language's invisible force."

I can't imagine a better end to my essay than to use her words about her desire in writing: "A tactile craving to wrap the mesh of language around the mystery of art-making."

Sillman's mind is full, her drive powerful, she does wrap, unwrap, make and unmake art, and in her essays, it is all here. ♦

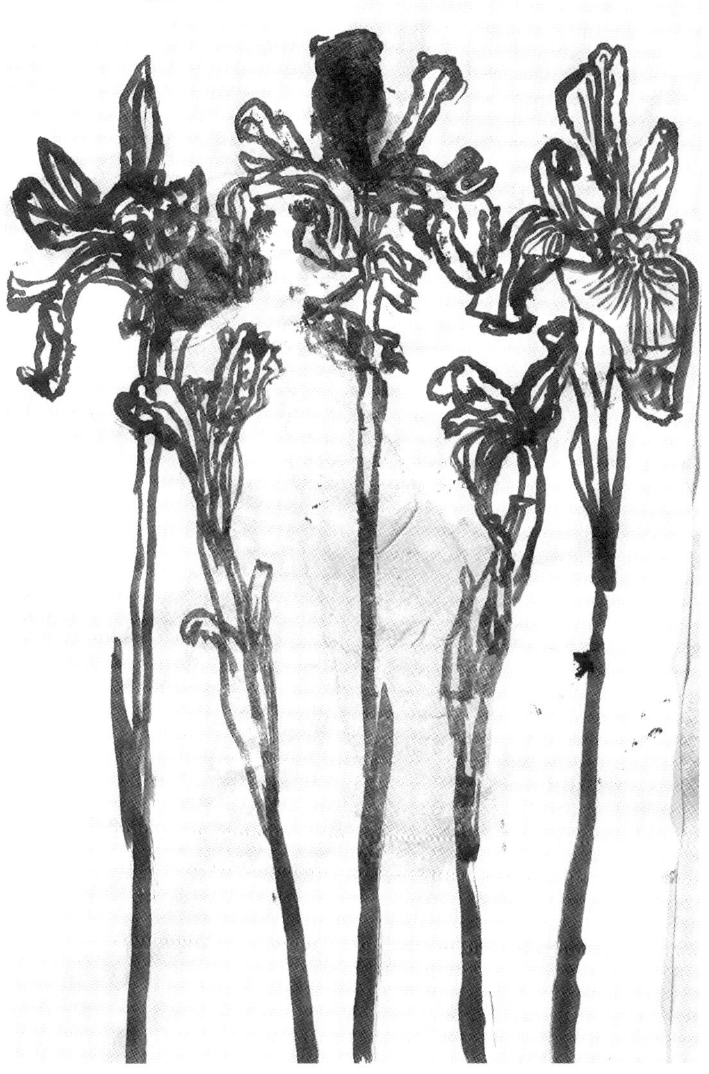

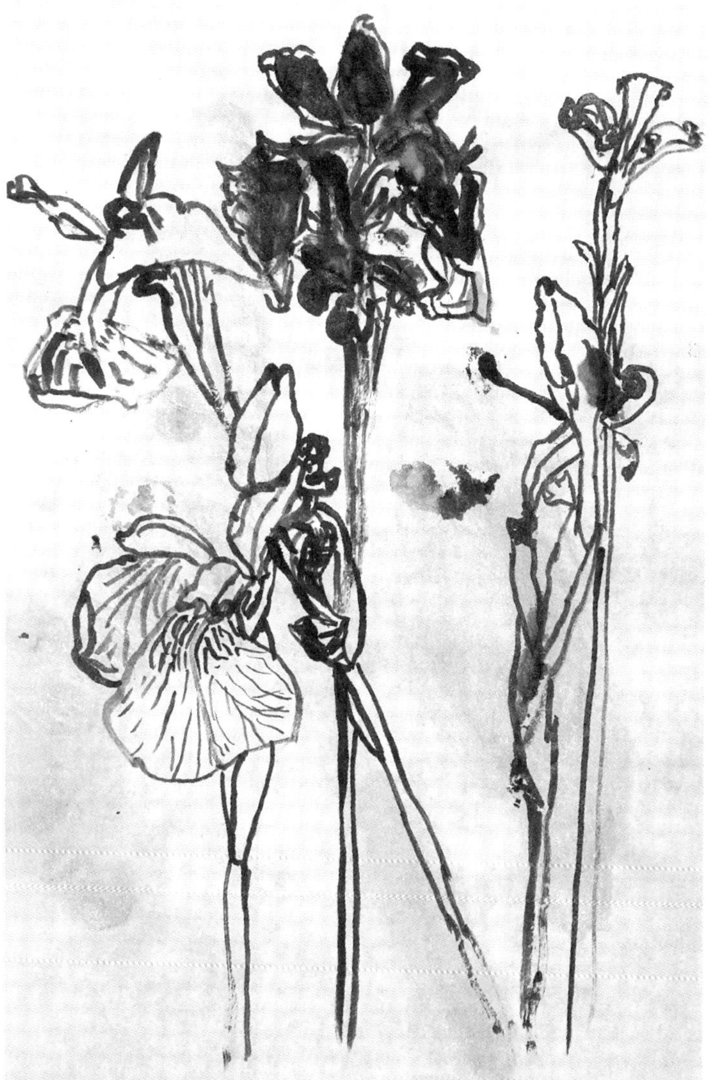

This interview between Amy Sillman and the editors of the book—Charlotte Houette, François Lancien-Guilberteau, and Benjamin Thorel—was realized over the course of three days, in Paris, in July 2019. It was then edited, and expanded, from May to June 2020.

Having a Voice: A Conversation with Amy Sillman

— *The texts gathered in the present book cover a period of time during which you have consistently nourished a writing practice, in parallel with your art—though you had written texts earlier. The last fifteen years saw you writing texts about, or for, other artists, as well as essays about art issues, dealing with your own work, and further questioning history, critical categories, or proposing new notions. How did you develop this writing practice? Was there a specific starting point?*
— I think that writing actually springs out of the experience I had teaching. Before that I simply never thought of myself as *having a voice*, literally. You don't have a "voice" when you're making a painting—you have a body. When teaching, you're doing crits, speaking to people, and it involves language. You're kind of working from the upper half of your body instead of from your torso.

I remember finally realizing that my work as a teacher and co-chair of a department at Bard was part of my art work: it was very empowering and really startling to think of my whole life as the expanded field of painting. The world shifted a little bit for me at that moment. It wasn't the first time I'd thought,

"Hey, I think like a conceptualist!" But since I work like a very conventional action painter in the studio, with an old-fashioned methodology, it was a great surprise to realize that my practice has this whole other shape that's not at all confined to the studio.

— *Teaching at Bard College meant meeting with a faculty of fellow artists, but also poets as well as theoreticians from other departments. Is this part of the "expanded field of painting"?*

— Totally, because if you work near a bunch of experimental poets you understand language as a kind of act. Plus, the difference between written language and spoken language interests me. I always liked difficult poetry, but at Bard I loved how the poets insisted on everyone's capacity to understand poetry. Even when your first reaction to poetry might be, "I don't understand it," they would always insist that you can of course understand it, and that you simply want to pretend that you don't get it, but you do, and you should respond. It's almost like it is your responsibility to engage in *responder*-ship—not because you "know" about it, but because you can. Talking is always a process of improvisation. Poets and experimental filmmakers changed my life.

Bard had a very radical dimension because we didn't have theoretician "experts"—or not very often. I helped create an environment where people were hired to teach painting because they were questioning it, not because we were trying to be better salespeople for painting. Yet I would look back now and say that even though the school had advanced thoughts on gender and critical language, it was overwhelmingly white, and there was very little consciousness about race, white supremacy, and anti-racism. That was almost totally lacking and it was a bad fault.

— *What place took language in your own art education, in the 1970s? Were you already writing and painting then?*

— By the time I moved to New York, in the mid-1970s, and by the time I got to art school, it was clear that painting was bad. Nobody would do it. Painting was riddled with a kind of uncritical romanticism that it couldn't shake, and was way too wrapped up with financialization; while language was seen as the way to *construct* new social realities, instead of laboring over compositions at easels. But though linguistic projects may have the appearance of criticality and resistance to the market, it's more complicated. I was sensitive, as a young art student, to how practices seem to offer proposals for accountability. I could see that painting was sort of a no-go, and I could also see that the idea that "words fix the problem" didn't really hold up either! Because you could sell words too. And the "bad" people were sometimes the "good" people, or the "good" people were the "bad" people. Some of its adherents were the "good guys," like queer feminists who had been left out of other radical politics. One of my ongoing questions has always been, who gets to be considered the avant-garde?

— *Were you thinking of yourself as a painter when you went to art school?*

— I just wanted to draw. Maybe paintings were "fancy" objects for sale, but drawings seemed pretty down and dirty. Anyone can do it. I was interested in the idea of recuperating painting with humor or low skills—like, if you just do it badly, you won't be a sellout? It's like the way George and Mike Kuchar were making films, or the *"Bad" Painting* show[1]: that DIY thing was

1. On this 1978 show at the New Museum, see "Shit Happens," note 3, page 164.

very important for my generation. I remember going to Holly Solomon Gallery—they showed all the funny art—and I saw William Wegman's drawings. He was very important to me because his work looked impossibly easy, like jokes, but was ironic, and hilarious—and it was shown in a gallery, in a frame! [LAUGHS] You're not supposed to have that in an art show. I was very impressed.

— *Would jokes, cartoons with punch lines, be the work with words that you were interested in then?*

— If it wasn't for Saul Steinberg I wouldn't be an artist. He didn't use punch lines, though. It was all visual play. He always did the cartoons of the covers of the *New Yorker*, which my mom subscribed to, so the magazine came in the mail when I was a kid. *Krazy Kat* was good, cartoons on TV were good . . . also I am from Chicago, where funny art has always been a big deal. The Hairy Who and the Chicago Imagists were important to me; though the whole generation of artists who are my age in Chicago were not into that grotesque slapstick humor. They wouldn't be caught dead making cartoons. But Mike Kelley was a huge fan of the older Chicago artists: he made a big difference in appreciating them. Anyway—I went to New York, where the painting was very serious . . . and I just couldn't understand how you could continue to be so serious about it, in the '70s.

— *In the text you wrote about Maria Lassnig, you allude to your life in New York in the late '70s, and you mention going to screenings, performances . . .*

— One of my closest friends when I moved to New York in '75 was C. Carr[2], the performance art reporter for the *Village*

2. C. Carr held the column "On Edge" in the *Village Voice*. See *On Edge: Performance at the End of the Twentieth Century* (Middletown, CT: Wesleyan University Press, 2008).

Voice. I literally went to everything with her, every week. I saw things like Jack Smith throwing empty beer bottles at Beth B. at Anthology Films Archive; people at 8BC,[3] the Kipper Kids, Dancenoise, Tabboo!. That's how I first saw Mike Smith's performances—his *Talent Show* and his *Puppet Show*.

— *How did you perceive the art world then?*

— I didn't know about a gallery scene in New York then, but rather an underground, or a counterculture of some sort, a downtown scene. But you could already tell that even though things looked cool, a lot of times they were pretty conventional. In *Before Pictures* Douglas Crimp recalls how, already in the '60s, when he was going to Max's Kansas City, the front room was all straight guys and the back room was all the queers[4]: that's just never spoken—nobody tells art history that way.

There was also a lot of renunciation in New York art schools at that time: people I knew were quitting art because they hated the art world. They became philosophers, rock musicians, etc. I didn't put any of these dots together then, but at that same moment when students were uninterested in the art world, there were also famous renouncers such as Lee Lozano, or Lee Bontecou. When I moved to New York the homeless person living on my corner outside was Valerie Solanas herself! I think that I was sensitive to the ideas of refusal, negation, and withdrawal. I've always been very interested in the underdog, the dropouts, the outsiders, people who choose an extreme path—almost à la Simone Weil—a refusal to compete.

3. 8BC was a music and performance venue and a nightclub in the East Village, active between late 1983 and late 1985. (Its name stood for 8th street between Avenues B and C.)

4. See Douglas Crimp, *Before Pictures* (New York: Dancing Foxes Press & Chicago: University of Chicago Press, 2016), 14–15. On Max's Kansas City, see "Dear Maria Lassnig," note 4, page 234.

— *The notion of an art "career" started to equal then success, visibility, and power . . .*

— Once in a while, you hear somebody boasting, "Fail better, that's our motto!" [SIGHS] There's this mythic, epic failure, and then there's real failure, actual obscurity. I'm interested in people who are really obscure. When I wrote the letter to Maria Lassnig I dug up all her old friends. It was all these women who were really cool, still working on great stuff, but quietly. In New York you can just disappear, or just say, in a very profound way, *you're not going to have access to me*. Engage in willful opacity. But that's only possible when there is a genuine idea of a subculture, an idea of the outside.

— *At the time you contributed to the feminist radical journal* Heresies, *didn't you? You are credited for putting together a compelling bibliography about lesbian art in one issue.*[5]

— I don't think I compiled this, I just wrote a little foreground. I probably collected information from everyone—the Lesbian Herstory Archives was super useful. I got involved in the collective through one of my teachers, May Stevens, who said they needed a paste-up girl for *Heresies*. I said I could do it! I brought my girlfriend, who knew how to do magazine production. Before computers there was paste-up: we would compose pages with glue and razor, paste everything up, and send it to the printer.

Heresies was probably a little above my head. I had no sense of myself as a practitioner of art so what they were talking about was mysterious to me. But I met all these painters, like Louise

5. "Bibliography on Lesbian Arts," *Heresies* 1, no. 3, "Lesbian Art and Artists" (1977), 115–17. Like the other members of the collective, Amy Sillman also contributed a "Statement" to that issue. See the online archive, www.heresiesfilmproject.org.

Fishman and Harmony Hammond . . . I was so blown away by their lives and their lofts! And Pat Steir—who was my teacher as well. I got a job with her when I left school: I was supposed to prepare her canvases and paint the first layer, all these things. I remember she had an Agnes Martin in her bedroom, and stacks of Wittgenstein books on a shelf. Her early work was amazing, beautiful—all charts and diagrams, with flowers, individual words, strips of colors . . .

— *You met them all at the School of Visual Arts.*

— I fell into this little pocket of feminism at SVA, with teachers such as Elizabeth Murray, Pat Steir, Susan Crile, Jennifer Bartlett, and Sylvia Plimack Mangold. Everybody taught there! Jon Borofsky, Joel Shapiro, etc. And a lot of people went to SVA: Mark Dion, Gregg Bordowitz, Tim Rollins . . . There was a conceptual class as well—Joseph Kosuth's.

— *Was this a context for writing?*

— Not really. But I was always sensitive to language—I love language. I took literature classes at SVA, and in the mid- to late-nineties, I took Eileen Myles' classes in writing poetry for artists. Three of them. It was at people's houses—one of them was at my place. You went every week, you had to read out loud. They would give you prompts. They would give you assignments. I loved those classes! And I would write little things about other artists when I was invited to.

— *What about that story saying you were trained as a Japanese interpreter for the United Nations?*

— That was my dream! I first studied Japanese because I wanted to learn a language that I felt nobody I knew could understand. (This was in the early '70s, it was pretty rare to study Japanese then.) What I had in mind was to do simultaneous translation: to hear one language and speak a different one. Through Japanese brushwork, I got into art. I went to SVA because a friend of mine told me, "You can draw cartoons there." Their illustration department was really famous, but I ended up in the painting department after all.

— *You didn't go to grad school after SVA.*

— I went to grad school later, in the '90s, at Bard College, where I later taught. In the '80s I had no clue what was going on—I was a disaster! I literally didn't know how to connect to the art world at all. My work was more '70s, when you do everything with your hands. The '80s were such a charged time: Reagan, AIDS, war . . . Money, power, empire, the beginning of neoliberalism—there was also a lot of coke. I just wasn't involved in those scenes. All I did during that decade was try to figure out how to paint—while I held day jobs working at magazines. It was for me a bridge between the '70s, where I was literally trying to figure out how to be an artist, and the '90s, when I actually started to do stuff.

— *Let's cross that time bridge, then, and go even further, to the twenty-first century, when you started to write more regularly. You also initiated a zine,* The O.-G., *in 2009, as an appendix to your shows. It has been an important vehicle for your essays.*

— I made the first *O.-G.* when I was living in Berlin; I had time on my hands; I was making a painting show and at the same time, I was making satirical seating charts for fun. I thought that in Germany my ideas about painting weren't entirely translatable; I wanted to make sure that I was situated right, so I decided to create my own context through writing. By chance the person randomly assigned to work with me at the gallery I was showing at was someone now a good friend of mine, Kerstin

Stakemeier, an art historian and writer who came out of left politics. She encouraged my idea for a zine . . . I called it "OG," which obviously means "Original Gangster," but also stood for the words *Objet* and *Gegenstand* in honor of the Russian/Berlin "zine" of the '20s *Vešč' Objet Gegenstand*, edited by Ilya Ehrenburg and El Lissitzky.

— *And you saw a connection between* Vešč' Objet Gegenstand *and today's zines.*

— A fanzine is basically a little teeny cheap thing circulated among the fans, and *Vešč'* was a little tiny thing circulated among cognoscenti. It was beautifully produced and designed: it is an art object, a conceptual art project, but one I'd say occupies a kind of fanzine "slot."

— *What resonates with the model of the zine is this idea of a publication that circulates between artists, in order to exchange ideas, works, words, and that creates a dynamics. Was it the first time that you were doing a zine?*

— Well, I made one when I was eighteen or nineteen and I moved to New York. Just really for myself. I started this zine about being ashamed by being too chubby. I named it honorifically after a Hawaiian queen. I think I just made one copy. It's in a box somewhere . . . I grew up in the time of underground comix so there was some notion of a zine that I was operating out of, in my drawings—but it was only in Berlin that it dawned on me that I could use that format to "explain" my paintings.

— *In* The O.-G. *you often share your sources, your influences, what you're reading and working with, etc. You're also sharing your personal research, proposing something like an alternative history—or herstory—of art and broadening the perception of painting.*

— *The O.-G.* is like a chronicle of footnotes, a digest of all of the stuff you think about during the day, and a kind of anti-professional gesture to create space for that stuff. The zines aren't intended to further aggrandize my painting; they might be about painting's limitations.

— *Is this more about the social dimension of writing and publishing then?*

— It's a way of communicating really directly. Asking to have a direct conversation rather than withdrawing into the framework of the painting. Once I had a show with just the paintings, no drawings that time, and I remember feeling very ashamed because all of a sudden, I realized the paintings were surrounded by a kind of frosty silence . . . which is how an abstract painting show can feel like if you don't open it up in some way.

— *It has to do with this authority of the painting.*

— Yes, exactly. It just becomes "important." Anti-pomposity is an extremely important principle for me.

— *In the first issue of* The O.-G., *there were these* Seating Charts *that mocked the art system and its rituals, but also a cartoon titled,* Artist Gives Talk, *depicting an artist in a pretty embarrassing situation . . . and it is actually* you.

— Yeah. Maybe that's how the zine is not more advanced conceptual art. Because it's still about me. [LAUGHS]

— *In your lectures some slides are DIY collages of yours, and you play with unexpected connections between one picture and the next. You deflate the speaker's position.*

— Because I want it to be funny. [LAUGHS] But I admit also to a fussiness inside of all this where I like things to be really good. I don't like them to just be messy, shabby, or just populist—I really love skill! Not always traditionally skilled: for example,

I know I'm really bad at design—but I still fuss endlessly over the zine designs. There's this part of me that wants everything to be super tight and good, even though I like it to look like it's breezy. But really, underneath, I don't like easy, dumb attitudes. What I'm trying to say is that there's a high-low, an informed openness at work here. I polish my texts intensely—I spend a lot of time fussing over the vocabulary—but I want them to look easy, straightforward, earnest, even dumb.

— *You use verbs and adjectives that are not part of the given vocabulary to speak about art, but account for its experience, in particular its making. It's stimulating—and one can guess there's pleasure in picking up certain words.*

— For me, language is like realism and painting is really abstraction. But I guess I'm trying to negotiate all those boundaries. I certainly work in a rhetoric of sloppiness, openness, and chance as a painter, but as a writer I tend toward precision—probably because I don't know how to let loose enough as a writer.

— *In your essays, you often talk about your situation as an artist in the studio; but, when it comes to writing, how do you work? Where do you write?*

— Oh, I can't write if I paint. It has to be one or the other. So I just stay home, like all other writers, in my pajamas, with crumpled paper. I write on the computer—and then I print out, read, and then throw it away. I think that's pretty common, no? But I can only do one thing at a time! Both painting and writing are immersive; they require using different parts of the brain that I can't use simultaneously.

— *You once said that writing the essay on Delacroix took you one month of research.*

— When I'm writing on a subject I really immerse myself in it. I think I read almost every single thing that was written about Delacroix—same thing for John Chamberlain.

— *In both these cases you articulate your own vision of the work; a discussion of the critical apparatus it has generated; and a very detailed approach to the lives of the artists, which allows you to have a new take on their work.*

— When I saw Chamberlain's work in Marfa, I was shocked by this bed where you watch this hippie movie of his. That's the part they don't usually show in New York! That was a real *way in*. So, when Lynne Cooke invited me to do a lecture at Dia, I said, "I would like to do Chamberlain!" She said, "Mmm, oh . . . Could you do Palermo?" and I said no . . . because I wanted to examine what seemed like the sore thumb in their collection, not the "cool" guy.

— *Do you mean the specific sensibility of Chamberlain—the very American dimension of his work?*

— Well, not the fact of ginormous metal sculptures . . . but I could understand Chamberlain as being wrong, garish, and vulgar—wrong within the Dia collection aesthetic. The same with Delacroix: the angle in for me was his problem. It wasn't really his painting. The great thing about Delacroix turns out to be that he was kind of a mess, actually. I got interested in the strange space in his work that isn't right. I guess a psychological approach is my only way of getting it.

— *Which would be forbidden, or ill-fitting for art critics or historians. Serious critics shouldn't care about psychology. Though for you, it* still *has to do with form.*

— With Delacroix it's all about the death drive. He just has this really out-of-whack violence and rage in him. You can formally feel it going on in the paintings. I would go back and forth between looking at the work and reading about him—and he does have some hateful politics! I came to understand an idea of formal aggression, with this kind of churning space his work has, and my intuition was amazingly confirmed by a description I found in a book of Delacroix at an orgy: apparently he would try to fuck three or four people at a time and he really couldn't get on top of them because he was so teeny. So he was always flailing and sweating and grasping, trying to get behind everyone and take over. I realized *he is* the swirl that always is in the center of his paintings, the tempestuous wind blowing everything around.

— *Beyond well-known artists like the two we just mentioned, you often write about artists from your generation, or whom you are close to.*

— Actually, sometimes I hesitate if I'm asked: I have to feel like there's something I can add to the discussion.

— *Is it a question of distance?*

— I just have to have had experiences with something, so I can explain a context, and not rest on the general. The Laura Owens article was about trying to describe, very specifically, the scene of post-1970s feminist painting in California, in addition to my feeling about her work. I knew all the people, a lot of her key friends and network associations. I felt confident that I could write about this very clearly.

— *One has to be an artist to really know a scene, and be able to talk about it.*

— Well, scenes are site-specific, local. Just like humor.

— *Funniness and humor are at the heart of the essay you wrote for Amelie von Wulffen . . .*

— Yes, and I got it a little bit wrong. Because I didn't quite understand her work as political in the way that she perceives it. I understood more why it was comic, but I didn't understand why it was ironic—its political dimension.

— *But it still allowed you to address this notion of humor that's often unacknowledged in painting.*

— I think everything I would write, is about trying to bring out something unacknowledged. Otherwise, why bother?

— *There's a notion you sometimes mention, and that you are at odds with: that of the dandy. Not the dandy in the nineteenth-century sense, but as a position in today's art field.*

— To me it has to do with opposing forms of humor. This writer Robert Garnett and I recently gave talks at a symposium called *Funny Peculiar*[6]: his talk was about humor that descends vs. ascends. His thoughts aligned with mine: dandyism takes this superior tone, ending up with what can just be a poseur's form of criticality, a smug silence, with no struggle. It reminds me of a talk a friend gave years ago at Bard about the "zero position." This wasn't about the dandy idea, but I remember responding passionately negatively: would a girl or a person of color or a queer or a disabled person ever celebrate being "a zero"? They're already legalistically a zero. It's not like something to try to attain—you don't have any privilege to negate. It's not even an option. I feel that now, productive critical positions are provided by feminism, queer theory, or initiatives like Black Lives Matter. In light of current-day discussions, the so-called dandy position is often just white men saying nothing new.

6. *Funny Peculiar*, at the Manchester School of Art, June 6, 2019, aimed at exploring "contemporary ideas in painting connected to shape, humour and diagrammatic thought." See *Painting: Funny Peculiar*, ed. Andrew Hunt (London: Slimvolume, 2020).

— *Nonetheless you're attentive to debunking binarisms. The figure you sometimes allude to as an anti-dandy, is the wrestler: its iconic embodiment by Mickey Rourke shows how weird—how queer—this hypertrophic, muscular body is.*[7] *Instead of getting rid of that arch-male figure, you seem to say, "OK, there's something in there. It doesn't have to stand for something terrible, fascistic, violent. There's other meanings to figure out."*

— I'm very interested in rethinking bodies, partly coming from years of friendship with trans people, and from what they have offered in rethinking everything. But I am also just really aware that, regardless of the digital, or the new biopolitical reality, we're all still gonna die. That hasn't changed one bit. Life and death are still the key. Every conversation that we have had since COVID-19 and the uprising that followed the many murders in the US these past weeks [of spring 2020] is about danger, struggle, the police, life and death. So many ways to feel afraid, so many ways to feel hideous, uncomfortable, lost, minimized. Or, I suppose, joyful or empowered. Anyway, I'm just looking at the enormous changes being called for in consciousness—changes that are political and also affect everyday life. In the everyday, ongoing dumb things of life continue, like food, longing, intimacy—and they can be joyful, painful or sometimes very funny. The intensity of it all is urgent. And I think that what is still funny is still urgent. ♦

7. *The Wrestler* (2008), directed by Darren Aronofsky. "I like art that struggles like Mickey Rourke in *The Wrestler*. Ugly. Vulgar. Hopeful. Intense," writes Amy Sillman in "Notes on the diagram, reworked. Version 2: not-knowing," *The O.-G.*, v. 1–2, "American Edition" (2009). (The reference isn't in the version of the text, "Notes on the Diagram," pages 143–153 of this book.)

ARTIST GIVES TALK

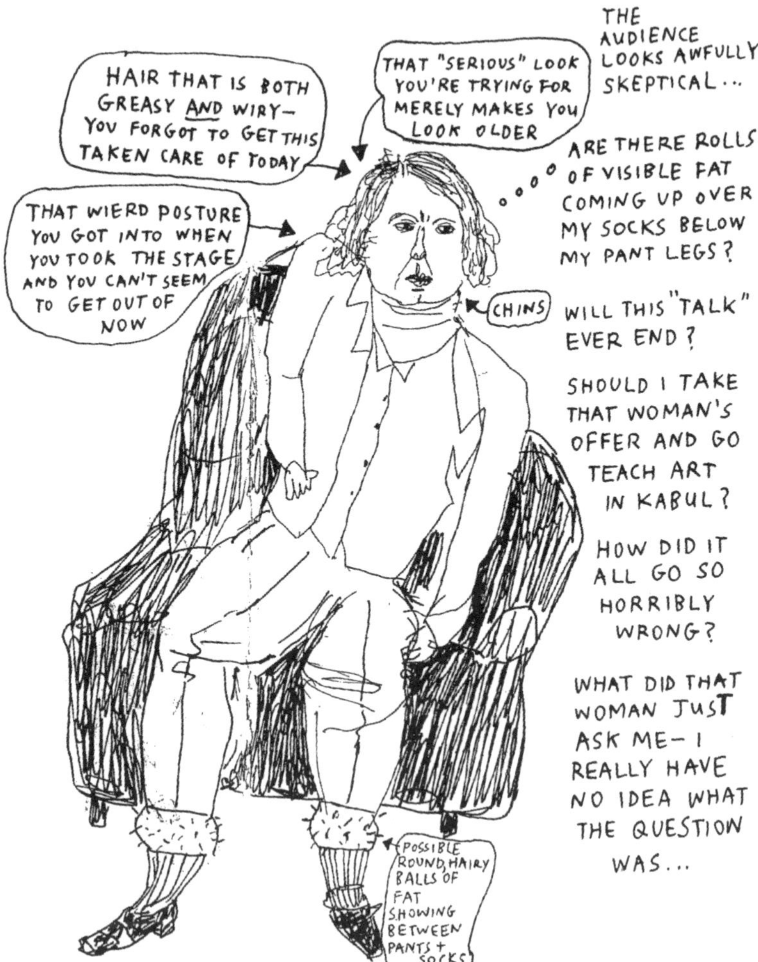

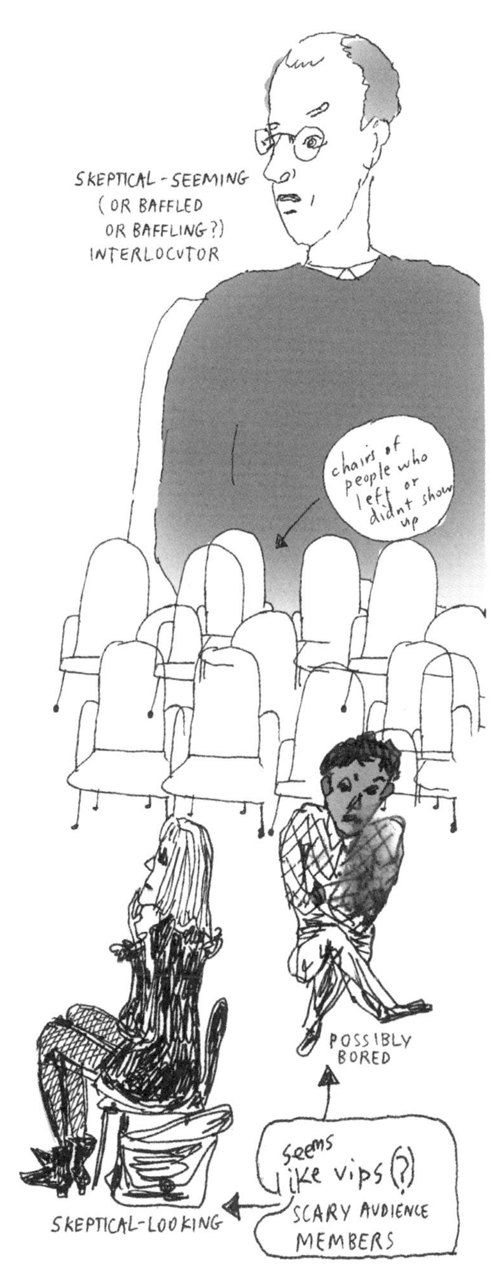
SKEPTICAL-SEEMING
(OR BAFFLED
OR BAFFLING?)
INTERLOCUTOR
chairs of people who left or didnt show up
POSSIBLY BORED
seems like vips (?)
SCARY AUDIENCE MEMBERS
SKEPTICAL-LOOKING

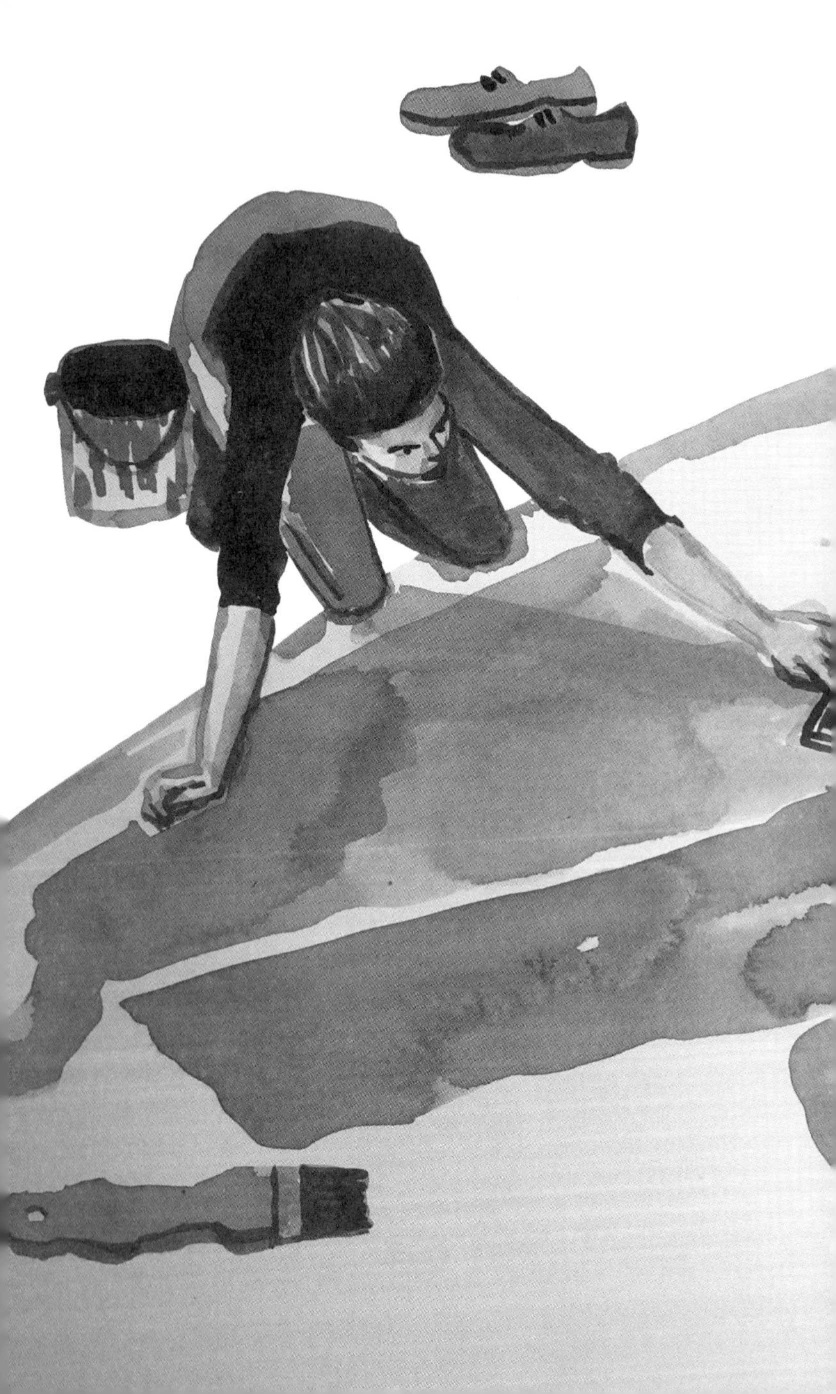

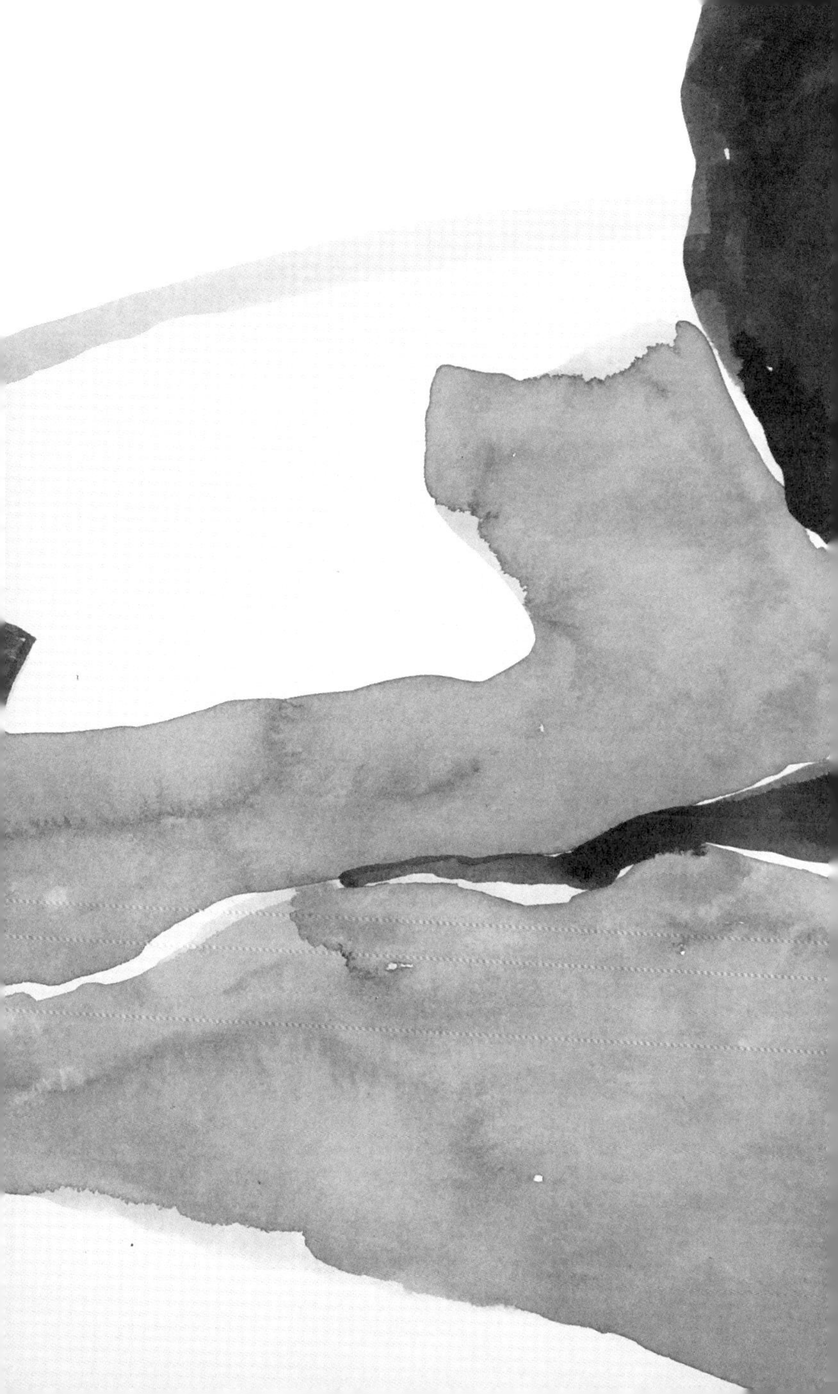

This essay is an expanded and revised version of a talk, originally given along with the screening of more than 200 images; the text has been edited to make their absence as painless as possible.

The lecture was first given at Harvard University, Cambridge, MA in 2013; then at the Whitney Museum of American Art, New York in 2014, as part of the talk series that accompanied the Whitney Biennial; and in the summer of 2017, at The Cheapest University, Paris. A different version appears in Painting beyond Itself: The Medium in the Post-medium Condition, *ed. Isabelle Graw and Ewa Lajer-Burcharth (Berlin: Sternberg Press, 2016), and* Bulletins of The Serving Library, *no. 11 (Summer 2016), under the title, "Drug, Poison, Remedy, Talisman, Cosmetic, Intoxicant."*

On Color

Handling

I was talking to a famous art historian recently, and I asked him if he knew that different pigments weigh different amounts; and that if a painter were blindfolded and two different tubes of paint were placed in her hands, the painter would know which hand held a tube of cadmium red and which a tube of cobalt violet. The art historian said no, he didn't know that. This was a shock: it never dawned on me that an art historian might have *beheld* color, but never *held* color. This simple difference between us expressed the schism that Josef Albers addressed fifty years ago in the introduction to *Interaction of Color* (1963). Albers declared that in his book he would be doing something radical: reversing the normal academic order—putting practice before theory, making subjective experience primary to understanding color.[1] So I guess I'll begin there too, taking up the subject of color as a manual thing.

1. "This book, therefore, does not follow an academic conception of 'theory and practice.' It reverses this order and places practice before theory, which, after all, is the conclusion of practice." *Interaction of Color: 50th Anniversary Edition* (New Haven & London: Yale University Press, 2013; first edition, 1963), 1.

I learned about color in art school in the 1970s, and through the usual post-Bauhaus, post-AbEx, post-hippie art school education of that period. The corporeality of color was simply primary; something to handle, pour, slosh around, feel, drip, smudge, tape off, and experience. We read Albers' color book more like notes from a test kitchen than like a bible of optical pedagogy, and in fact *Interaction of Colors* is both of these. To learn color from Albers, to do his exercises, you first have to gather color swatches like ingredients, splice and dice them, layer them and shift them around, test them out on your own eyeballs. Albers' empirical tradition came down to us via the idea of *push-pull*, Hans Hofmann's wrestler-like term for the muscular dynamics of color in paintings.[2] At art school, we talked about color the way baseball players would discuss the feel of different pitches, or like butchers would talk about how to cut up slabs of beef. So I can only begin any discussion of color with this kind of practical shoptalk.

When I say the practice of color, I really mean the nuts and bolts, its tactility and handling, where you get what it feels like. In fact, I often fail to make a distinction between color as pigment and paint as material in my own daily life. (In German, too, the word *Farbe* is used for both color and paint.) In a sense, my starting point is a pun: the German word *Handlung*. *Handlung* can mean act, action, deed, or plot line; it can also mean a store, a place for transaction. *Buchhandlung* means bookstore.

2. The work and teaching of German-born, American painter Hans Hofmann (1880–1966) was highly influential in the development of abstract painting in the US. The notion of "push-pull" is at the center of his conception of abstraction: it refers to the way colored shapes interact with each other on the canvas, opening to an expressive, intuitive, and dynamic use of paint. See *The Search for the Real, and Other Essays*, ed. Sara T. Weeks and Bartlett H. Hayes Jr. (Andover, MA: Addison Gallery of American Art, Phillips Academy, 1948; reprinted by Cambridge, MA: MIT Press, 1967). [Editors' note]

In the same way, I would like to talk about just that: *Farbehandlung*, color handling, and art supply stores. Before color becomes the mysterious and complex force it has been theorized to be, before it is a philosophical or alchemical problem, or a socio-economic demarcation, color is a material, a tool, the ready-at-hand colored *stuff* that you wield in making a painting.

To paint is to handle color by hand, to take hold of its plot line; painting *for a painter* is an inherently synesthetic experience that merges the senses of touch, smell, sight, and even sound while the painter makes the painting. I once asked a conceptually-minded curator why she loved Richard Serra's work. She said, "Because his work is phenomenological." I was like, "What?" For the artist there is no kind of art that is not essentially phenomenological, since artists always *feel* their work as it is brought into being. Any art student, even a freshman in

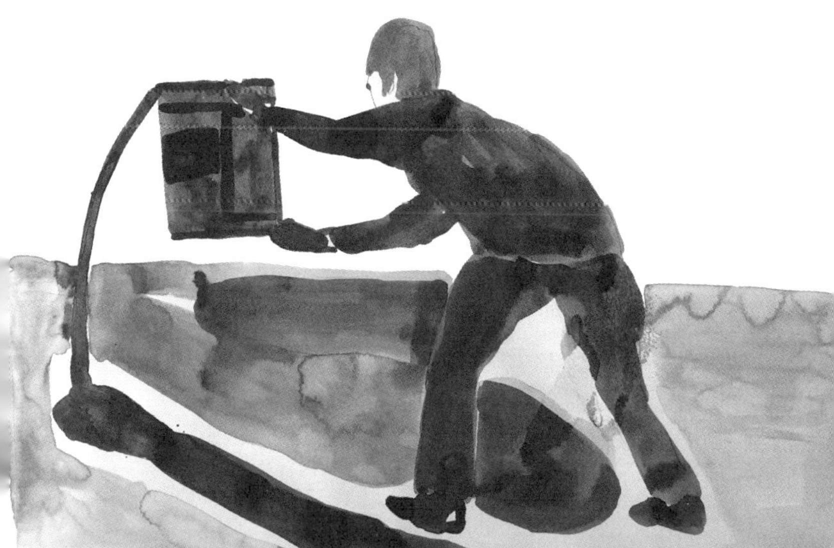

first-year class, would already know what the famous art historian didn't know: the weight of things, how heavy pigments are. They can even figure out which *brand* of paint they are handling by its very texture: Williamsburg paint has grain, Rembrandt paint is sleazy, Old Holland is creamy, Gamblin is dull, Utrecht doesn't weigh enough, Lefranc & Bourgeois weighs too much. After handling the various pigments for a short time, you get to know them almost as characters: Naples yellow is turgid; chromium oxide green is overbearing; flake white has a dry indifference; phthalo blue seems a little sleazy, and then ends up dominating everything else; king's blue looks good at first but is kind of tacky.

But first things first: how do you get the color? The art supply store—the *Handlung*. The painter Peter Saul once said that modern art was the triumph of art supplies over art.[3] If so, it is because the purchase of color at the art supply store is entirely capricious, a hedonist's paradise. Make no mistake about it: these places are pure fetish—color isn't called *pharmakon* for nothing. As you probably know, *pharmakon* in Greek means color, drug, poison, remedy, talisman, cosmetic, or intoxicant. Art supply stores are supermarkets for all these things simultaneously, and the good metropolitan art supply is often two, three, or four stories tall and packed with products that the customers can touch and put into their baskets.

Here I must add an RIP for two near-mythic art supply stores in New York City: Pearl Paint and New York Central Art

3. "Main thing I think about artistically for the last couple of years is getting the 'idea' . . . or the literary content or whatever you call it out in front of the art supplies." Peter Saul, letter to Robert Storr, quoted in Storr, "Peter Saul: Radical Distate," *Art in America* 73, no. 1 (January 1985), 99. [Editors' note]

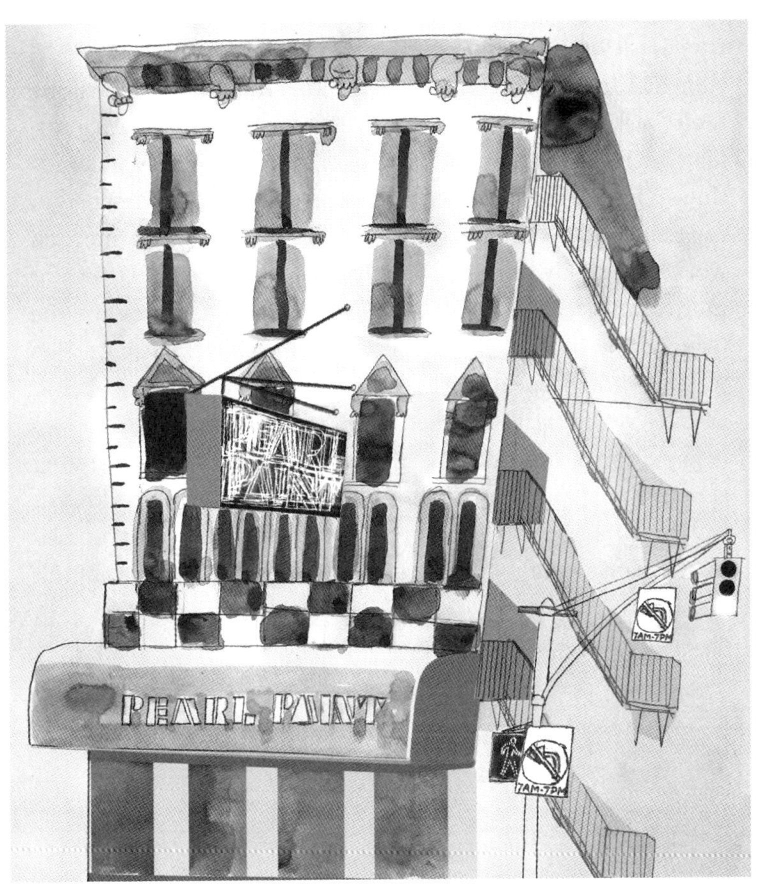

Supply, both formerly downtown, both having served the needs of entire generations of New York expressionists, Pop artists, and Minimalists. Both are now closed. Pearl, with its red-and-white checkered facade, was the queen of Canal Street; New York Central, in the East Village, was the esotericists' favorite. Both of them defined art supply experiences for the artists who were basically born and raised in those stores. We would see art stars like Julian Schnabel and armies of students in there filling their baskets with goods; we endured condescending clerks, long queues, Pearl's vertical climb up the stairs and their byzantine system of getting a personal check okay'd. Pearl opened in 1933 and closed on April 7, 2014, in the end firing 39 unionized workers illegally, some of whom had worked at the store for more than a decade, giving them only 10 days' notice before the termination of their employment, with no layoff package. The workers' union Local 169 has filed charges against Pearl Paint, charges which (last I checked) were still pending. The building is listed for rent or for sale, and advertised as an outstanding condo opportunity at fifteen million dollars.[4] New York Central, my other beloved store, was in business since 1905, owned by the same family for 111 years. Benjamin Steinberg found-

4. One of the buildings on Canal Street has since been repurposed as a luxury store; the other is still waiting for renovation. [Editors' note]

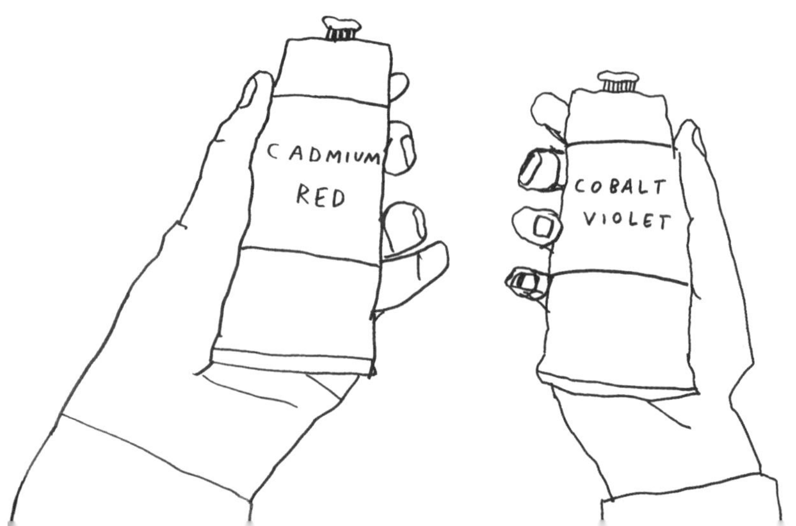

ed it and the Steinbergs ran it until the end, in 2016; you still saw Steve Steinberg sitting behind the desk and could discuss paint brands with him. Warhol was their customer, as were De Kooning, Kline, Basquiat, Haring, etc. These stores, unlike some art supply stores I've been to in European cities, are set up in such a way that you can touch and smell everything, feel it with your hands, because the smart store owners know that if you can pick it up and feel it, you will get what you like, whatever you can afford: that new gold lacquer finish, that little jar of metallic lilac, that new kind of creamy modeling paste. You cannot NOT be a gear-head at a good art supply store—*nothing* is more satisfying than this equipment. And it is so linguistically specific: the nomenclature of paint is all beautiful adjectives. You don't say "pink," you say *dianthus* pink, *hematite* purple, *flake* white, *turkey* umber, *Hooker's* green, *Egyptian* violet, *cinnabar* green, etc. As I said earlier, *Handlung* means an act, but it also means an exchange. And as the poet Lisa Robertson wrote: color, "like a hormone, acts across, embarrasses, seduces. It stimulates the juicy interval in which emotion and sentiment twist."[5] We can barely control ourselves in the aisles full of this profligate luxury item. We throw as much as we can into our baskets and hemorrhage the money to pay for it.

Value

So let's take a look at the weird economy of color: here I have made a chart with the relative cost of color in time and dollars, compared to other luxury goods. An ounce of cadmium red light costs the same amount as an ounce of the best caviar

5. Lisa Robertson, "How to Colour," in *Occasional Work and Seven Walks from the Office for Soft Architecture* (Astoria, OR: Clear Cut Press, 2003), 149.

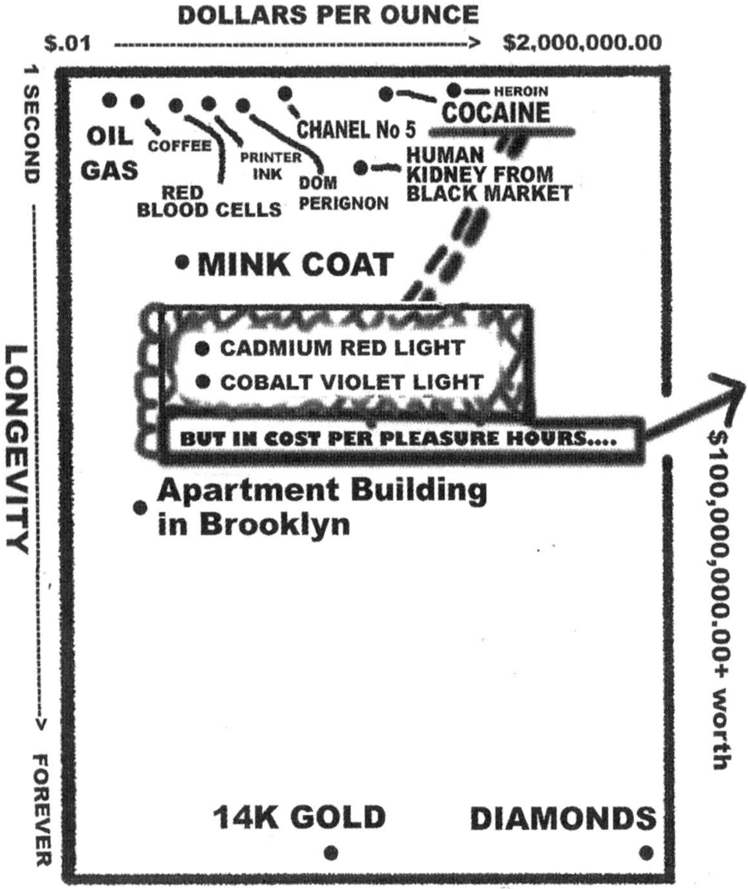

DOLLARS PER OUNCE

$.01 --> $2,000,000.00

1 SECOND ------------ LONGEVITY ------------> FOREVER

OIL

GAS

COFFEE

RED BLOOD CELLS

PRINTER INK

DOM PERIGNON

CHANEL No 5

HEROIN

COCAINE

HUMAN KIDNEY FROM BLACK MARKET

MINK COAT

CADMIUM RED LIGHT

COBALT VIOLET LIGHT

BUT IN COST PER PLEASURE HOURS....

$100,000,000.00+ worth

Apartment Building in Brooklyn

14K GOLD

DIAMONDS

CONCLUSION:
IF YOU FIGURE A PLEASURE HOUR IN TERMS OF THE COST AND LONGEVITY OF COCAINE, THEN AN OUNCE OF CADMIUM RED OIL PAINT IS WORTH ONE HUNDRED MILLION DOLLARS OF COCAINE.

available on the Upper East Side; the same red costs as much as an ounce of cold-packed human red blood cells. With what I spent in the last tax year on color, I could have bought a BMW or a mink coat. A small tube of cobalt violet costs the same as a bottle of Dom Pérignon. (A quarter ounce of cadmium red will cover a square meter of canvas but if Barnett Newman painted it, it would cost the same as a bar of gold.) A large bag of the same pigment will cost you as much as a very large bag of cocaine. But note: if you figure oil paint by the time vector, in longevity rather than dollars per ounce, paint is way better than drugs. An ounce of cocaine costs about sixty times more than an ounce of oil paint, but it only lasts for an hour, while cadmium red lasts hundreds or thousands of years. So if you figure it backwards, in pleasure hours, a tube of oil paint is equivalent to a hundred million dollars of cocaine. And like a crack addict, I often find myself up late at night with a razor blade, desperately scraping the last miserable speck out of an exhausted tube of color because *I just need more of that substance*—and the store isn't open. Color is a "market," said Lisa Robertson.[6]

To add further luster, consider the esoteric feeling when working with stuff like the color carmine, a pigment that is made from acids extracted from the body and eggs of female cochineal insects that live on prickly pears; or Indian yellow, a color that comes with a legend about being made from the piss of cows who are fed on mango leaves (though I've heard this is mythic); or Tyrian purple, a dye substance made from secretions drained from the glands of predatory sea snails. All pigments need to be diluted with special lubricants made from

6. *Ibid.*, 142.

the oils of seeds, herbs, and flowers, or raw melted beeswax. And even more arcane, add in the fact that these substances are poisons. A painting studio is a kind of haphazard chemistry lab where non-scientists work like medieval alchemists, with little protection from treacherous metals like lead, copper, aluminum, oxides, arsenic, or cobalt. To work with these materials, one *should* really wear protective masks and latex gloves, though we often don't (just as we really *shouldn't* smoke, but it still looks sexy). The work requires ventilation systems, metal storage cabinets, and industrial waste removal. Paint needs terrible volatile solvents to dilute it, like naphtha, benzene, and Gamsol. These precious poisons are applied to the finest textile surfaces, which are stretched and prepared fetishistically as though one were rubbing a papyrus for a pharaoh; sized with glues, which may be made from pulverized rabbit skins that have been warmed twice to exacting degrees in double boilers, and then layered, sanded, and layered again with such things as milk proteins, marble dust, chalk powder, or polyvinyl acetates. And all this stuff I am describing is just run-of-the-mill stuff, which any normal fetishist-aka-painter will have and use. Most painters have their own special recipes and techniques for these artisanal preparations, all to create *just* the right kind of ground for their colors to lay down on. Painters constantly discuss these surfaces, touch them, caress them, go over them with special sponges and scrapers, with brushes made of the hair of goat or mink or mongoose, with handles of hardwood or bamboo. The best brush is called Kolinsky sable: I always thought Kolinsky was a Jewish brush man, someone like Steve Steinberg at New York Central, but it turns out that Kolinsky is a kind of weasel that lives in the snow in Siberia.

Paradoxes

Making a painting is so hard, it makes you crazy. Before even the vicissitudes of color, you have to negotiate tone, silhouette, line, space, zone, area, layer, scale, speed, and mass while interacting with a meta-surface of meaning, thought, text, sign, language, intention, concept, and history; you have to go your own way, to cut away from your heroes and influences, and still be utterly conscious and literate about the discourse. You have to simultaneously diagnose, predict and ignore the past, present and future, all at once; you have to remember and to forget at the same time. You have to both deny and embrace all your impulses toward romanticism *and* irony; you have to both love and hate your objects and your subjects, to believe every shred of romantic and passionate mythos about painting and at the same time to cast a gimlet eye upon it. Color is even harder to negotiate. You embrace the vicissitudes of this toxic, expensive, and unpredictable substance, while trying to keep it looking fresh, maintaining the illusion that it is effortless. When someone talks about color as decorative, I just don't know what they are talking about. Try mixing oil paint: ninety-five percent of the time it's hideous. Those beautiful shimmering powders from the paint store turn immediately into pasty slop buckets of sickening green or hemorrhage-y brown tones. This is where the fetishism goes horribly wrong. All painters speak regularly of their colors becoming "mud." The pigment itself is reverse alchemy, a gold that becomes shit in our studios, and our task is to try to turn that shit back into gold. Often, surrounded in my studio by buckets and paper towels, I wonder what kind of Freudian mistake has been made to turn me into a painter.

This brings me to one of color's primary paradoxes: the schizophrenic nature of its rhetoric. On the one hand, color represents all the good things on Earth: beauty, awe, surprise, romance, freedom, innocence, gay politics, civil rights. First there is light—then there is the rainbow. Color begins as the primordial signal of everything right and true: the rainbow flag is carried at both gay pride marches and Jesse Jackson marches. Color is freedom to an extreme, a wild card, the joker, a destabilizer. Julia Kristeva says color is "the shattering of unity."[7] The Fauves are the wild beasts who overthrow the rational order of the Renaissance. Iridescence is contingency, colors are feelings, in shape-shifting newness and alterity. Who forbids color? Men in control, men with homosexual panic, Stalinists, prison guards. (A woman who grew up in a Communist country recently told me an anecdote about the ultimate color buzzkill. When she went to art school, only one color was issued to all the artist comrades: chromium oxide green. All the paintings in the school were painted by chromatic fiat in tones of this one dull pigment, and she talked about how the art students longingly gazed at flowers and imported German candy in rich purple and pink wrappers.) Against such forces of joy-killing, color is a powerful force, a feminine or anarchistic other who is resistant to the language of law. Walter Benjamin writes that color is the very essence of childhood imagination, a form of innocence that can subvert the logic of capitalism.[8]

7. Julia Kristeva, "Giotto's Joy," (1972) in *Desire in Language*, trans. Thomas Gora, Alice Jardine, and Leon S. Roudiez (Oxford, UK & Cambridge, MA: Blackwell, 1982), 221.

8. See Walter Benjamin, "A Child's View of Colour" (1914–15), trans. Rodney Livingstone, in *Selected Writings, Volume 1, 1913–1926*, ed. Marcus Bullock and Michael W. Jennings (Cambridge, MA: Harvard University Press, 1996), 50–51. Benjamin notably contrasts "productive adults [who] derive no support from color," with how, "in a child's

On the other hand, there is the color production. At the heart of capitalism's dark mechanisms is the dye industry, which infiltrates our homes, our clothing, our tastes and surroundings, becoming natural and *heimlich*. Color is marketing, color is big business, color is meted out in bite-size Pantone swatches, for our drapes, our walls, our clothes, our food. To wring color out of the earth requires the worst and most oppressive systems in the world, a story that extends from mining to plantation work to Nazis to child labor.[9] When you think of color, think of the chemical industry, of colonialism, indigo plantations with laborers working in vats. Think of the IG Farben company, the biggest German manufacturer of dyes in the first half of the twentieth century, simultaneously producing the colors for sofa cushions and the Zyklon B gas used in concentration camps; its former headquarters in Frankfurt are an oppressive-looking building, informally known as the Pentagon of Europe and now a part of Goethe University. Think of the iPhone in your pocket, and how that device is made in Foxconn factories, where thirteen-year-olds kill themselves working on its wonderful color settings of "millions."[10] Think of Walt Disney, whose animations

life, color is the pure expression of the child's pure receptivity, insofar as it is directed at the world." [Editors' note]

9. This story is chronicled eloquently by Esther Leslie in her book *Synthetic Worlds: Nature, Art and the Chemical Industry* (London: Reaktion Books, 2005).

10. Foxconn is a Taiwanese company that manufactures electronic products for companies including Apple and Amazon. In 2010 a spate of suicides drew international attention to the dire working conditions in its largest factory, located in Shenzhen, where iPhones are made. See Brian Merchant, *The One Device: The Secret History of the iPhone* (London: Bantam Press, 2017). Suspicions regarding child labor at Foxconn were confirmed in 2019, when leaked documents showed that teenagers, classified as "interns," were employed and required to work nights and overtime. See China Labor Watch report, *Amazon's Supplier Factory Foxconn Recruits Illegally: Interns Forced to Work Overtime*, August 8, 2019, https://chinalaborwatch.org/ amazons-supplier-factory-foxconn-recruits-illegally-interns-forced-to-work-overtime (last accessed July 5, 2022). [Editors' note]

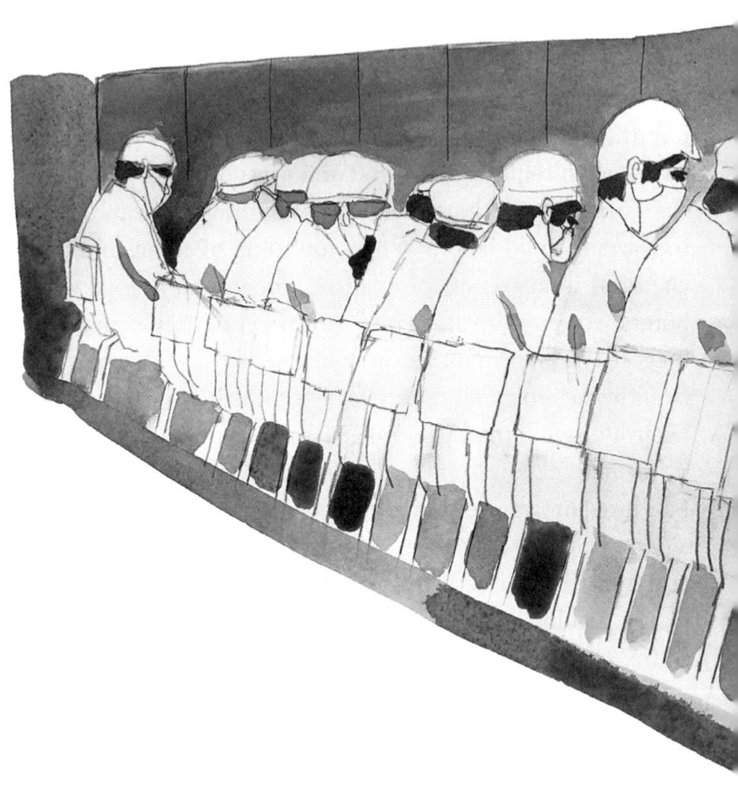

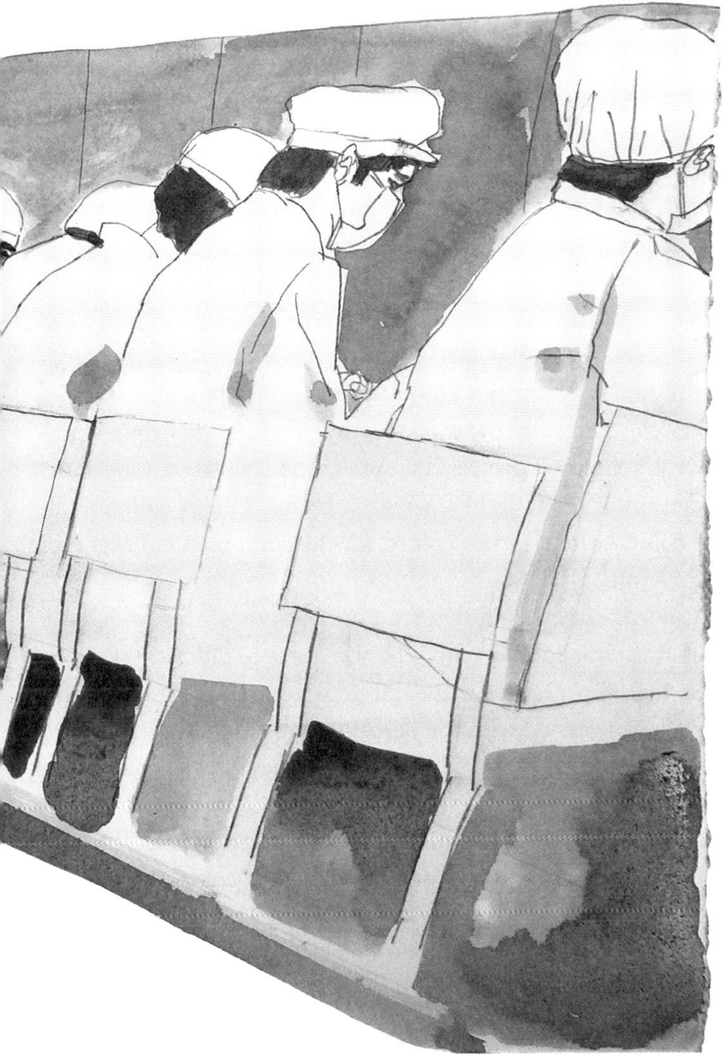

were regularly outsourced to India and China to maximize profits. Think back on that rainbow that unfurls in the beginning of every Disney movie.

Meanwhile, with a kind of transcendent indifference, the *representation* of color in the form of the same old color wheel, steady as the sun, has been the largely unchanging visual theorem for color from the seventeenth century onward, no matter what ideological system toils below. Color since Sir Isaac Newton, who first devised a picture of the color wheel in 1704 in his *Opticks*, has been depicted as a nice, clean pyramid or circle, pleasingly divided into uniformly sized slices, grading neatly into one another in a kind of rounded rainbow made into a full circle. The rainbow was of course literally its origin, since Newton's theory was based on optics, on his observations of the refraction of white light through a prism. This is called additive color—when all the colors, all the rays, blended together make white.

Color theory was updated a hundred years later by Johann Wolfgang von Goethe, whose book *Theory of Colours* (1810) on color theory presented a radical departure from Newton's approach. Concerned with the perception of color, the senses and the sensuousness of it, Goethe associated color with earth/pigment/ground/physicality/tactility. It is called subtractive color—when all the colors mixed together make black. Goethe's big update was to add red-violet to the list of colors. By moving color from heaven to earth, he "humanized" it, adding desire, feeling, psychology, and mood—Goethe's colors have human characteristics: red is beautiful, orange is noble, green is useful, etc. It could also be considered the beginning of a semiotics of color, in which names capture and locate meaning.

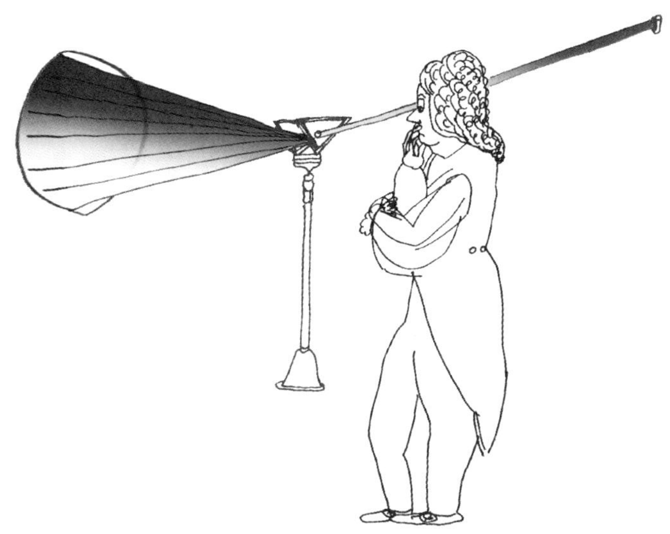

One thing that has always fascinated me is that almost all the various theorists and teachers of color use essentially the same wheel or system. Let's consider three famous artists / art teachers renowned for their courses in color theory in the same general time period: Gustav Klutsis, a Latvian productivist artist who taught color courses at the VKhUTEMAS in Moscow in the early 1920s (in all other ways, Klutsis was a revolutionary and anti-bourgeois activist, but not with his color wheel); Johannes Itten, the complete opposite of Klutsis, a robe-wearing Swiss painter leaning toward mysticism, who taught color at the Bauhaus around the same time; and Itten's student, Josef Albers, who in 1933 emigrated from Germany to the United States and became the head of Black Mountain College in Asheville, North Carolina. Though their politics and methods diverged entirely, all three utilized the same basic color wheel and followed the same basic principles as Isaac Newton's in the seventeenth century.

Occasionally there have been attempts to reinvent the color wheel. In the early twentieth century, H. G. Maratta devised a spectrum color chart that deployed a system of numbers and letters to indicate what he called "radiating intensities," which was used by various American painters like Robert Henri and John Sloan. At roughly the same time, Professor Albert Munsell—who taught color in Boston at what is now the art school called MassArt—also devised a color system with number/letter indications, and went further to identify chromatic intensities. Munsell declared the traditional color names "foolish," and offered a new decimal system and a new pole-shaped model. The colors were now merely called by their first letters: red was "R," yellow-red was "Y-R," yellow was "Y," and so forth. Gradations of hue, value, and chroma were introduced, with updated scientific color names like "7.5 B-G" or "1.5 P-B." The Munsell system didn't really make its way into the domain of art education; by the time I got to art school, the details of this math-y approach were largely forgotten or ignored. Instead, Munsell's system was employed as a kind of antiquated index of quasi-scientific data for governing color operations in business and technology. Nowadays, you can find Munsell-based guidebooks in thrift stores, which recommend color schemes for the offices of male vs. female executives, or Munsell color standards in the US Department of Agriculture guide outlining, for instance, the possible gradations of golden brownness required in the preparation of frozen French fries.

Palette

So by the 1970s, to paraphrase a Rihanna song, we at art school found color in a hopeless place. The pedagogic trajectory was schizophrenic. In Painting 1, a freshman was instructed in an outdated method of laying out a brownish palette on a piece of heavy glass, really only useful for someone rendering nudes in a wooden academy in Philadelphia. Then in Painting 2, you met Kandinsky, and picked up some crypto-informational tips that boiled down to a kind of color astrology, like that red wants to come forward and blue wants to recede—the same way that Geminis are fun and Pisces are moody. If you got any further, you learned that French people taught us to build space with color, yet that by the 1960s, to be vanguard you would withdraw from color altogether. What were we to make of this mishmash of theory and practice? Furthermore, we painted in the light of fluorescence and TV screens—that is, if we painted at all, since painting was dead. Our world was lit with signs, bulbs, televisions, and eventually the infra-thin space between pixel and monitor. All color was essentially a compromise formation. And who was the standard viewer anyway? We were Americans, we had Pearl Paint, so we went shopping.

We found our readymades at the art supply store. We found our radiating intensities by feel, and put our colors in buckets and cups any which way we wanted, rejecting color theory altogether, except as a kind of stimulating experience in an aisle of the cultural supermarket. An earnest poststructuralist student-friend said to me: “Color is the name given to forces that allow us to confront the uneasy task of marking difference.” He was right, of course: color marks value, regional art, gender, pathology, lust, shame, humor, camp, excess, vulgarity,

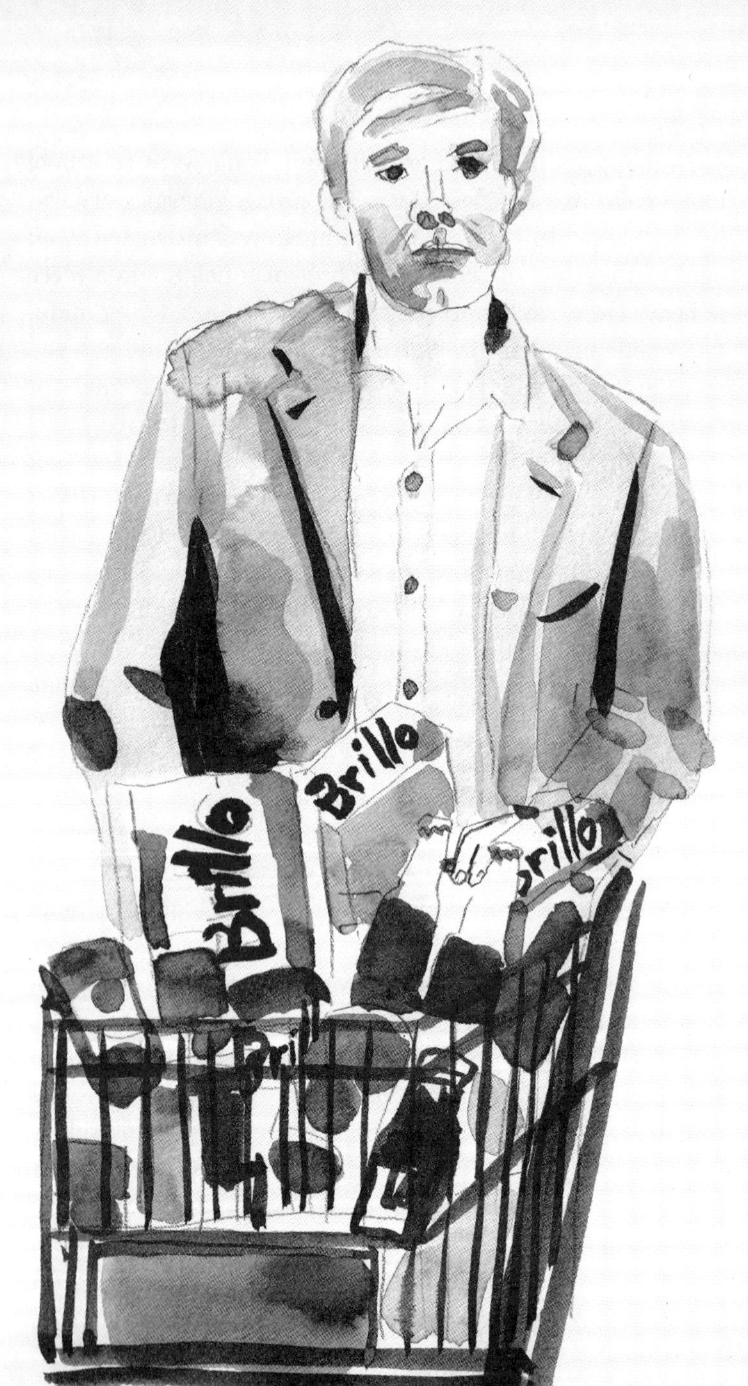

Brillo
Brillo
Brillo

and bad taste. But who could understand this in relation to color's physicality, its actuality as a thing that you can hold, or buy? There was no color theory but there were gusts of chromatic experience, to which one yielded, and there was fatigue, many catastrophic mutations, clumsiness, and productive misunderstandings.

Color Operations

To illustrate this point, I spent one afternoon trying to examine the actual method of color in the practices of various painter friends—just anyone who came to mind with interesting color in their work. In this casual overview, I realized that each one uses color in a different way, that there is *no* particularly coherent or systematic approach to color among a random sample of my contemporaries. Here are twenty-three quick examples of this manifold: first, a nod to Justin Lieberman, who arranges a palette of "Who Wore It Best?" pages from the magazine *Us Weekly*; Cameron Martin, who sometimes uses no color, but in whose monochromatic work one finds the color of the spectral glow of monitors, cathode rays, or nuclear winter; Jacqueline Humphries, whose colors are both harsh and sensitive, who uses silver, gray, and Day-Glo to accentuate her surfaces with extremely tactile markings; R. H. Quaytman, whose colors speak of mirrors, windows, scrims, and illusions, and who insists on shadow when she knows that shadow is impossible in modernism; Cheyney Thompson, who purposefully imbricates systems into each other, like time and taste and color, to make a parody of order—and ends up with something impossibly excessive; Stephen Westfall, who mixes the tonalities of signs in civic space with the jazzed-up jitterbug of geometries; Stanley Whitney, whose polychromatic sequences are like languages, scales, and harmolodic rainbows, interactions of the free-form and the systematic; Odili Odita—color literally woven like textiles, and applied directly to walls and surfaces of sometimes-architectural-scale immersions; Rodney McMillian's reduced palette of symbolic reds, browns, blacks, whites, describing a desperate kind of social space with images wrought in desolate reds of desire and despair; Glenn Ligon's corrosivity—colors that start as symbols but which degrade and become illegible or impossible through systematic reproduction; Dona Nelson, wrestling action painting into an absurdly insistent material form; Charline von Heyl, consistently countering the logic of the move before or after with a sequence of interrogative color responses; Rochelle Feinstein's unreliable narrations, color that literally demonstrates the feelings of distrust and falsity—off-colors, fleeting colors, impossible colors, like pastel fluorescents, or queasy incandescences; Jennifer Packer's inflammatory colors (crimsons, lakes, madders, violets, magentas, buttercup yellows) which insist that color is primary in seeing the world with feeling—her work is a testament to seeing, feeling, knowing and remember-

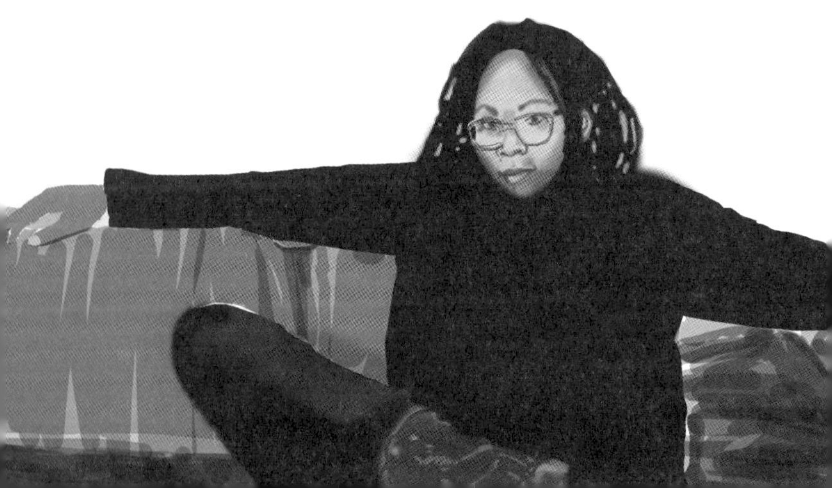

ing the world through a prism of stains, patches, zones, and environments of color; Jutta Koether—both historic and hysteric color acting as a kind of psychic signal beam to shine a light on history, as though plugging the Poussin monitor into the crazy beam; David Reed, whose filmy overlays and techniques of Technicolor bespeak of film; Bill Jensen, with gestures, washes, and wipes rendered in pure chroma; Halsey Rodman's time-as-space—color used to distinguish between repetitions and displacements from one stroke to the next, almost like an absurd version of Monet's haystacks; Laura Owens' graphic colors mashed-up with digital space, in all their glowing emptiness and distraction, each screen bleeding into the next in a kind of hyperspace; Thomas Eggerer's "artificial sweeteners," a post-camp negotiation between the desire for mysterious feelings and the feelings of pictures; Rachel Harrison, complementary/uncomplimentary colors that resist logic, offering moments of trash and belligerence in stains, jabs, and strokes; Kerry James Marshall's color-zone theory, reconfiguring the entire world from high to low, with all the colors of comic books, maps, people, and social spaces cunningly deployed to reveal both love and resistance; and David Salle's peacockery, things seen in an illuminating and compulsive light, like an appraising eye cast on a window display.

What I find here, if there is an overview to be made, is color in a consistently denatured or unnatural form; color as a chronicler of critical moods of subversion and humor; color in overt interaction with the digital, with screens, displays, and other modern circulation systems; color not applied to surfaces or describing light so much as bringing its own synthetic force to bear.

A Brief Mention of Problems in the Age of Digital Reproduction

"Color is the shattering of unity," writes Kristeva, and in mechanical reproduction what is shattered is any idea of a dependable or original experience. Digital delivery systems bring a new hall of mirrors to color, a new set of mishaps between systems in which every color is basically just an approximation, a compromise formation. The tensions between the systems of additive versus subtractive color are merely amplified by digital processing, and the reproduction of color is always a translation, usually a bad one.

For many years I regularly painted with a particular mixture of cadmium lemon and cinnabar green—in person, this was an acidic yellow-green color that hit your eye in a pleasingly acrid way, but this same color was basically un-seeable in slides. The color simply could not be represented in the photographic spectrum of analog photography. On all Kodak film it went to a warm ochre; in the coldness of Fujicolor it just went straight greenish. I have had more luck reproducing that same color now in the digital age, because acidity is more easily rendered with various gamma settings, but given all the differing viewing platforms, this color, and all colors basically, are already approximate before they must skulk further back down into the limitations of CMYK printing. Since art is mostly experienced these days in reproduction, the very specifics of my palette are lost as they go out into the world. The experience of my work is only to be had in so-called "real life." Is this different from old times? I don't think so; you always had to be there. But artists can now *choose* to focus on the unphotographability of their work, the requirement to experience their work first-hand, like Ryman, Martin, or most other monochromists famously did;

or conversely, artists can choose to work specifically with the logic of color's contemporary circulation, such as the early 1996 Rachel Harrison work, *5 × 7's*, in which the artist took a photograph of an anthill to various commercial photo printers, and assembled the highly varied results.[11] But whether the artist ignores or highlights mechanical reproduction, color points inescapably to subjectivity. Who *is* the standard viewer, and how can you ever know what colors they see? There is simply no way to measure it. As Albers said fifty years ago on the very first page of his book on color: even if the same standardized Coca-Cola-red sign is proposed to a thousand people, they will all still be *thinking* of a thousand different reds (not to mention a thousand different ideas about Coke).[12]

Time

"So how do you use color?" people ask me all the time. An impossible question, as though I were to "know" something about time, sex, sound, scent, heat, touch, emotions, how color performs like sex in language. Color is something that I can only describe, which lives in the memory and sensation of the skin, the feelings of touch and handling itself. I love the painter Jim Nutt, who once said, "My work isn't even close to an idea. It's just something that I'm doing."[13]

11. The complete title, *5 × 7's (A&R Quality Photo, Aurora, Duggal, Emulsion, Foto Print, Image Studio, Pro Photo, R&B Color Labs, US Color, Victoria Photo)*, provides the names of the different printers Harrison worked with; the work consists in a wall display of the ten prints in a line. [Editors' note]

12. See "Color recollection—visual memory," the first chapter of *Interaction of Colors, op. cit.*, 3.

13. Carroll Dunham in conversation with Jim Nutt, in *Jim Nutt: Drawings and Paintings*, ed. David Nolan (New York: Nolan/Eckman Gallery, 2003), 7. See also, "The Writings of Carroll Dunham," page 250. [Editors' note]

Maybe what I'm most interested in, anyway, is *time*; how in painting, time merges with materials to form constant changes. We know from Albers or Matisse that color can only be measured by the color next to it, and when things keep changing, color will be in ongoing flux. As a painter who uses color as a material, I could describe color as simply the flesh of these changes—the way I mark the negations and negotiations of painting-time. I just keep going until I find a weight and a surprise that tells me something I don't already know; it's more a process of *détournement* than of progress. Colors block each other out, contradict each other; they live and die in an ongoing process of destruction and reconstruction.

I mix paint more than anyone I know, to find a palette as I go along. It starts with everything I look at: people, paintings, iPhone apps, cartoons, magazines, flowers, clothing, buildings, trees. I am doomed to use the colors of the oil paints and sticks that I can buy, too: it's a palette that is half-predetermined, chosen for me by guys like Richard Frumess, who owns R&F Handmade Paints, the manufacturer of one of the brands of paints that I like. I noticed at some point that my palette contained an element of 1980s kitsch, a vulgar pink for example. And I realized that my palette is not necessarily *my* palette, but choices that might be made by Richard. Who knows? He might also wear a nylon windbreaker in shades of purple and green? My work is partly determined by the colors I can buy, and then the weird way I mix them, mulching around not knowing exactly what I am doing. I basically work the colors until they are ruined, and then I rescue them with solvents, in pots and buckets, and then eventually bring all the sludgy browns, grays, and intermediates that I have scraped off a painting to mix together with the vulgar readymades that I bought new.

Here is an example: in 2007 I started a painting that became more than a one year-long struggle. After about eleven months, I accidentally took a palette knife to this painting, and in a horrifying moment of technical disaster, half the painting peeled off the surface under my palette knife, because of my mistake in primer application. That night, in a state of painter's despondency, I glumly had dinner with a painter friend, Robert Bordo. I asked him how to deal with this loss, both how to rescue the painting and how to deal with the loss I felt for a surface I had been in a relationship with for a year. My friend said, you take your stethoscope and place it on the painting's surface and ask it: "Painting, what do you need to regain your light?" So I went back, and found a way to reconstitute the blue/gray light of its former background. I was able to get the painting from the brink of the dumpster and it went to a show at the Hirshhorn Museum.[14] I don't claim that this is anything special. All of this is completely normal for a painter—in my case the engine of this work of constant adjustment, dissatisfaction, emotional struggle, is color, and yet it has nothing whatsoever to do with color theory. This is what interests me the most about color: that it has its own problems, vexations, and characters. Color theory is not really a theory at all; it is merely a description for the protean world of our sensations, or an attempted prediction of what might happen next. ♦

14. *Directions: Amy Sillman, Third Person Singular*, curated by Anne Ellegood at the Hirshhorn Museum, Washington D. C., March 13–July 6, 2008. [Editors' note]

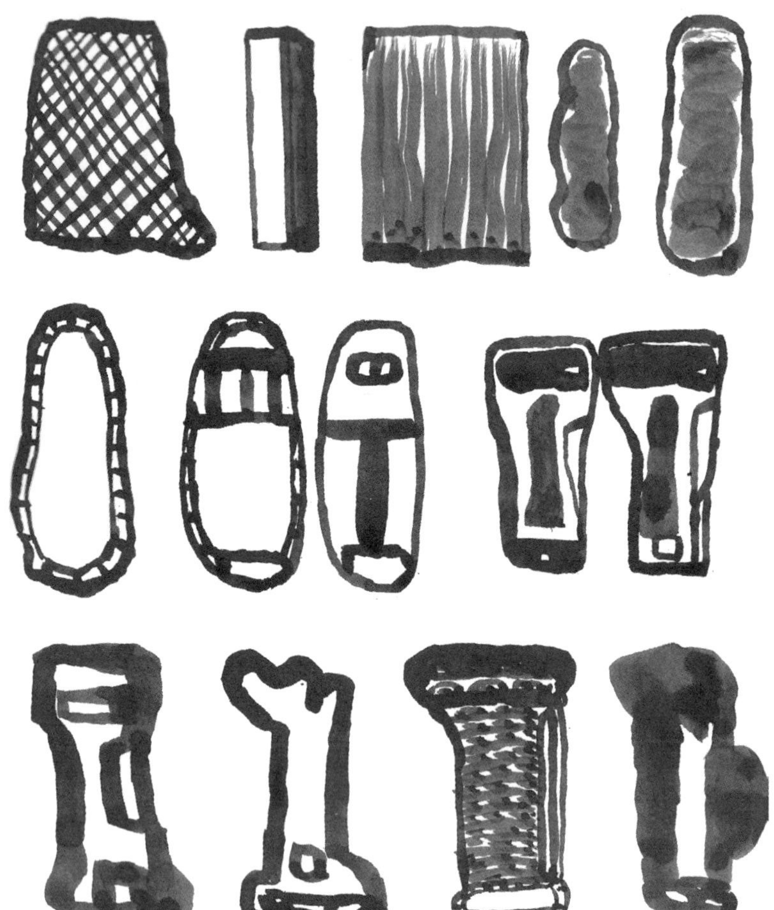

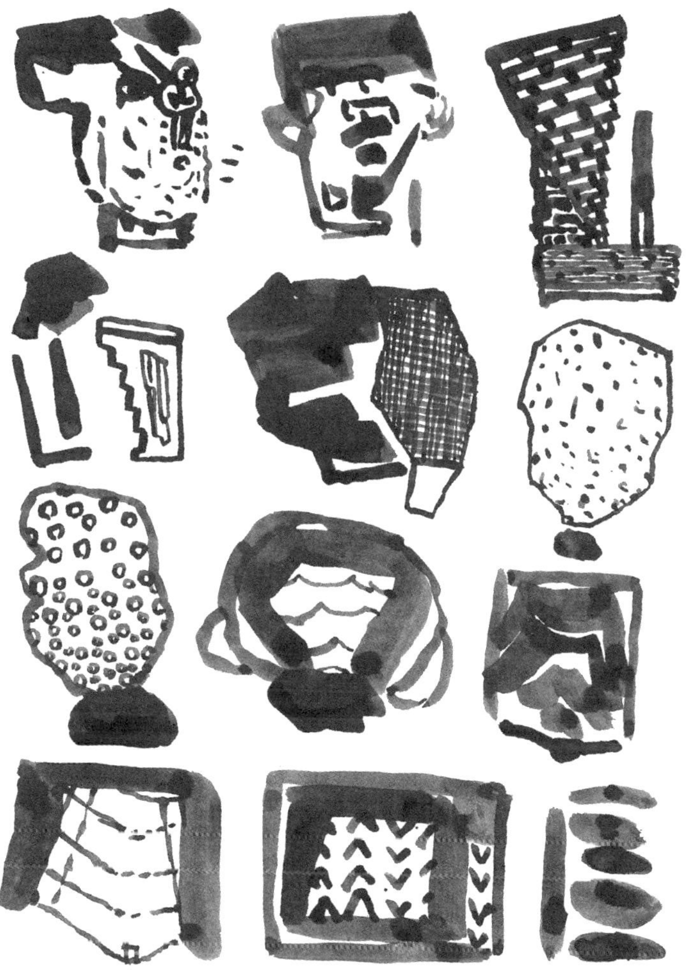

The following text is a revised version of a talk given at the symposium, "Figures of Conjunction: Experience and Interest in Politics, Theory, and Art," a "temporary free academy" organized by Helmut Draxler and Monika Baer, at the Kunstverein Nürnberg, November 18–21, 2014, with the participation of a dozen art professors and their classes from different schools in Germany. Sillman delivered this talk again on January 13, 2017, at the Menil Collection, Houston, TX, as part of the Menil Drawing Institute series, "Draw In: Conversations and Lectures on Drawing and Its Resonances." This previously unpublished essay is an edit of the 2017 text; it condenses the second and third parts of the original talk, which relied heavily on the use of images.

Some Notes on Drawing

I have never understood myself as a painter, but really only as a draw-er, and I think there's a huge difference between the two. In the philological task of dividing the world into neat groups, there have been a lot of binaries made, some of them useful: the Greek poet Archilochus divided knowledge into two groups, fox vs. hedgehog. ("The fox knows many things, but the hedgehog just one big thing.")[1] The artist/writer Manny Farber divided art into "White Elephant" art vs. "Termite art." ("The clogging weight of a masterwork" vs. "the 'small sensation' . . . the tingling, jarring excitement where he nibbles away.")[2] For me, you can divide painting and drawing into eagle vs. beaver. A painter is like an eagle, a canny and noble bird who soars above us, doing something enlightened, getting the big picture. A draw-er is more like a beaver who builds a dam from the ground up stick by stick, without an overview, but just with an animal urge to keep going until the thing becomes a form. Henri Matisse, a

1. William Harris, "Archilochus: First Poet After Homer" (2002), *Research Resources* 48, 96; available online at https://fordham.bepress.com/phil_research/48 (last accessed July 5, 2022).

2. See Manny Farber, "White Elephant Art vs. Termite Art," *Film Culture*, no. 27 (Winter 1962–63). About this text, see "Further Notes on Shape," note 5, page 95. [Editors' note]

real draw-er, once said: "I threw myself into it like a beast that plunges towards the thing it loves."[3] If painting is "an expensive hunk of well-regulated area,"[4] as Farber says, then drawing is a literal underdog. It's a promiscuous, mongrel form, the whole medium an inherently expanded field.

Literally *everyone* draws—but then, people are always claiming that they "can't" draw. Yet everyone with a pencil in their hand is doing some form of drawing. Handwriting is a kind of drawing; you're drawing when you idly doodle on a scratch pad, diagram directions to your house on a cocktail napkin, or play Pictionary or hangman. You're drawing if you furtively scrawl a message on a bathroom wall. Robert Rauschenberg did it by doggedly erasing a drawing he got from Willem de Kooning's drawers. Joan Jonas did it standing in front of a projector, tracing the tip of a long stick on the ground. Carolee Schneemann did it with gravity, swinging like a pendulum in a hammock and letting a piece of charcoal bang against the wall. Trisha Brown did it lying sprawled on large pieces of paper on the ground with the charcoal between her toes.[5] Tibetan monks sit cross-legged on the floor and delicately tip sand out of their palms to make a shape.[6] Drawing's procedures include so many different

3. "From the moment I held the box of colors in my hands, I knew this was my life. I threw myself into it like a beast that plunges towards the thing it loves." Matisse quoted in Hilary Spurling, *The Unknown Matisse. A Life of Henri Matisse: The Early Years 1869–1908* (London and New York: Knopf, 1998), 46.

4. See Farber, "White Elephant Art vs. Termite Art," *art. cit.*

5. Sillman alludes here to Rauschenberg's *Erased de Kooning Drawing* (1953), also mentioned in "AbEx and Disco Balls," page 134; to Jonas' *Reanimation* (2010/2012/2013), a performance now presented as an installation; to Schneemann's *Up to and Including Her Limits* (1973–76), a performance turned into an installation as well, mentioned in "AbEx and Disco Balls," page 139; and to Brown's work with drawing, that she developed in close connection to her dance practice from the early 1970s. [Editors' note]

6. The creation—and destruction—of mandalas made of sand is a tradition from Tibetan Buddhism. [Editors' note]

kinds of actions that you can attach a different verb to everyone's drawing, which is why when I originally delivered these notes on drawing as a lecture, I began with a list of hundreds of verbs, each verb attached to a different artist with a different action that showed how expansive drawing might be.[7] *Everyone draws*—until around puberty, and after that for some reason they either announce that they can't draw, or they *keep* drawing. Maybe the only thing that marks an artist is the presence of a double negative: an artist is someone who *doesn't* claim that they *can't* draw.

For me the ground zero of drawing was marked by a twist of fate: I traveled to Japan at age 19 and found myself washed over by an exhilarating waterfall of cryptograms, curlicues, and sonic particles that I could not decipher. It was easy to pick up the sonic alphabetic parts of Japanese, the kana: "kah," "kee," "koo," "keh," "ko," etc.—but it was nearly impossible to learn the complex constructions of the kanji. It reminded me of the vivid time as a child when I already knew how to read block letters but I could only stare dumbly at a blackboard of cursive, a delirious set of Twombly-like loops that only older people knew how to read. Going to Japan meant something like that, a place where language was deliriously unhinged from its regular tasks and more visually alive than ever. The first line of Roland Barthes' book on Japan, *Empire of Signs,* is: "The dream—to know a foreign (alien) language and yet not to understand it."[8]

7. This part of the talk was adapted and published under the title, "To Do List," in *The Drawings of Susan Te Kahurangi King*, ed. Tanya Heinrich, exh. cat. (Miami: ICA Miami, 2016). [Editors' note]

8. Roland Barthes, *Empire of Signs* (1970), trans. Richard Howard (New York: Noonday Press, 1989), 6.

This feeling of forgetting knowledge and starting fresh came in handy later as equipment for loving abstract art, that other great site of wonderful alienation. But first I passed through the study of Japanese language and calligraphy.

Calligraphy is a composite of drawing + writing: like writing, it's done with a brush and ink on a blank background; like drawing, it's a visual language based on shape, gesture, and tonality; and, like drawing, it's usually done on a blank surface, a negative space that is taken into consideration in its overall composition. The scale of drawing, like writing, is generally based on the size of the tool, which means usually that it fits into your hand, though any body part could really do the mark-making, from the foot to the hair. (The eighth-century Chinese calligrapher Zhang Xu, known as Mad Zhang, famously drew with his hair while drunk; 1300 years later the Bahamian-born artist Janine Antoni thought of doing the same thing in her 1993 piece, *Loving Care*.)

Kanji is an aggregate of ideograms and phonemes, to which calligraphy adds the writer's own personal style, their signature, to an already-composite situation of picture + text, image + not-image. A glut of calligraphy-based painting emerged in postwar American art, especially in New York. When asked what "painterly painting" was, De Kooning said bluntly, "it's done with a *brush*."[9] Generations of painters have had the calligraphic urge to tilt their brushes against their surfaces like writing tools, making asemiotic squiggles, slashes, stains and

9. De Kooning, interview by Emile de Antonio for the film *Painters Painting* (1972), quoted in Richard Shiff, "Willem de Kooning: Same Change," in *Late Thoughts: Reflections on Artists and Composers at Work*, ed. Karen Painter and Thomas Crow (Los Angeles: Getty Research Institute, 2006), 37.

jots, from Franz Kline to Joan Mitchell to Ed Clark to Joan Snyder to Keith Haring to Joanne Greenbaum. Likewise, generations of writers and artists have had the reverse urge, to work against meaning in writing, to transcend meaning and change texts into calligraphic drawings—notably the artists from the Russian Cubo-Futurist movement, like Olga Rozanova and Aleksei Kruchenykh, who made little booklets and illustrated pages, as well as writers like Henri Michaud, Antonin Artaud, or the Lettrists Isidore Isou and Gabriel Pomerand, who explored how wide the boundaries of language can be. All of this enterprise of scrambling the space between painting/drawing/writing establishes the aliveness in the grain of the urge to write.

In ancient Asian calligraphic traditions, value was literally placed on life itself, on the breath, and how well the calligrapher incorporated breath itself into the work. François Cheng, in his book *Empty and Full: The Language of Chinese Painting*, writes that "failure to capture the breath is the very sign of mediocre painting."[10] The brush and ink in Chinese painting were described anthropomorphically, like intimate partners in a sexualized relationship; and the marks or lines of the calligraphy were alive in partnership with the paper like a three-way. The ink, brush, and paper worked together, or in a familial division of labor, and the artist was a kind of switchboard operator, hooking up lines between mark making and meaning-making.

Eventually, in a long twentieth-century mishmash, specific medium distinctions between painting and drawing were blurred, and I came into art when this attitude was at its height,

10. François Cheng, *Empty and Full: The Language of Chinese Painting* (1991), trans. Michael H. Koh (Boston & London: Shambhala, 1994), 63.

learning painting in college in the 1970s from older teachers who came from action painting and embraced this tradition of working from instinct and the body, and from younger artists whose work was organized around newer "time-based" forms like modern dance and performance art rather than the composition of easel paintings. But you can still look at what constitutes a drawerly thing to do. You could even decide, as I did, to be a draw-er, not a painter *per se*. Drawing, done at the site of that feverish thing, the body, was down and dirty. While painting requires canvas, oil paint, and expensive real estate, drawing, painting's cheaper cousin, can be done with nothing but paper and pencil. So it could be done in the throes of a complicated encounter between substance, surface, and your body, seeing what emerged in an improvisational activation of haptic relationships between eye and hand, hand and tool, body and surface, the page and whatever lay beyond the page. Drawing was residue, surplus, a mere recording of whatever happened while doing it. It was of-the-moment, fragile, yet flexible enough to be erased, redone, *détourné*, changed, and therefore available to fluidly go backwards in time as well as forward. A friend of mine stated that "drawing is the thinking of painting." That is true if you conceive of thinking as something that the body does, not just the brain. I always say I can only think with a pencil in my hand, and maybe draw-ers are people who need to feel something in their hand while thinking the world into existence. While making a drawing, you are looking down, out, across, around, and shifting boundaries between what is inside and what is outside, because as you draw your consciousness moves from inside your body toward the outside world, but you also simultaneously drag the outside world into your hand and eventually down onto your page. So drawing serves as a kind of liminal thinking machinery, a kinesthetic field where limits are felt, re-negotiated, re-presented. Drawing, then, is a living thing, a go-between, a genuine medium. As Jean-Luc Nancy writes in his book *The Pleasure in Drawing*, "all pleasure aims toward the coming together of an 'outside' and an 'inside' whose distinction and relation are opened by *feeling*."[11]

Drawing feels its way both backwards and forwards in time. Far from being a preparatory or preliminary act, a sketch or a rehearsal, drawing is a constant respooling of chronological time and circular time, where "knowing" builds up over time, but also loops back onto itself. Drawing is a particular time-based art because not only can you see self-reflexively from both inside and outside simultaneously, but you might also be thinking about something else entirely. Nancy's book constantly underlines process rather than the drawing object; he keeps saying that drawing is a form that is forming, a form opening by forming itself. There is an ecstatic pleasure of this simultaneity, this shimmer of something uncertain coming into being. All drawing is in this sense aleatory. You cannot memorize a drawing's steps and recreate them exactly: to draw is never the same as to simply repeat or copy, just as when you walk, each step is not a copy of the step that came before, but a new step. The drawing emerges from the body as the moments of time unspool, each with its own little pulse or heartbeat. Therefore all drawing is a kind of free drawing. Drawings are propositions, posited in the present, iterated by its ground, its literal soil, negative space.

11. Jean-Luc Nancy, *The Pleasure in Drawing* (2007), trans. Philip Armstrong (New York: Fordham University Press, 2013), 86.

John Berger wrote: “Drawings are only notes on paper . . . The secret is the paper.”[12] Paul Cézanne went even further: “There is no such thing as line, no such thing as modeling, there are only contrasts.”[13] So a drawing can boil down to nothing more than a kind of pulse in a forcefield.

Farber again, on “Termite art”: “A peculiar fact about termite tapeworm-fungus-moss art is that it goes always forward eating its own boundaries, and, likely as not, leaves nothing in its path other than signs of eager, industrious, unkempt activity.”[14] Recently I heard a scientist on the radio playing a field recording of a caterpillar scraping chlorophyll off a leaf. It was an almost inaudible, even-paced thrumming sound, and the scientist explained that in biology, this tiny rhythmic beat has the almost magical correlative effect on the plant to make it want to grow back more vigorously. I think drawing provides something similar on the human consciousness: seeing the network of lines, the strokes and rubbings of a handmade drawing brings us to the edge of something, a little bit of energy or moment of time unfurled. What we get from drawing is in its small particularities, and the tiny jolt of sensation, of desire, as the drawing communicates something across from one body to the other. Drawings, “whether graphic, vocal or colored, tactile or verbal,”[15] as Nancy says, come from out of the body and stay close to the language of the body that makes the drawing. This

12. John Berger, “To Take Paper, to Draw. A World through Lines,” in *Drawing Us In. How We Experience Visual Art*, ed. Deborah Chasman and Edna Chiang (Boston: Beacon Press, 2001), 123; first appeared in *Harper's Magazine* (September 1987).

13. See Maurice Denis, “Cézanne” (1907), trans. Roger Fry, *Burlington Magazine*, XVI (January–February 1910); reprinted in *Art in Theory, 1900–1990*, ed. Charles Harrison and Paul Wood (London: Blackwell, 1992), 40–47.

14. See Farber, “White Elephant Art vs. Termite Art,” *art. cit.*

15. Nancy, *The Pleasure in Drawing*, *op. cit.*, 39.

makes drawing an impulse-driven thing. Like living in a body, it can be seductive, secretive, dirty, fun, ragged, uncertain, full of bloopers and gas and emission and decomposition. In finding form, drawing *in*-forms, *re*-forms, and *trans*-forms.

Thinking about termites and beavers, I looked for an essay from the world of biology or entomology that would extend my ideas about drawing. I found one from 1995, by the philosopher and feminist theorist Elizabeth Grosz, entitled "Animal Sex: Libido as Desire and Death." In this essay, Grosz describes the actions of mating praying mantises. Her description of the sex lives of these strange insects perfectly matches what I would say about drawing, so I took a paragraph from her essay, and replaced the words "desire" or "sex" with the word "drawing." Here's how it goes: "DRAWING experience is uncertain, non-teleological, undirected. It upsets plans, intentions, resolutions; it defies a logic of expediency and the regimes of signification. Its temporality is neither one of development nor that of investment. Nor is it a system of recording or memory; the memory of 'what happened' may be open to reminiscence, but the intensity of DRAWING, the sensations of voluptuousness, the ache of DRAWING [has] to be revivified in order to be recalled."[16] Doesn't this sound just like that promiscuous thing that we all love, that thing called drawing? ♦

16. See Elizabeth Grosz, "Animal Sex: Libido as Desire and Death," in *Space, Time and Perversion. Essays on the Politics of Bodies* (New York: Routledge, 1995), 187–205.

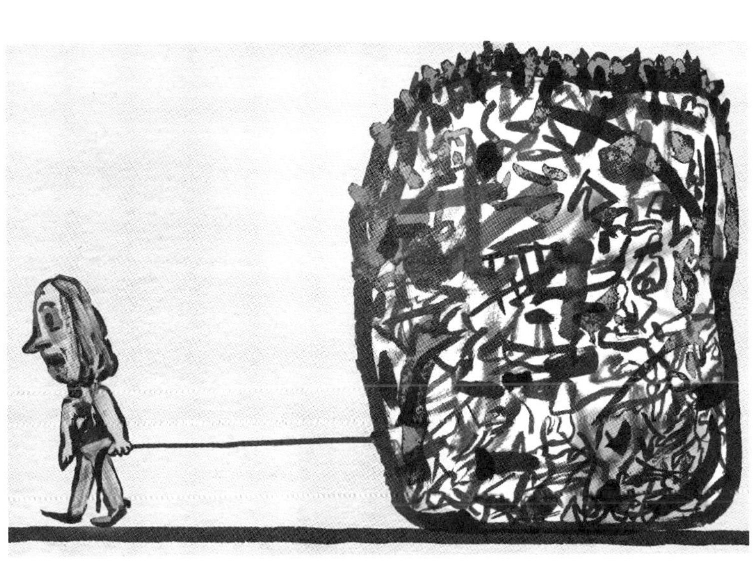

This essay was first published in The O.-G., *v. 14, "Shapes" (Spring 2020), produced in collaboration with the Museum of Modern Art (MoMA), New York, on the occasion of the exhibition* Artist's Choice: Amy Sillman—The Shape of Shape, *organized by Amy Sillman with Michelle Kuo and Jenny Harris. The exhibition—that comprised 71 works—opened on October 21, 2019; as MoMA temporarily closed to the public in spring 2020, due to the COVID-19, the exhibition was adapted to an online version, accompanied by this issue of* The O.-G.

Further Notes on Shape

O my body, make of me always a ~~man~~ PERSON who questions!
—FRANTZ FANON[1]

Part One

A couple of years ago, I realized that I barely knew anything about *shape*. I didn't even know where to begin reading about it, aside from a few books on still life and one on the psychology of perception. This was odd, because shape seems just as fundamental to vision as color—but there are tons of books about color: color theory, techniques, optics, dyes, rocks, rays, anthropology, RGB/CMYK, politics, etc. My favorite was always Josef Albers' *Interaction of Color*,[2] because it demonstrated that color is not absolute but relational, dependent on the beholder. And, it turns out, that's also the case with shape, since basically everything in the world is a shape. It's so mundane and so

1. Frantz Fanon, *Black Skin, White Masks* (1952), trans. Charles Lam Markmann (London: Pluto Press, 2008), 181. This is the last line of the book—Fanon's "final prayer." [Editors' note]

2. Josef Albers, *Interaction of Color: 50th Anniversary Edition* (New Haven & London: Yale University Press, 2013; first edition, 1963). See also "On Color," page 51 sq. [Editors' note]

ubiquitous: every edge, corner, blob, form, silhouette, or negative space is something you have to navigate to get through a room. If you think of shape as figure/ground, then every shape is a figure and the ground is the whole world. Shapes are how you make distinctions, get the lay of the land, or even tell time. And doesn't everyone have two shapes, really? The first is your own body, which you can't get out of, and the second is your shadow, which you can't get rid of. Shadows don't talk back and don't cast shadows themselves, they just do whatever you do and go wherever you go. (Only in noir films and spook houses do shadows really rise up with their own agency.) Your shadow is your personal shape, your silent companion, your own flat echo. It's worse than your ego, it's your creep—always just *there*. In the mythology of shadow, the devil can snip yours from your feet and make off with it, but if he takes it away, you miss it terribly. In a way, then, isn't your shadow kind of like your subjectivity?

So why was there comparatively little written about shape (let alone shadow)? There were books on geometry and topology, but those are fields based on shape *ideals*, not shape *experience*. But then again, maybe "experience" is TOO shiftily subjective to organize into a grand theory anyway, which would account for why the books I found on shape were mostly about gestalt and psychology. Maybe shape is just too vast to talk about, or resistant to language. Is it just that shape doesn't have a specific substance—a commodity—attached to it, like color and pigment? Is there a poetics of shape? (Is that what still life is?) Shapes are essential to modern art, but had there ever been a show specifically about the topic? And was there possibly even a kind of historical bias against shape, or against artists who work with shape, that had kept the whole subject a bit unspeakable, under wraps? Art historian Michael Fried wrote about shape, but he wrote about the issue of its "viability,"[3] setting up highbrow standards for success and failure among a handful of advanced modernists, whereas I wanted to look around elsewhere, and I didn't really care about sticking with the "advanced." Fried wrote about winners, but what about all those others creeping around in the shadows—the weirdos, outliers, those relegated to a B-list?

About that B-list: all artists I know carry with them their own personal genealogies. We all have a list of favorite, loveable, off-the-radar artists, the "off-modern," the knight's move, the not-quite-right, the great ones who never got credit. (To wit: artists especially loved the *Outliers* show, curated by Lynne Cooke at the National Gallery of Art in 2018.)[4] To use the painter / film critic Manny Farber's term, this is the realm of "Termite art" as opposed to "White Elephant art."[5] You know how everyone loves the Paleolithic? Wouldn't you take Antiquity over the Enlightenment any day? Like freak folk over stadium rock, doesn't everyone love the Sienese more than the Florentines, the Medieval over the Renaissance, going to the movies over trudging through hallways of history paintings?

3. "Frank Stella's new paintings investigate the viability of shape as such." Michael Fried, "Shape as Form: Frank Stella's Irregular Polygons" (1966), in *Art and Objecthood: Essays and Reviews* (Chicago: University of Chicago Press, 1998), 77.

4. *Outliers and American Vanguard Art*, National Gallery of Art, Washington, D.C., January 28–May 13, 2018.

5. See Manny Farber, "White Elephant Art vs. Termite Art," *Film Culture*, no. 27 (Winter 1962–63). In this essay (that deals mostly with film), Farber famously sets up a contrast between, on the one hand, works whose conception is bound to the notion of the masterpiece and that painfully seek meaningfulness, and on the other, works that are marked by a sense of the present and self-involvement, "[going] forward eating its own boundaries." See also "Some Notes on Drawing," pages 81 and 88. [Editors' note]

(I know I would, and I'm not alone: the one year I hung out with medievalists, they whispered conspiratorially, "You're one of us!" and assured me that mimesis was the most overrated thing in art history.) The B-list of art history, the artists' artists, the alt-canon, the roster of artists' favorites is an almost predictable one, running from James Ensor to Chaïm Soutine to Giorgio Morandi, Florine Stettheimer, Jacob Lawrence, Milton Avery, Myron Stout, Joseph E. Yoakum, Saul Steinberg, George Sugarman, Jack Youngerman, Alice Neel, Jim Nutt, Shirley Jaffe, Carol Rama, etc. And, I wondered, since MoMA seems like the ultimate White Elephant venue, who are the Termites in its storehouse? Who of the B-list was in the collection, and who might be missing entirely from view? Certainly some shape-artists are fully canonical—for example, Hans Arp or Henri Matisse or Frank Stella—but, given the apparent difficulty of discussing shape, did that make their work harder to be written about? Anyway, who doesn't love poking around in the holes of art history—there are so many cracks in it already that at some point it dawns on you that art history might just be *wrong*, or a mythic fiction made up by certain people, like a religion with its own Kool-Aid.

For a long time I'd been nurturing a second idea, too, that somehow got nested in these thoughts: that you could divide artists into draw-ers versus painters, and that draw-ers were a subculture. Painters, it seemed like, work from an idea, moving deductively from the big picture down to the details in order to produce or construct an image they have in mind. Draw-ers, on the other hand, work from the weeds outward, building up from particulars, inductively, scratching and pawing at their paper with tools the scale of their hands. OR maybe they never get to a bigger picture at all, but move sideways, abductively, from particular to particular. This made drawing itself seem like an activity not founded on logic but made up of contingencies, overflow, stray parts—a process that might be described as working blind, like a mole, or like a beaver building a thatch, rather than like someone with an overarching worldview. Maybe working this way means not necessarily making a truth-claim or asserting a "master" narrative, or getting anywhere at all. Maybe a practice like this by nature stays on the B-side, staying at the grassroots, in the inchoate experience of the body as the organ of knowing. (Incidentally, I've heard a million talks by artists who fall into the draw-er category, and when the Q-and-A gets to questions like "How do you begin?" or "How do you know when you're done?", they routinely claim that they don't know.)

So when I was invited to curate an "Artist's Choice" show at MoMA from their collection, I had all these things on my mind. I began burrowing in the dark, but with one single question like a lightbulb over my head: what would a show look like if *shape* prevailed over all other considerations—shape *over* language, shape *over* system, shape *over* nameable image or subject? I quickly accumulated an enormous list of 800 things. So there was no dearth of shapes, but I soon perceived MoMA's general conceptual tilt, which went in the other direction: works and movements related to language, organized around theories or systems, or having a manifesto seemed to WIN OUT over works without *a grand plan*. For example, Russian Constructivism over Symbolism, Minimalism over Pattern & Decoration, almost anything over Funk, etc. [NOTE: This wasn't an accident: for example, the founding director of MoMA, Alfred H. Barr, Jr. visited the Soviet Union in 1927 and met with members of the Russian avant-garde; he then famously championed their work in the 1936 MoMA show *Cubism and Abstract Art*, arguing that Russian Constructivism was critical to the very invention of abstraction. The radical strategy of *construction* was based on necessity, on rigorous system, and on truth to materials—a revolution in perception that would lead, in theory, to political revolution. —MICHELLE KUO] And to add to this, Aleksandr Rodchenko and Kazimir Malevich, who made great shapes, are well-known, but I wanted to look at harder-to-classify people. One of my all-time favorites, Aleksei Kruchenykh, *did* make it into the new MoMA hang, but what about great shape-makers and non-household names like Ksenia Ender and her family of painting teachers, Il'ia Zdanevich and Serge Charchoune, who left Russia for France, or the intriguing Mikhail Matiushin, who you just don't hear much about?

A lot of artists *don't* have a manifesto. Maybe someone who has worked all their life on shape-perception, shape-fussing, doesn't have what feels like a radical rhetoric to offer. I understand it this way: people who sit around *composing* are, in part, inheritors of a Romantic ideal. They are often artists in small rooms, sitting at tables or workbenches or in bedrooms, imagining, noodling, editing, and shaping with nothing much to go by but their own experiences. This still requires a room of one's own, time and space and the privilege, perhaps the detachment, to consider that one's own imagination is of enough value to warrant investigation. But in the avant-garde circles of the early twentieth century, the conditions required for contemplation were pitted against more worthy-seeming radical acts. Wassily Kandinsky, one of the few people who actually *did* try to write a book about shapes,[6] was excoriated by his colleagues for being part of a putrid older regime, and thrown out as head of the Institute of Artistic Culture in Moscow in 1921. As Varvara Stepanova wrote in 1920, "We, formalists and materialists, have decided to . . . to make an explosion by founding a special group for objective analysis, from which Kandinsky . . . [is] running away."[7] Kazimir Malevich said: "Freedom can be obtained only after our ideas about the organization of solids have been completely smashed."[8] To *compose* was to re-inscribe the values of a privatized bourgeois class, whereas to *construct* was the way to make a new society.

This image of radicality was inherited in modern Western art, consecrated by MoMA, incorporated into art history, and taught at art schools ever since. Even if the very idea of a singular position is precisely what early radicals would have argued against, the result was the establishment of an ideological position, and by implication a kind of conceptual backwardness or naiveté seemed to settle over those artists who did other things, even though their work might involve other skills, other criticalities, other forms of resistance. I was taught this in school in the 1970s and it has been repeated to me throughout my life as

6. See (of course) *Point and Line to Plane*, trans. Howard Dearstyne and Hilla Rebay (New York: Solomon R. Guggenheim Foundation, 1947); originally published in the Bauhausbücher series as *Punkt und Linie zur Fläche* (Munich: A. Langen, 1926). [Editors' note]

7. Varvara Stepanova's diary, November 25, 1920, quoted in Maria Gough, *The Artist as Producer: Russian Constructivism in Revolution* (Berkeley & Los Angeles: University of California Press, 2005), 32.

8. Kazimir Malevich, "Futurism-Suprematism" (unpublished manuscript, 1921), quoted in T. J. Clark, *Farewell to an Idea: Episodes from a History of Modernism* (New Haven & London: Yale University Press, 1999), 234.

a painter ever since. Sitting around fussing over shapes is not revolutionary. Still, everyone likes play, the carnivalesque, or some idea of care. Perhaps this was why certain shape-based-artists were beloved but described in slightly lesser terms: "personal," oddballs, offbeat, playful, etc. Morandi was "poetic," Eva Hesse made "eccentric abstraction," Alexander Calder, Sugarman, and Niki de Saint Phalle were "child-like," Forrest Bess was a hermit. Even Louise Bourgeois made the "kook" category, cemented in place by the famous Robert Mapplethorpe photograph of her with a sly smile and giant plaster phallus tucked under her arm. And you've never even heard of a million others who don't quite fit the mold, like the German artist/performer Lavinia Schulz, whose costume designs for her dances look like an earlier Mike Kelley. But how do we deal with the idea of a beloved B-list, or otherness, without mythologizing marginality itself?

Obviously these questions are political, the precise point of decades of struggle. Whom does history validate, deem a radical or a reactionary? In 2019, visiting London, I saw in two packed days four exhilarating survey shows by four great and formerly marginalized artists, three of them older women—Dorothea Tanning, Natalia Goncharova, and Lee Krasner—and the fourth the Guyana-born painter Frank Bowling.[9] What really struck me was how all these artists had been making work all along that was just as formally invested as it was politically savvy. When I say "formal," I mean they worked with

9. *Dorothea Tanning* was presented at Tate Modern, London, February 27–June 9, 2019; *Natalia Goncharova* at Tate Modern as well, June 6–September 8, 2019; *Lee Krasner: Living Colour* at Barbican Centre, London, May 30–September 1, 2019; and *Frank Bowling* at Tate Britain, London, May 31–August 26, 2019. [Editors' note]

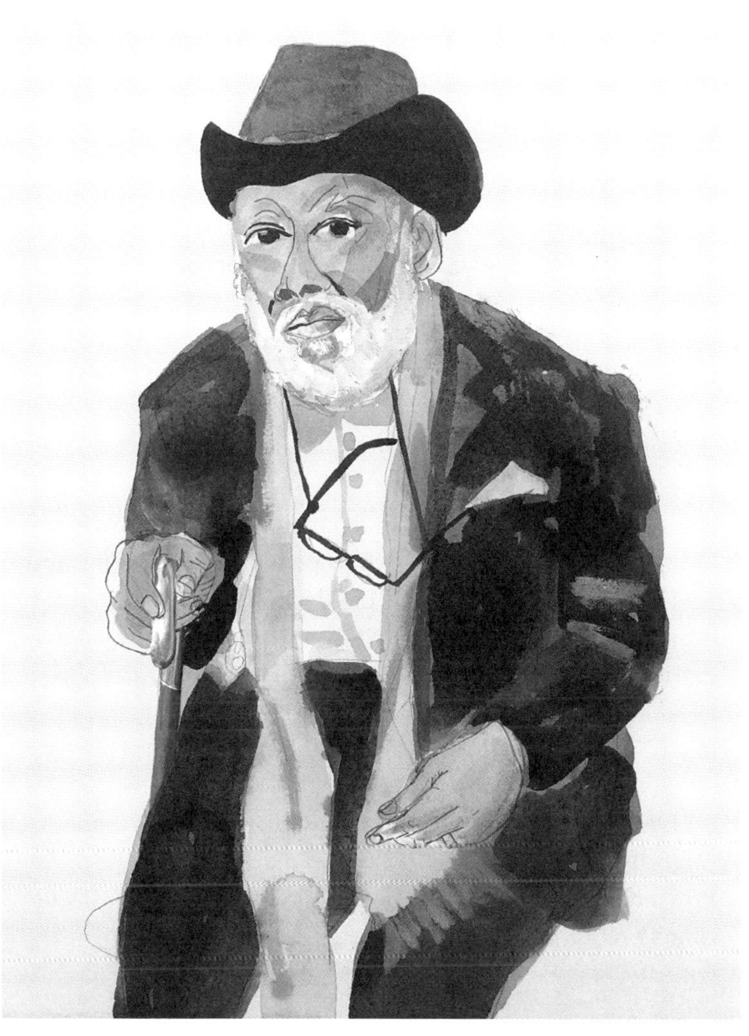

form permissively and inextricably from content, freely using new materials, synthetic pigments, polychromaticism, mixing painting with language, photo, craft, fabric, and mechanically produced shapes—and they all worked overtly with composition. What was common to their otherwise very different works was a refusal to separate art into "politics" vs. "form." Or you could say that all worked on the threshold between "language" and "body": as *speaking bodies*, to paraphrase Frantz Fanon, a body that questions. Their works all involved impure negotiations, ideals that are in conflict with pleasure, and intensities that are in dialectical relation with ideology.

Part Two

Poking around art history to find out more about these dynamics, I looked in particular at two contentious scenes of postwar art in the 1950s. The first: an English postwar abstract painting scene based in and around St. Ives, particularly the painters Patrick Heron and Prunella Clough.[10] The second: the chronicles of the conversation being held simultaneously in downtown New York City in the pages of the art magazine *It Is*.

St. Ives is a seaside outpost in Cornwall, and it was a hub for English artists with an outlier vibe, maybe equivalent to the Provincetown scene in America in the 1950s and '60s, a loose confederation of slightly lesser-known artists, including many fantastic shape-artists (Marlow Moss, Peter Lanyon, Patrick

10. Amy Sillman dedicated one issue of her zine to this scene: see *The O.-G.*, v. 13, "Shape" (Fall/Winter 2018–19), published on the occasion of her exhibition *Landline* at Camden Arts Centre, London, September 28, 2018–January 6, 2019. A short piece by Sillman on Clough also opens the book, *Prunella Clough: a small thing edgily*, ed. Camila McHugh (Berlin: Floating Opera Press, 2021). [Editors' note]

Heron, William Scott, Barbara Hepworth, and others). These artists were not self-declared radicals: they identified with the School of Paris and Cubism, and had some overlaps with the burgeoning American AbEx painting scene. Old photos from the 1950s show Clement Greenberg and Mark Rothko visiting and taking tea in the gardens of the St. Ives painters. Through these connections, the painter/critic Patrick Heron was appointed as London correspondent for the New York journal *Arts Digest*, and, in turn, I read about my favorite shape-y English painter, Prunella Clough, in texts by Heron and John Berger.

In the '50s, Berger praised Clough's work as "machine-life painting"[11] and in the '80s, Heron wrote that her paintings were "machines for seeing" that possessed an "electrifying strangeness."[12] Revisiting Clough's work recently, while thinking about shape and outliers, I was struck by how she seemed like a "conceptual painter" *avant la lettre*; her moves reminded me of the much later R. H. Quaytman and Charline von Heyl, with a bit of Shirley Jaffe thrown in. I researched Clough's life: born in 1919, she grew up in an artistic milieu, with a Sunday-poet father and a close relationship with her aunt, the designer/architect Eileen Gray. Clough was known and appreciated in her day, taught for many years at the Camberwell School of Arts & Crafts (now Camberwell College of Arts), had important shows, and won influential prizes. But she suffered (or perhaps occasionally enjoyed the privacy of) what I'd call a "female career." (Do I really have to explain that?) After her death in 1999, Clough fell into

11. See John Berger, "Machine-Life Painting," *New Statesman and Nation* 45, no. 1154, April 18, 1953.

12. See Patrick Heron, "Prunella Clough: Recent Paintings, 1980–89" (1989), in *Prunella Clough*, ed. Ben Tufnell, exh. cat. (London: Tate Britain, 2007).

relative obscurity, especially outside England, but I could now read her entire life's work as one long, persistent experiment with shape. In her paintings, she gleaned and transformed images from the world at large, taking the shapes of everything from vacuum packs to zigzags, animal skins to power grids, rock formations to plastic toys. She then emptied these forms out, flattening and rearranging them as fields of puzzling signs, working in an idiom that Berger deemed abstract still life. Clough exemplified a formal position to which I'd always been instinctively drawn: an artist whose work is radically quiet, innovative but slightly aloof, removed from its own time. Clough said she wanted to "say a small thing, edgily."[13]

For his part, Heron was a champion of slow, thoughtful paintings and anachronistic positions. He began in the '50s as an advocate of the New York School, but by the '60s he was increasingly critical of American painting's "systematic advance towards the extremes of flatness, emptiness and bigness."[14] By the '70s, he'd suffered a bad breakup with American art, and in 1974 Heron published the world's longest poison pen letter to the art world in a bilious three-day-in-a-row screed published in the *Guardian*. "As with the stock market, so with the art market: the client public . . . needs to have its confusing medley of investment choices weighed, determined, and given a reassuring 'objectivity.'"[15] Paradoxically, this champion of Picasso,

13. Prunella Clough's statement, "Seven Artists Tell Why They Paint," *Picture Post*, March 12, 1949, 15.

14. See Heron, "The Ascendancy of London in the Sixties," *Studio International* (December 1966); quoted in *Patrick Heron*, ed. Andrew Wilson and Sara Matson, exh. cat. (London: Pavilion Books, 2018).

15. Untitled essay, Arts section of *Guardian*, October 10, 1974, 12. The other parts of the essay were published on the October 11 and 12 issues of the *Guardian*. [Editors' note]

the old boys' club and its old-school values, came out swinging against the art world's clubbiness and money, advocating instead for a politics of the personal, and tying this ethical process to the work of composition, to the realm of intimacy, care, and feelings. For Heron, this kind of art-making was a form of resistance in itself: "Even the crankiest, wobbliest pots, the lumpiest cloth and the dottiest pictures are all effective in one single respect: that they register *protest*."[16]

Protest is what Heron calls the linkage of process and form, a call to arms against "success" and a commitment to craft and the handmade, to fussy details, editing, glitches, attention to small-bore problems, embodied work, like managing the weight and density of a painting, or struggling with its edges. And this struggle is a metaphor for working against collapse, for art as a kind of non-alienated labor rendered in the delicate intricacies of surface, color, layers. I recognized this earlier attitude I had picked up at art school in the '70s, too, both from old-school AbExers and from feminists and queers. It is an attitude that circles back to that theory I was nursing about marginalized versus top-down processes, about draw-ers versus painters.

I had a hunch that this all connected with the postwar scene in America. So I went to the MoMA library to dig out all six issues of *It Is*, the artist-edited magazine from the '50s.[17] It was a contentious grab-bag of musings, exhortations, and even

16. Heron, "Submerged Rhythm: A Potter's Aesthetic," in *The Changing Forms of Art* (New York: Noonday Press, 1955), 61–62.

17. *It Is: A Magazine for Abstract Art* was published in New York by Second Half Publishing; the first five issues were published between 1958 and 1960, and the last one in 1965, after a four year gap. [Editors' note]

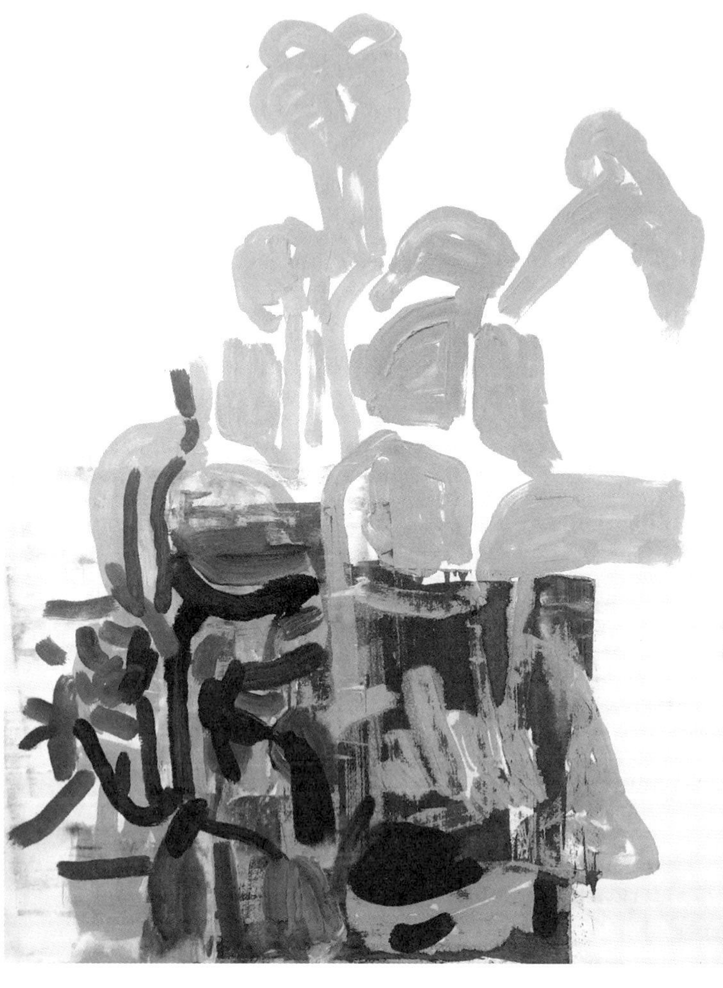

nonsense, with a soul-searching intro to each issue by the magazine's editor, the sculptor Phillip G. Pavia. I wanted to see how shape was tackled by the artists who hung out at the 8th Street Club in New York and literally got into fistfights about the artist's responsibilities to form and politics.[18] Their problems were not with *composition* vs. *construction*, but with subject matter, which lay somewhere between public nuisance and felony (depending on who was talking). In a panel discussion from 1960, Ad Reinhardt squabbled over it with Philip Guston and Jack Tworkov, with Reinhardt declaring, "Good artists have no need for content, nor any shape or form," and Guston and Tworkov retorting that such an idea was ridiculous, and that painting was merely the adjustment of impurities.[19] From the first issue in spring 1958, Pavia set out the central dilemma as something he called "The Problem." Pavia's concerns surpassed the simple binaries of construction vs. composition, or form vs. content: the studio was a total struggle, and artists were engaged in a kind of existential wrestling match just by making art, posing ur-questions like *what are we doing here, why*, and *how*?[20]

As Pavia lays it out, drawing is the answer to The Problem. By "drawing," he didn't mean a preparatory act or rehearsal, a sketch, doodle, plan, or cartoon. Drawing was a mythic and materialist form of engagement, the bones of thinking itself, the tool for stripping down, the exercise and the equipment

18. The 8th Street Club was founded in fall 1949 in a loft at 39 East 8th Street, New York by a group of artists committed to abstraction, as a self-organized "club" where meetings, parties, talks, and lectures were held. Pavia was informally the person in charge of the Club. [Editors' note]

19. Philip Guston, Robert Motherwell, Ad Reinhardt, Harold Rosenberg, and Jack Tworkov, "The Philadelphia Panel," *It Is*, no. 5 (Spring 1960), 34–38.

20. See Phillip G. Pavia, "A Manifesto-In-Progress. The Problem as the Subject-matter," *It Is*, no. 1 (Spring 1958), 2–5.

for getting into shape. Drawing was "attitudes become form" way before that phrase existed: it was a dialectical procedure of propositions made, then scraped down, then rebuilt. In Pavia's view, only through "drawing, drawing and more drawing"[21] could an artist perform a vanguard inquiry. A large group of American artists worked with this belief system, a group that included women as well as men. Reinhardt, Tworkov, Motherwell, William Baziotes, Helen Frankenthaler, Guston, Mercedes Matter, and many others of their generation saw drawing as part-event and part-object, a way to look both inward and outward. They traced their roots back to James Joyce and Cézanne, and attended the New York Studio School on 8th Street to learn the techniques of Cézanne-ist space. Their lineage included heavy hitters like Arshile Gorky, Lee Krasner, and Willem de Kooning, but also stretched out to experimental new forms and B-sides, like modern dancers whose own bodies assumed the shapes of The Problem. Matter described this as working with "resistance and dissension," echoing Heron's idea of how form registers protest.[22] Drawing imparted both an attitude and a sense of time, which they called "freshness" rather than "newness" (Motherwell likened "freshness" to fresh air, or the opposite of artificially packaged meat).[23] In other words, something surprising, never completed, never final, but circular, a looping act in a continuous present, like the one Robert Morris later wrote about as "altered daily,"[24] or the one Gertrude

21. *Ibid.*, 3.

22. See Mercedes Matter, "Drawing," *It Is*, no. 3 (Winter–Spring 1959), 12.

23. Guston et al., "The Philadelphia Panel," *art. cit.*, 35–36.

24. See Robert Morris' installation, *Continuous Project Altered Daily*, at the Leo Castelli Warehouse, New York, March 1–22, 1969. The work inspired Yvonne Rainer to initiate a piece with the same title, evolving over 12 months from 1969–70. [Editors' note]

Stein described decades earlier in "Composition As Explanation": "A continuous present is a continuous present."[25] I'd also argue that the looping, repetitive sensibility of the comic, of slapstick, of drawing cartoons and funnies, is probably not that far from this shape impulse (something Reinhardt knew well).

Reading *It Is*, it struck me that my show at MoMA was as much about drawing as it was about shape. Almost all the artists in the show flirted with modernism's dictates (as shadows do) by employing flattened spaces and slices of form, but they arrived at their hybrid composition-constructions through procedures that were often uncertain, experimental, close to the body, driven by urges. All follow the urge to define a figure against a ground with pencil or tool, making form both privately and publicly, in rooms where the clock is ticking and the newscasts are coming in on the radio, grappling with the reality of looking both within and outside, from the consciousness of one's studio table to the political demonstrations and jobs and greater relations that everyone is negotiating. Maybe artists fussing over shapes are not the same people we first think of when we think of political art. But they make lumpen form that registers protest, they make gestures of care and repair, or they merely try to beam out an electrifyingly personal and strange signal that wakes up the receiver for a moment—one weird moment that could shift the sense of things, and thereby alter the world, even if only slightly. This sounds urgent to me.

Can we really afford *not* to think about composition now, when we seem surrounded by the *de*composition and deformation of

25. Gertrude Stein, "Composition as Explanation" (1926), in *A Stein Reader*, ed. Ulla E. Dydo (Evanston, IL: Northwestern University Press, 1993), 498.

bodies and social structures? We are in a time of political catastrophe, destitution, doom. We live in a heightened sense-time that feels like it's both spinning backward and outward simultaneously, when the terror and tragic palpability of political events and illness provokes a constant sense of precipice, of exhaustion, the rattling of ongoing crisis. It's so weird and extreme that, if not tragic, it's like a kind of horrible slapstick, something veering way out of control. The scholar Lauren Berlant has written brilliantly about comedy as a "tableau of repair . . . that's always teetering on reversal, exposure, and collapse back into raveling and unraveling at once," and as "flooding . . . flow, then blockage, then flow"; "anxiety to be taken in as a successful arrangement of ill-fitting parts."[26] To be honest, this is exactly how I have always seen painting, or art in general: as the sensation of ill-fitting parts. That points back to the idea of shapes, and the intimacy of parts and labor, of staying close to the body and working from the grassroots, from detail to fussy detail. And in trimming, adjusting, editing, messing around with shapes, one works not only from the individual expressive body, but with body politics—a politics that, like shapes, includes *everything*: our ambiguities, our dysphoria, our skin tones, our histories and consciousnesses, all the uncertainties, dangers, ugliness, eroticism, absence—the nights, fogs, dreams, and depth perceptions of our rhythms, losses, laments, and even our senses of humor, as we approach a kind of limit condition at the dead end of seriousness. ♦

26. Lauren Berlant, "Humorlessness (Three Monologues and A Hairpiece)," *Critical Inquiry*, no. 43 (Winter 2017), 307 and 313.

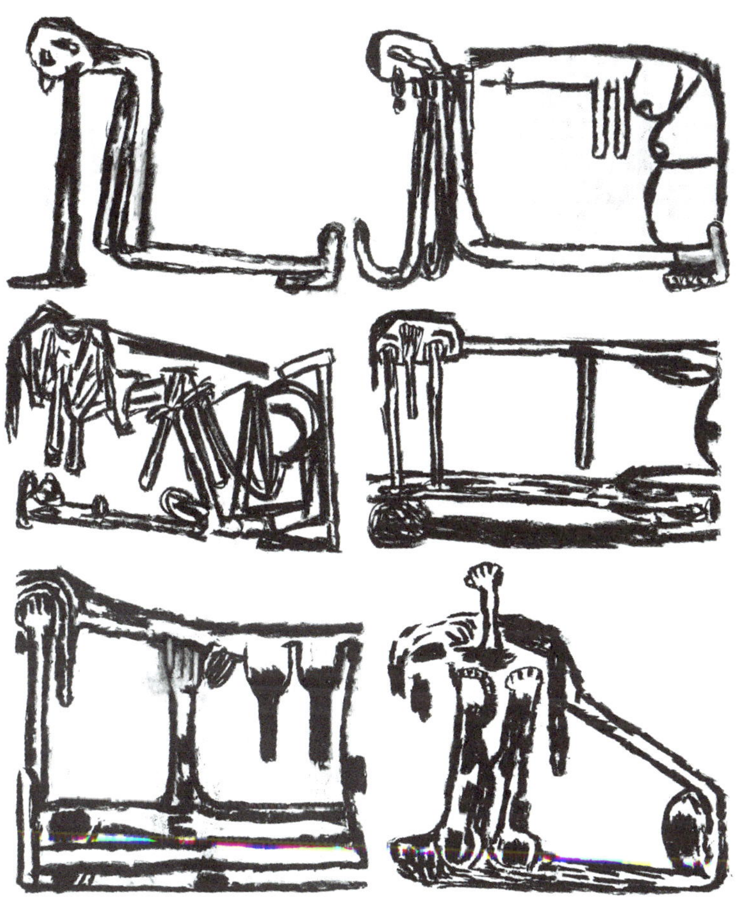

A. MEANING OF SYMBOLS

1. BODY PARTS / PART-OBJECTS

(1) = one arm with a small roll of fat under it, and one breast (signifies the split between one side of the body and the other – or an unnatural psychodynamic splitting-feeling)
[note: no nipple is customary — bulges and shapes are more important than specific functional parts, or parts-to-the-whole]

(2) = two legs, on a slant – (signifies the enlarged psychic experience of encountering a giant but neutered body – perhaps the legs of a parent removed at a young age — someone in pants – also the TWONESS of legs – the fact that the BODY itself contains the uncanny repetition of form (TWINNING)

(3) = EITHER two Legs with no apparent sexual organs – OR – one leg with a Large phallus above it – The continuation of which is a new jointed Body part – which is in itself conceived either as:

a) a calf of a leg (But which has bulbous exaggerations)
b) a column or prosthetic section of a leg
c) a RAY coming out of the sun (which relates to an ejaculatory expulsion from the phallus) (or A Kind of reference to A PHANTOM LIMB)
d) an EYE WHICH SEES (perspective is therefore (somehow) related to spray.

a)

b)

c)

[THIS WHOLE IDEA IS VERY IMPORTANT BECAUSE IN IT, ANYTHING CONICAL IS A DOUBLE-SYMBOL — ONE FOR A "VANISHING POINT" AND THE OTHER FOR A POINT OF EXPULSION — one going away and one emerging.]

→ (which leads to the idea of the VISIBLE and the other which relates to the INVISIBLE)

From The O.-G., *v. 1, "Zum Gegenstand / Das Diagram" (2009), published for Amy Sillman's solo show* Zum Gegenstand *at Carlier-Gebauer, Berlin, May 2–June 13, 2009.*

B. INTERRUPTIONS - ERASURES - TIME FUNCTIONS

4

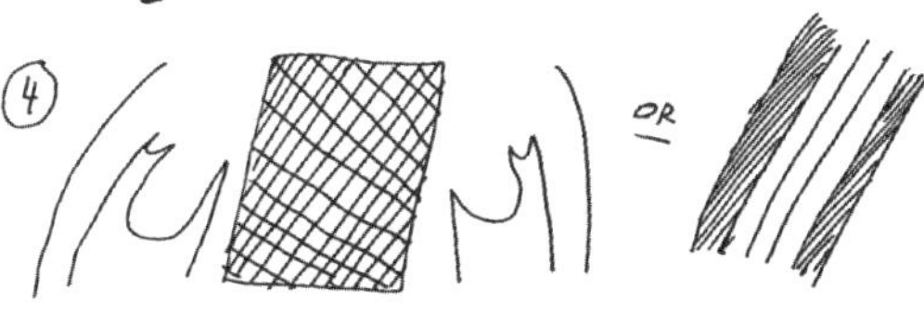

= something that comes between -

(anything that interupts OR comes between does a few things at once:

A) creates a THIRDNESS

(there B) implies a phallus or a false-phallus

fore —) c) implies a PHANTOM LIMB, a psychically-constructed presence-of-absence (this may be related to the idea of a FETISH)

→ this also means BLOCKED ENERGY, STILTED, STUMPED OR MADE-ASYMETRICAL BODY (i.e. a kind of ~~uncanny made~~ canny made uncanny -

(I.E, the two-ness of body/uncanny made into a stumped one-ness)

5

THE APOPHATIC

= something scratched out or scribbled over -

willfull act of erasure, anger, negation, disgust, hate, embarassment, shame, or a wish to make invisible or to obliterate.

6

- something that REACHES ACROSS A PAGE, which usually goes from lower left to upper right, and which therefore indicates BOTH TIME and SPACE -

- it goes "back" into "perspective" (if the picture plane is "front" -)

and,

- it goes "back" into "time" (if the foreground is "present" -)

- And furthermore if the front of the painting is the "here" and "now" then to move something behind OR back moves it into the MEMORY (OR "PAST")

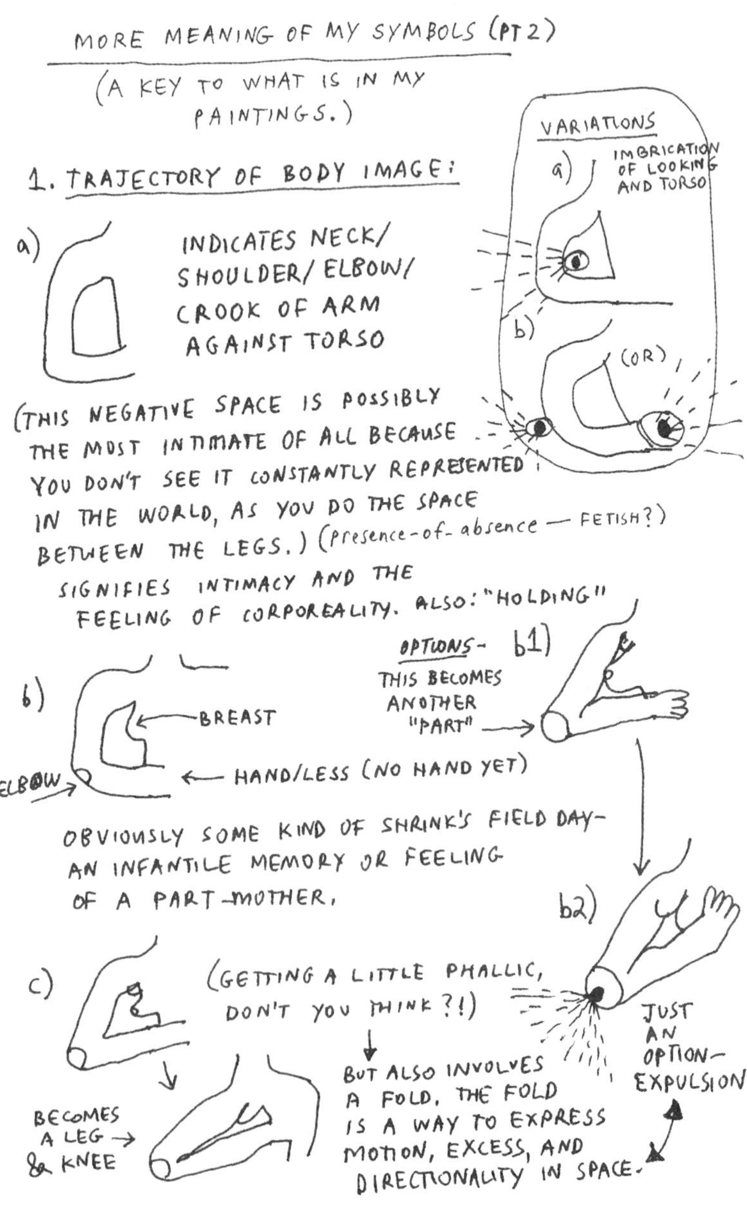

From The O.-G., *v. 1–2, "American Edition" (2009), published for an exhibition by Amy Sillman at the Sikkema Jenkins booth, Art Basel Miami Beach, 2009.*

2. IMPLICATIONS OF TWINNING, DOUBLING, +/OR ERASING:

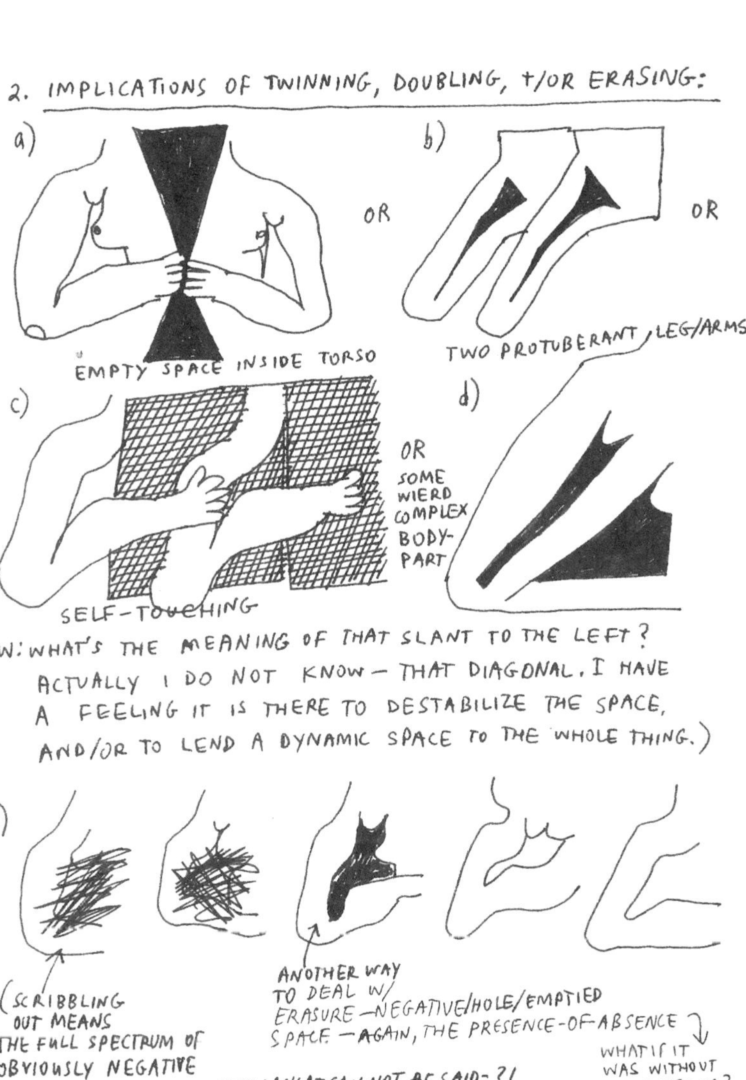

(BTW: WHAT'S THE MEANING OF THAT SLANT TO THE LEFT? ACTUALLY I DO NOT KNOW — THAT DIAGONAL. I HAVE A FEELING IT IS THERE TO DESTABILIZE THE SPACE, AND/OR TO LEND A DYNAMIC SPACE TO THE WHOLE THING.)

(SCRIBBLING OUT MEANS THE FULL SPECTRUM OF OBVIOUSLY NEGATIVE EMOTIONS →) ⟵ ALSO: WHAT CAN NOT BE SAID-?!

ANOTHER WAY TO DEAL W/ ERASURE — NEGATIVE/HOLE/EMPTIED SPACE — AGAIN, THE PRESENCE-OF-ABSENCE

WHAT IF IT WAS WITHOUT THE EXTERIOR? SHAPE-ALONE?

SHADOW-SILHOUETTE- WHAT IF IN COLOR?

THIS SHAPE-IN-COLOR THAT REACHES ACROSS A PAGE FROM LEFT TO RIGHT COULD BE A SPACE-TIME OBJECT — OR A RAINBOW.

This text was written for The O.-G., *v. 11, "Metamorphoses" (Winter 2017), a zine Amy Sillman published in conjunction with the exhibition,* Amy Sillman: After Metamorphoses *at The Drawing Center, New York, January 20–March 19, 2017. A slightly different version was published on Artforum.com, on January 5, 2017, as part of a series of artists' responses to the election of Donald Trump as President of the United States on November 8, 2016. In her introduction to the text on Artforum.com, Sillman noted: "I was shocked by the election results, and had no idea how to process the news or how to make art for a show. . . . But a zine is a fast and furious public/private form of address, so I just knew I should write* something, *a kind of letter, about how to approach this new time."*

Unpresidented Times

A few years ago we were knocked out by the first line of Ovid's *Metamorphoses*: "I want to speak about bodies changed into new forms."[1] What the hell? That was written in, like, the year 8 AD, and it's still totally up our alley. So we read the book and made a list of the changes that occur in order in it: this became our "score" for an almost readymade animation, *After Metamorphoses*.[2] We are on the same wavelength with Ovid in at least one sense: total fascination with a structuring logic of endless change.

But meanwhile, this work is being shown, dismayingly, on the literal eve of the inauguration of you-know-who, and we face a global rise of neo-fascism.[3] Changes have to be made—but

1. "*In nova fert animus mutatas dicere formas / Corpora.*" Ovid, *The Metamorphosis*, trans. Anthony S. Kline (s.l.: Poetry in Translation, 2000), 9.

2. The "animated drawing" *After Metamorphoses* (video animation with iPad drawings, 5 min, 2015–16; music by Wibke Tiarks) was shown at The Drawing Center in the exhibition of the same title. It followed three animation videos by Amy Sillman: *Triscuits* (video with ink drawings, 12 min, 2011–12); *Pinky's Rule*, in collaboration with poet Charles Bernstein (video animation with iPhone drawings, 7 min, 2011); and *Draft of a Voice-Over for Split-Screen Video Loop*, on a poem by Lisa Robertson (video animation with iPhone drawings, 6 min, 2012). [Editors' note]

3. The opening night at The Drawing Center was on January 19, 2017; the inauguration of the 45th President of the United States happened on January 20. In case you didn't get it. [Editors' note]

how exactly to refuse and resist now as artists, citizens, educators, people? How to split up one's time, how to keep going to the studio—to go defiantly, or not go at all? Should we not be in shows, not sell work, not go to art fairs? (Call us old-fashioned, but personally we really don't understand why artists go to art fairs anyway—networking while someone sells your work from a booth, don't get why this is a thing—but whatever . . .) What changes are required? What do we do right now? Our desires are conflicting and ill-fitting. Do we re-tool our art practices, or just keep going, pulling the anger into the work? What would be the point of abstraction now? Our immediate answer was refusal, but does that refusal actually function to do anything except turn us against our own methods? After a few days the answer seemed to be: don't allow them to take away your sense of humor. Keep making that awkward, slow, funny, unaesthetic, non-product-oriented, skeptical, passionate, complicated thing you want to make with all your heart, *and with the anger*. Gang up with your friends. Don't be silenced. We enjoyed the weirdness of the Agnes Martin show at the Guggenheim Museum (an artist whom we respect, but at whose altar we have never worshipped),[4] and noticed that we could see it better—rather than asking why Martin was making abstract paintings of grids during times of political crisis. The work beamed out its stoic, clear-headed, purposeful, classical, stubborn weirdness . . . good qualities even in those extreme times. But we don't care about "the grid"—we are committed to something different: something scrappy but complex, earnest but smart, ironic but not cynical—a strange FORM! We're not

4. *Agnes Martin*, presented at the Solomon R. Guggenheim Museum, New York, October 7, 2016–January 11, 2017.

in it for the money and *WE'RE NOT MONEY*. We're not coins of the realm, easily identified by our denominations; we're definitely not thin paper currency meant to slip inside a wallet. We don't make sense. We have rough edges and contradictions. What the fuck is "thing theory" anyway—we're like things that *talk back*.[5] Where is emancipation located? Should we split our time between art and politics? Is art enough? Is it possible that our work, our love, our beliefs, our symbolic gestures, our senses of humor, can amount to any meaningful resistance? Does resistance come in different lengths: a long game and a short game? Does everyone have to do it the same way? We haven't figured it out but we love art that offers *change above all*: insistent, unremitting change that won't resolve into finality or finesse. We don't know quite what to do but the qualities that mean something have shifted: knowingness is out, a goddamn "good" painting seems irrelevant, smug . . . we don't need someone to tell us which painting is "better." Fuck that. Plowshares? We need to sharpen our senses of humor into swords. We need to know what we love and what to toss out. We need to not normalize. We need to stick together. We have no answers. We have questions. We send these questions out with love to the people with whom we're walking home. We refuse to be stripped of our complications.

With love,
Amy

5. Thing theory defines things in opposition with objects, by the suspension of function or use, and proposes to study their agency—focusing, so to say, on the liberation of things from human constraints. [Editors' note]

Amy Sillman made the works on the following pages in response to an invitation to participate in the project DYKWTCA (Do You Know Where The Children Are?), *initiated by activists and visual artists Mary Ellen Carroll and Lucas Michael. More than 100 artists were invited to make works that incorporated excerpts of interviews with children who were separated from their families and detained by the US federal government. These interviews, conducted in June 2019, were made available through the public awareness initiative, Project Amplify.*

At its peak in 2019, the number of unaccompanied children (UACs) seeking asylum in America who were separated from their families and detained by the US government reached over 14,000 children. The detention of these children and the conditions in which they were being kept was illegal, inhumane, and still has no end in sight. Per the Health and Human Services report from January 31, 2022, 746 minors are confirmed as having been previously subjected to the Migration Protection Protocols policy (according to which they and their families were forced to remain in Mexico) and to have subsequently re-entered the US alone.

The works made for DYKWTCA *were shown in the 2020 exhibition,* When We First Arrived . . ., *curated by Ruth Noack and on view at The Corner at Whitman-Walker in Washington, D.C. The artworks were sold in a random access online sale, with 100% of the proceeds benefiting four organizations: Innovation Law Lab, Team Brownsville, Safe Passage Project with Terra Firma. More information about the immigration situation in the US can be found on their websites: www.innovationlawlab.org; www.teambrownsville.org; www.safepassageproject.org; www.terrafirma.nyc.*

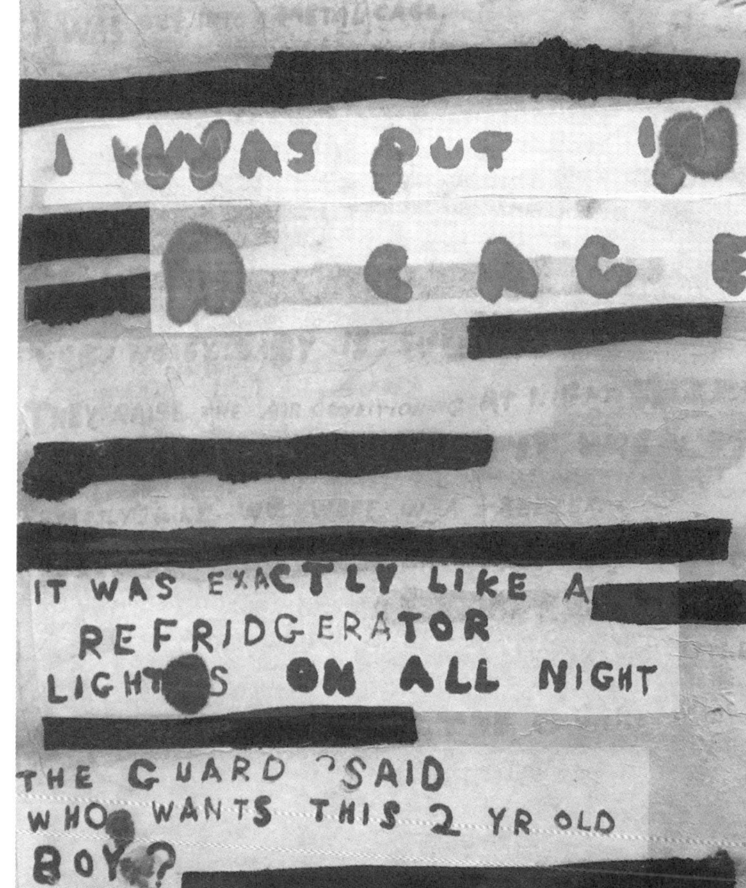
I WAS PUT IN
A CAGE
IT WAS EXACTLY LIKE A
REFRIDGERATOR
LIGHTS ON ALL NIGHT
THE GUARD SAID
WHO WANTS THIS 2 YR OLD
BOY?
HE NEVER SPEAKS
I HAD TO
CRUMPLE INTO A BALL

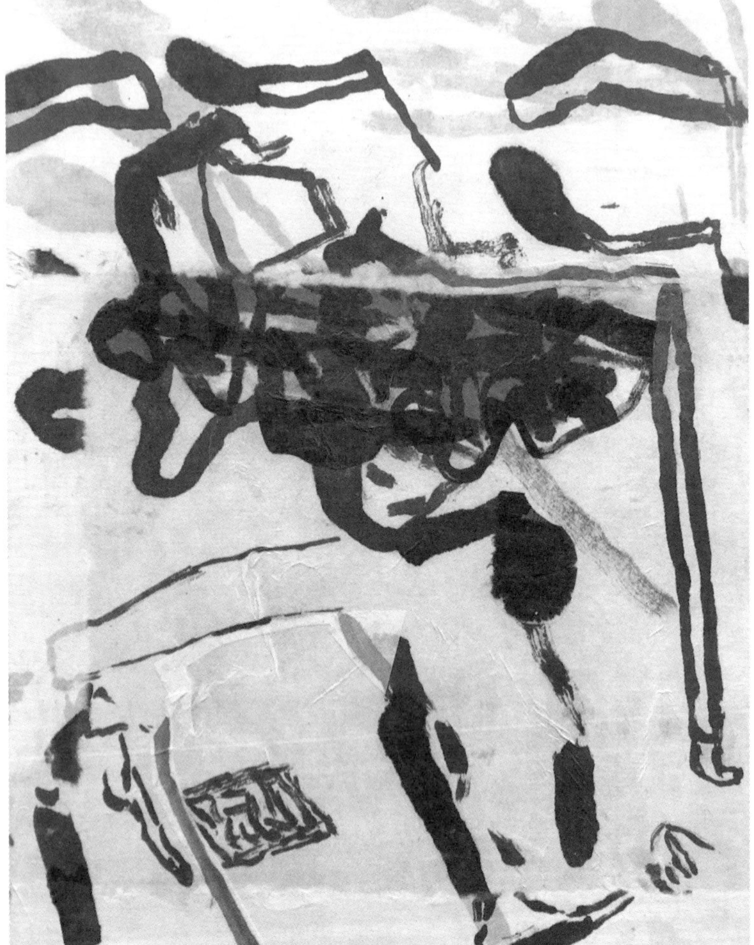

I WAS PUT
A CAGE WITH 60 OTHERS IN
IT'S EXACTLY LIKE A FREEZER

I HAD TO CRUMPLE UP INTO A
BALL

THE GUARD SAID WHO WANTS
THIS 2-YEAR OLD BOY?
HE NEVER SPEAKS.

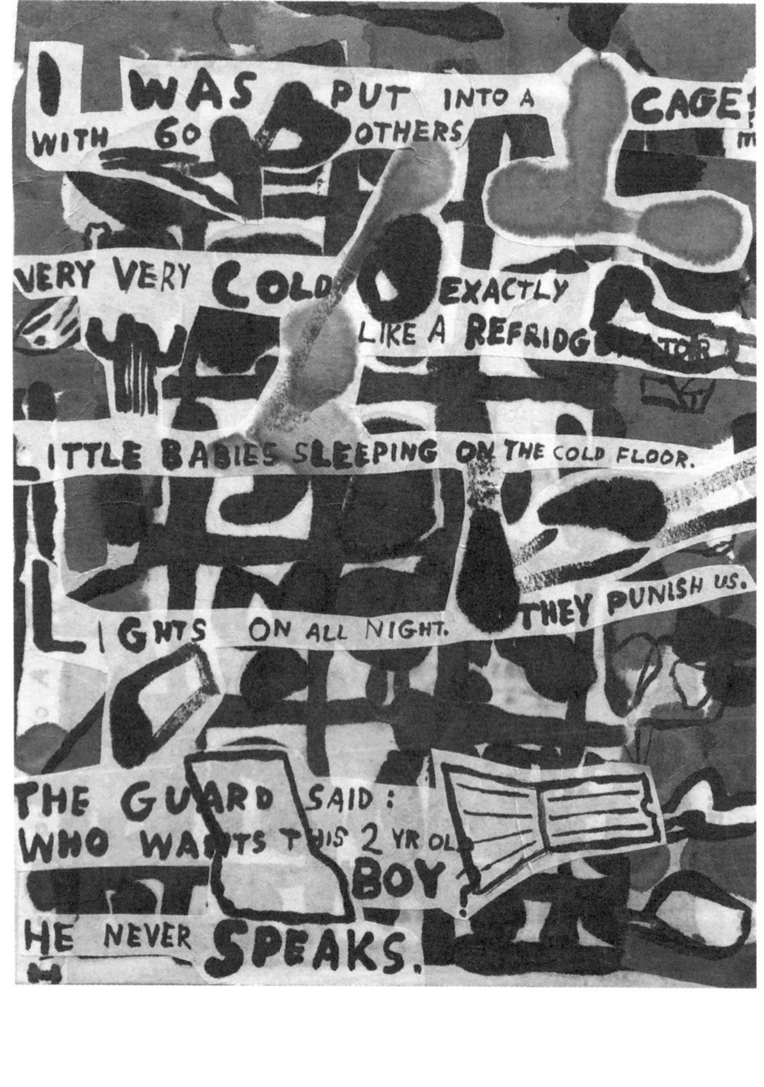
I WAS PUT INTO A CAGE!
WITH 60 OTHERS
VERY VERY COLD EXACTLY
LIKE A REFRIDG
LITTLE BABIES SLEEPING ON THE COLD FLOOR.
LIGHTS ON ALL NIGHT.
THEY PUNISH US.
THE GUARD SAID:
WHO WANTS THIS 2 YR OLD
BOY?
HE NEVER SPEAKS.

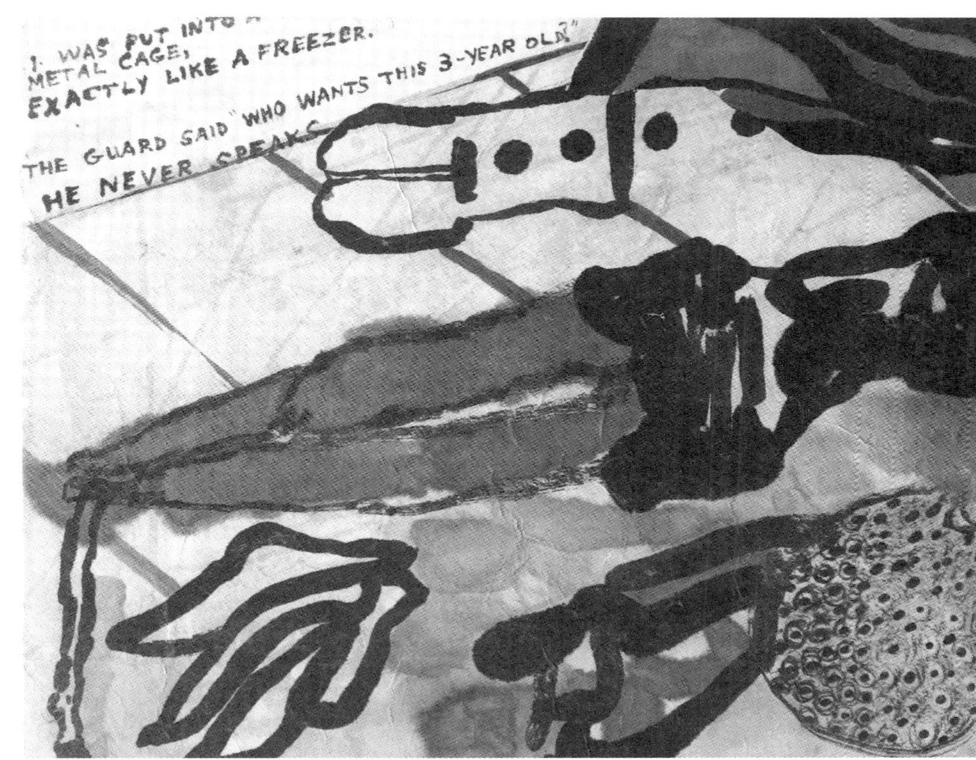
I WAS PUT INTO A
METAL CAGE,
EXACTLY LIKE A FREEZER.
THE GUARD SAID "WHO WANTS THIS 3-YEAR OLD?"
HE NEVER SPEAKS

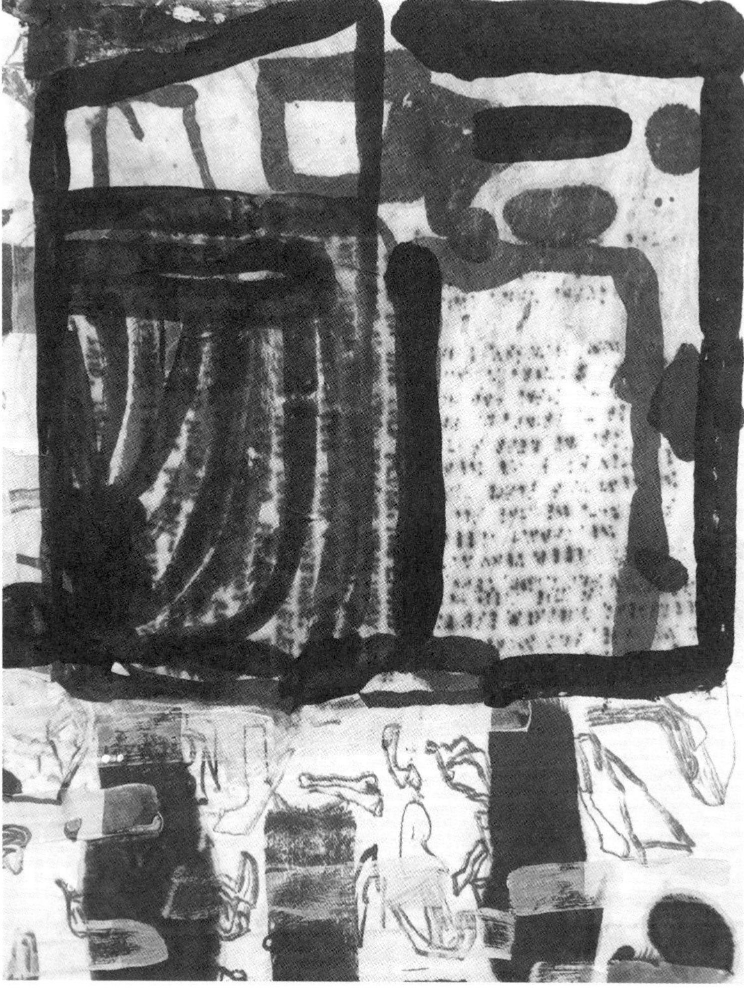

I WAS PUT IN A
CAGE, WITH 60 OTHERS.
IT WAS EXACTLY LIKE A
REFRIDGERATOR.
THE GUARD SAID WHO
WANTS THIS 2-YR-OLD BOY?
HE NEVER SPEAKS.

I HAD TO CRUMPLE UP
INTO A BALL.

This essay was originally published in Artforum *49, no. 10 (Summer 2011), as part of a feature section titled, "Acting Out: The Ab-Ex Effect," conceived in the aftermath of the exhibition,* Abstract Expressionist New York *at the Museum of Modern Art, New York, October 3, 2010–April 25, 2011.*

Throughout the text Sillman uses "AbEx" as the nickname for Abstract Expressionism.

AbEx and Disco Balls: In Defense of Abstract Expressionism II

I feel kind of bad for AbEx. At sixty-something, the old bird's gotten the gimlet eye from just about everybody: it's vulgar, it's the phallocracy, it's nothing but an empty trophy, it celebrates bourgeois subjectivity, it's a Cold-War CIA front, and, well, basically, expression's really embarrassing. A dandy wouldn't be caught dead doing something as earnest as struggling, or channeling jazz with his arms. An *old-style* dandy, at least. T. J. Clark's 1994 text "In Defense of Abstract Expressionism" made AbEx's connection to the vulgar perfectly clear, rendering it bathetic in all its ridiculous glory.[1] But his writing touches only briefly on one of the most important aspects of this vulgarity—the fact that it is gendered. And it's precisely the gender vicissitudes of AbEx that I'd like to examine here: I would draw the dotted line back to 1964, when Susan Sontag mined this

1. See T. J. Clark, "In Defense of Abstract Expressionism," *October* 69 (Summer 1994), 22–48. In this untimely essay the art historian proposes an alternative interpretation of Abstract Expressionism, against its modernist eulogists and its postmodernist adversaries as well. Clark notably insists on the "vulgarity" of Abstract Expressionism, an ambivalent quality that he links to the notions of taste and subjectivity, to the question of the body, and to class issues. See also "Some Notes on John Chamberlain," pages 214–15. [Editors' note]

territory in her "Notes on 'Camp,'" declaring: "The old-style dandy hated vulgarity. The new-style dandy, the lover of Camp, appreciates vulgarity."[2]

How is it, exactly, that we forgot the new-style dandy? How is it that, despite the complexity of AbEx, its reputation has boiled down to the worst kind of gender essentialism? Its detractors would have it that the whole kit and caboodle is nothing but bad politics steel-welded around a chassis of machismo—that the paint stroke, the very use of the arm, is equivalent to a phallic spurt, to Jackson Pollock whipping out his dick and pissing in Peggy Guggenheim's fireplace. (This sexualized reading is itself, of course, a reversal of Clement Greenberg's earlier—but no less testosterone-driven—notion of AbEx as a pure and transcendent optical experience.) Meanwhile, AbEx's legacy presents us with a tangle of still more gender clichés, a strange

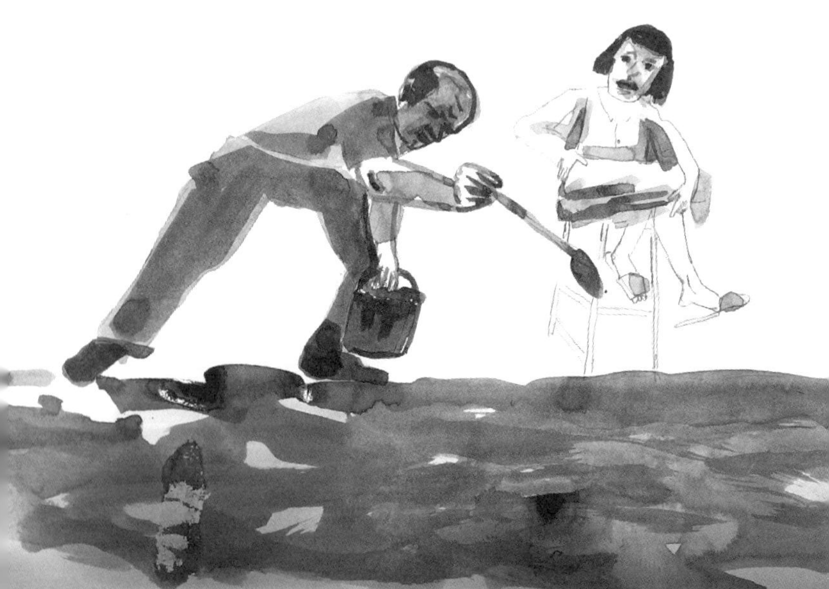

terrain inhabited by fake-dude-women like Lee Krasner and Joan Mitchell, wielding their paint sticks like cowboys; and Pollock and Willem de Kooning operating as phallic she-males, working from their innermost intuitive feelings, a "feminization" that introduces another twist in this essentialist logic.

I thought we were past simple butch and femme role-playing by now. The current acronym for queers alone has stretched out to six options, LGBTQQ (lesbian, gay, bi, trans, queer, and questioning).[3] But with AbEx, it's always the same old, same old. This kind of simplification wipes away the possibility of looking at all the really interesting vagaries and conflicts within AbEx, like the fact that Krasner actually *was* man enough to bend hot-pink planes with her bare hands, and the fact that Mitchell was no feminist. Maybe it's possible for me to look at AbEx through rose-colored glasses because I came along too late to actually have to date any of those artists and I didn't have to sit on their laps at the Cedar Tavern.[4] I'm sure they all probably *were* horrible in real life. But I'm still gung ho about looking at their work and finding in it tenderness, tragedy, contingency, and inverted color schemes; I'm still inspired by the rhetorical position of speaking from the gut, Walt Whitman style, by the AbExers' work with reimagined relations between parts and between forces, Gertrude Stein style, but in an anti-Platonic, improvisational, real-time mode of production.

2. Susan Sontag, "Notes on 'Camp,'" in *Against Interpretation and Other Essays* (New York: Farrar, Straus & Giroux, 1966), 289; first appeared in *Partisan Review* 31, no. 4 (Fall 1964), 515–30.

3. Up-to-date term is LGBTTTQQIAA (lesbian, gay, bisexual, transgender, transsexual, two-spirit, queer, questioning, intersex, asexual, ally) or LGBTQIA2+. [Editors' note]

4. The Cedar Tavern was a bar and restaurant at the Eastern edge of Greenwich Village; in the 1950s, it was a hangout of many prominent Abstract Expressionist painters—who lived or had their studios nearby—and Beat writers and poets. [Editors' note]

Meanwhile, the only people worse than AbEx's haters are its defenders. And I agree, it makes you feel a little clammy to clap your arm around a form that seems to wear an American flag on its lapel, that is constantly being hailed as an American Triumph on public television and in bus shelters. AbEx: Saw it? Loved it! Got the tote bag—and it came with a free Charlie Parker record! (Poor old jazz, it's going through the same thing, but AbEx seems to have suffered a fate worse than jazz: jazz with money.) Of course, we know that the original AbExers were also horrified by the coming institutionalization. Art historian Serge Guilbaut cites a letter by Clyfford Still to his dealer, Betty Parsons, as early as 1948, in which Still writes: "Men like Soby, Greenberg, Barr, etc. . . . are to be categorically rejected."[5] Once AbEx was thoroughly under glass, everyone involved tried to get away as fast as possible, either by acting irascible, or by fouling the "high" of AbEx by courting the low, or by screwing up the "Ab" part by embedding it with pictures, or by just moving away from New York. This evacuation left the entire property available for simplistic, ideological essentializing. But it also left us with a very nice plot of foreclosed real estate that, several generations later, younger artists could make use of—especially those who were supposedly barred from the place to begin with, as if we were squatters in Peggy Guggenheim's house.

5. Serge Guilbaut, *How New York Stole the Idea of Modern Art: Abstract Expressionism, Freedom and the Cold War*, trans. Arthur Goldhammer (Chicago: University of Chicago Press, 1983), 201. Alfred J. Barr was the first director of MoMA; James Thrall Soby was an art collector, and a curator at MoMA. Guilbaut's book shows how the international success of Abstract Expressionism was closely linked to the postwar political and economical context, insofar as supporting the avant-garde and putting it to ideological use was an integral part of the cultural Cold War. [Editors' note]

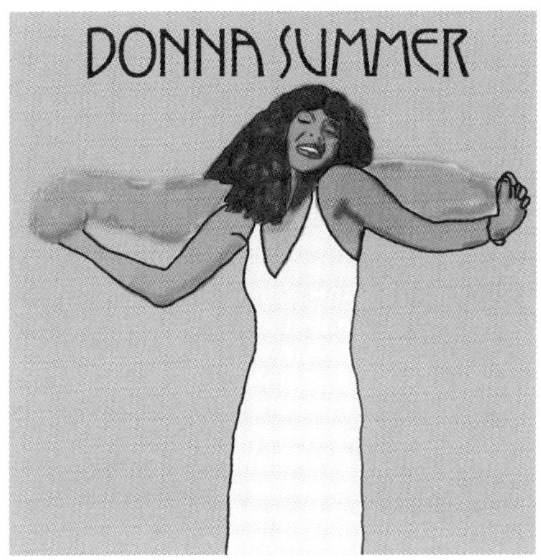

Actually, the fear and loathing that AbEx arouses reminds me of that '70s punk button DISCO SUCKS. But disco *didn't* suck, and the injunction against it was perhaps more about homophobia and racism than about musical taste. What do you think they were listening to over at the Stonewall, anyway?[6] I spent my youth at bars watching high femmes in gold-belted slacks do the hustle with thick-waisted girls in mullets. They *liked* Donna Summer. Disco wasn't just a corporate shill; it was the soundtrack for getting down with your marginalized pals.

Throughout the same decade that disco did or didn't suck, the mid-'70s to mid-'80s (before the birth of homocore clubs, where they played both punk *and* dance music), I was a little undergrad painter-girl with a can of turpentine and a kneaded

6. The Stonewall Inn—the gay bar that was the site of the Stonewall riots of 1969—opened in 1967 at 51–53 Christopher Street; not that many blocks from the Cedar Tavern actually, that was still in operation then, at 83 University Place. [Editors' note]

eraser, an earnest student with an old-guard teacher. If you attended art school in New York in those days, your teacher would most likely be one of these former AbEx party members who had gotten himself a teaching gig. I didn't like him, and he warned me in return that I would certainly fail as an artist, but he was the only painter I knew, and he played Sinatra in class and called AbEx "action painting," which sounded exciting, and I wanted to have his clichés and eat them, too. AbEx was great, in other words, because it involved erasure. And Robert Rauschenberg's *Erased de Kooning Drawing* (1953) was a downright lifestyle choice, a physical embodiment of uncertainty, a praxis of doubt. It wasn't just a defacement of AbEx—it was a recognition that a kind of negative capability was already there in De Kooning.

It pains me to admit how naive I was then, how little of the big theoretical picture I could see, but at the time, the art school system was completely divided between those who studied critical theory and those who studied studio art and painting. They studied the Soviet avant-gardes. *We* studied the School of Paris. Sontag's famous list of qualities for camp—"the exaggerated, the fantastic, the passionate, and the naive"[7]—were the ones we studio students leaned on, and we were alive to the slightly outmoded feeling of AbEx, its sense of condemnation and failure. We didn't really know much about art, but we knew what we liked. AbEx was something grand lying around the dollar bin at the secondhand-book store, something to be looked at, cut up, and used as material, like punk music or underground movies or other sloppy, enthusiastic things made by a lineage of

7. Sontag, "Notes on 'Camp,'" *op. cit.*, 283.

do-it-yourselfers and refuseniks with a youthful combination of awareness and naiveté. As Sontag says: "In naive, or pure, Camp, the essential element is seriousness, a seriousness that fails."[8]

I wouldn't call this negative way of working deskilling,[9] though; it was more like an active embrace of the aesthetics of awkwardness, struggle, nonsense, contingency. For better or worse, we didn't glean the mythic aspect of AbEx, and therefore we were not limited by its ironclad gender identity, its masculine grandiosity. Since we weren't selling anything ourselves anyway, the commodity critique of AbEx was also lost on us. I didn't want to limit myself with the critical rhetoric around either disco or AbEx, because to do so would leave me—where? You have to ask yourself, what do you want to do all day and night, and how are you going to make a painting practice, anyway? AbEx was simply one technique of the body for those dedicated to the handmade, a way to throw shit down, mess shit up, and perform aggressive erasures and dialectical interrogations. If you want to make something with your hands, if you want the body to lead the mind and not the other way around, you may likely end up in the aisle of the cultural supermarket that includes painterly materials and AbEx delivery systems: canvas, oil sticks, fat paint brushes, rags, trowels, scrapers, mops, sponges, buckets, and drop cloths. And it's not that you're going to be working "like" an AbExer, but that the tools themselves will mandate a certain phenomenology of making that emanates from shapes, stains, spills, and smudges.

8. *Id.*
9. On this notion, see "Shit Happens," note 5, page 164. [Editors' note]

Later on, I could perform a more sophisticated maneuver by doubling back on and reversing the injunction against AbEx, performing a critique of the critique, one that allowed me to appropriate AbEx as a practice back into my own hands and twist it into the form I wanted it to assume. Camp is alive to a sense of the doubled, and same-old-same-old AbEx was ripe for double *détournement*. This reclamation amounted to reversing the reversal of its fortune.

AbEx was a form for the defiant optimism of our own remodeled and low-to-the-ground culture. Its very sentimentality and ridiculousness proposed a rich archive for future "conceptual painting," painting that used the bad taste and bad values of the art world as springboards rather than as end points. Like disco, AbEx could be reclaimed as a Foucauldian materialist-discursive practice, connected to the "bodies, functions, physiological processes, sensations and pleasures" described in Michel Foucault's *History of Sexuality*.[10]

And, of course, AbEx was already undone while I was still studying it. Andy Warhol's piss paintings, Robert Morris' cut felt, and Rauschenberg's erasure—all the now canonical work that came on the heels of AbEx—had been doing a thorough job of referencing, reversing, and emptying out AbEx's rhetoric and techniques. But still, in art-making, things don't necessarily happen in order. They happen simultaneously, or they circle around and repeat, or they are incomplete, or people realize things backward or feel a fondness for forms of obsolescence. In fact, while AbEx was already debased, deskilled, materialized, and sexualized twenty years after it began, other people

10. Michel Foucault, *The History of Sexuality. Volume I: An Introduction*, trans. Robert Hurley (New York: Pantheon Books, 1978), 151–52.

had been working adjacent to it all along, or just recently realized that they might do so. You might kill the father, but you don't have to kill the already dead uncle.

So I don't find it odd that AbEx practices have now been vitally reinvigorated by a queered connection of the vulgar and the camp. Many artists—not least of them women and queers—are currently re-complicating the terrain of gestural, messy, physical, chromatic, embodied, handmade practices. I would argue that this is because AbEx already *had* something to do with the politics of the body, and that it was all the more tempting once it seemed to have been shut down by its own rhetoric, rendered mythically straight and male in quotation marks. AbEx's own deterioration into cliché was a ripe ground, a double-edged challenge that, to quote Sontag again, "arouses a necessary sympathy."[11] AbEx was like a big old straight guy who had gone gay.

Speaking of rolling in my grave, when I saw Leidy Churchman's videos, I thought, I can die now; my message to the world has been received, and gestural art is in good hands again. In Churchman's "painting treatment" pieces, which were shown in *Greater New York* at MoMA PS1,[12] Churchman and associate Anna Rosen performed improvisational acts of painting upon

11. "This is why so many of the objects prized by Camp taste are old-fashioned, out-of-date, *démodé*. It's not a love of the old as such. It's simply that the process of aging or deterioration provides the necessary detachment—or arouses a necessary sympathy." Sontag, "Notes on 'Camp,'" *op. cit.*, 285.

12. *Painting Treatments* (two-channel color video, 20 min, looped, 2010) was exhibited, along with an installation of paintings by Churchman, in the 2010 edition of the quinquennial exhibition *Greater New York*. The two videos in *Painting Treatments* show different performances, and have different durations, so that their pairing isn't fixed. [Editors' note]

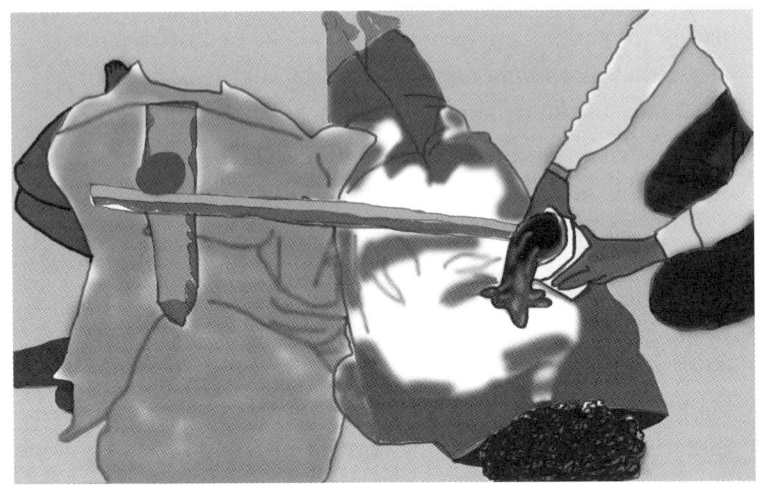

friends' bodies, flaunting carnal pleasures via one of their most commonplace forms—as "treatments," as in spa treatments. Even critical theorists like a rubdown, right? We who participated in the creation of Churchman's videos were invited to come in, take off our clothes, and lie down under towels while Churchman-plus-Rosen did things to us. As they worked horizontally across our prone bodies, we lay languorously in an increasingly spaced-out, spa-like state of mind, and the camera recorded a cropped image of the proceedings, *Flaming Creatures* style. They did excessive, polychromatic things to our bodies, like dipping a banana into a can of orchid-lavender paint and pressing it against our asses, or dragging a rake with green and brown paint in its combs across our legs, or letting chrome-yellow enamel dribble off random pieces of plywood onto the smalls of our backs, or tossing some green-gray grit on us.

As Sontag noted, "Camp is a *tender* feeling,"[13] and it was nice being prodded, touched, stroked, and dribbled on with the warmish liquidity of paint. And meanwhile, the supposedly manly, authoritative, and triumphant discourse of AbEx had been displaced, not by a parodic emasculation or a cynical recapitulation, but with a newly enthusiastic form of painting as a nudie activity. It was a way to spend the afternoon with your friends and do something both tender and sloppy. I actually liked the "paintings" formally, too, not so much the towels themselves, which were fairly arbitrary (and which Churchman judiciously did not exhibit), but the way the painting process and detritus looked on the video monitor, in a state of discarded materialist excess. These images reminded me of the films of Austrian filmmaker Kurt Kren, whose orgiastic and abject throw-downs are more fertile than they are masculine, with images of feathers, milk, eggs, and plant life falling on breasts, nipples, and lips. And that put me in mind of the party scene in Kenneth Anger's *Scorpio Rising*, and then the sight of Carolee Schneemann in her holster wielding crayons on the walls in her '70s performance *Up to and Including Her Limits*. The list goes on: most of Paul Thek's work, Yayoi Kusama's '60s film where she is shown painting dots on everything from her friend's back to the surface of a pond, Hélio Oiticica's street actions and *Parangolés*, etc. All of these are acts of sensuous and repellent aggression by artists responding to the AbEx vocabulary, artists for whom AbEx was essential as a reclaimed template for their own promiscuous and unessentialized surplus. And these works are slightly different from, say, Warhol making his piss

13. Sontag, "Notes on 'Camp,'" *op. cit.*, 292.

paintings, because they seek not just to mimic or dismantle AbEx, leaving it as a sardonically depleted trace of itself, but to engage it in a dialectical conversation, with a sense of inquisitiveness, openness, and even the risk of actual delight—not undoing but redoing, if from an oblique angle. Even now, as we pass into a time when pencil smudges themselves are an increasingly exoticized thing of the past, the world is still tactile and material. To touch it is to know it.

Things have changed, but I still hear AbEx characterized fairly regularly as just a bunch of macho gestures, now collapsed and out of use. It reminds me of an occasion about a decade ago, when I went to give a talk somewhere in America at a university art department that was populated by self-described "content-driven" students and faculty. "Content-driven" was how you said it back then—meaning, "we work with politics and abhor the (supposed) emptiness of formalism." So I naturally insisted extra hard on the *form* in my work, taking a certain perverse pleasure in describing myself as a kind of formalist. This didn't go over too well with the crowd, who became audibly disgruntled. Afterward, though, some bearded guys came up to say how much they *loved* the talk, and when they walked away, I found out that they were trans men. It was funny for me to realize that the people who loved my formalist rap the most were the ones who had gone the furthest in their own personal lives to make specific changes to their own forms. We were both committed to an idea of the inseparability of form and content, and we were working with their interactions, their malleability; if you could change one side, you could change the other. This made for a funny alliance—funny ha-ha and funny peculiar. ♦

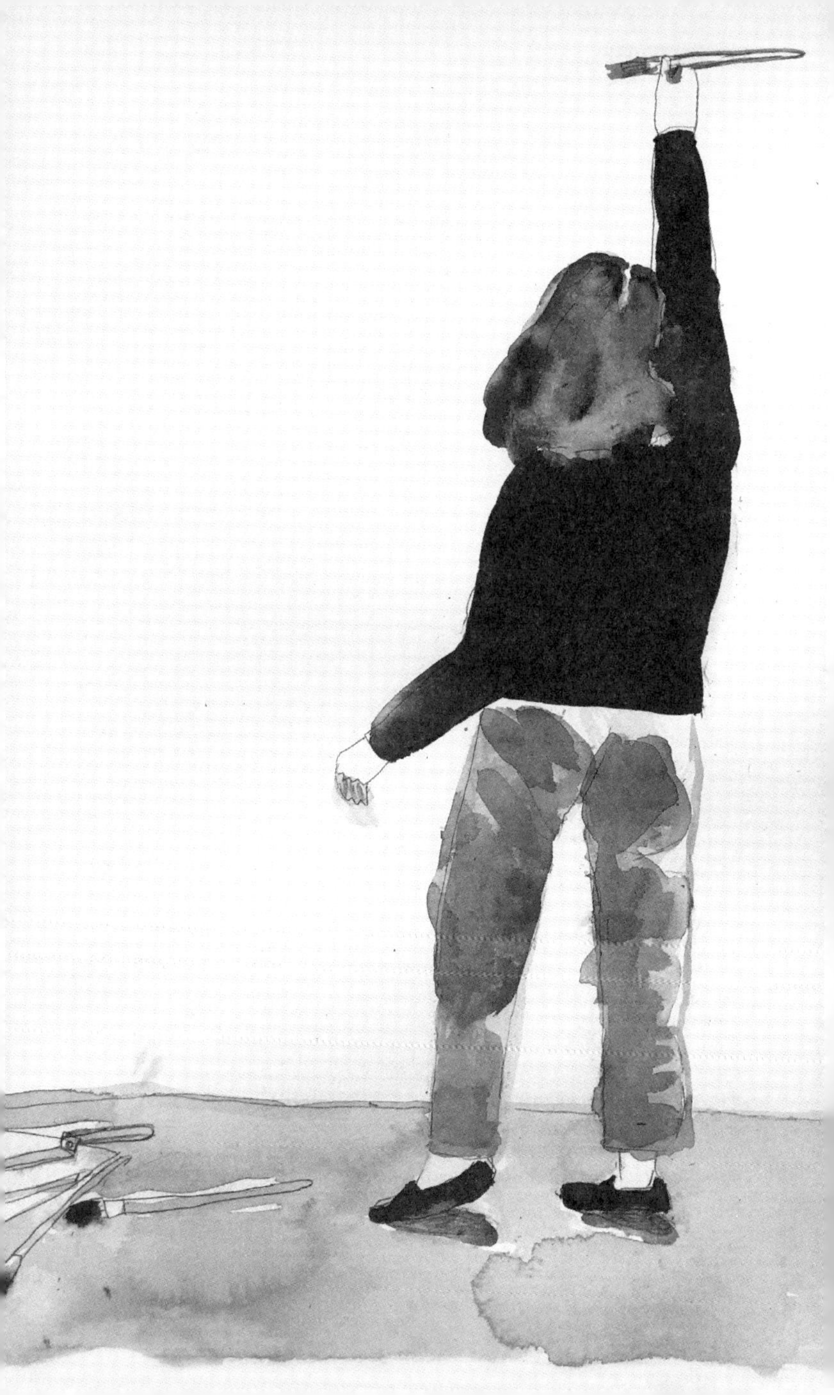

This is the third, previously unpublished version of “an endlessly revised essay,” that Amy Sillman started in 2009, during a residency at the American Academy in Berlin. The first version was published in The O.-G., *v. 1, “Zum Gegenstand / Das Diagram” (2009), that Amy Sillman elaborated in parallel with her solo exhibition,* Zum Gegenstand *at Carlier-Gebauer, Berlin, May 2–June 13, 2009; the second in* The O.-G., *v. 1–2, “American Edition” (2009), published on the occasion of a presentation of drawings by Sillman at the Sikkema Jenkins booth, Art Basel Miami Beach, 2009.*

Notes on the Diagram

In this sense, a subject is "a nothingness, a void, which exists." (Lacan)
—SLAVOJ ŽIŽEK, *ORGANS WITHOUT BODIES*[1]

A virtual particle is one that has borrowed energy from the vacuum, briefly shimmering into existence literally from nothing.
—DAVID KAISER, *AMERICAN SCIENTIST MAGAZINE*[2]

The Higgs boson is apparently the most powerful particle on Earth, but it has never been seen.
—WIKIPEDIA ARTICLE ON THE HIGGS BOSON[3]

Look who thinks he's nothing.
—PUNCH LINE OF A JOKE ABOUT A PRIEST AND A JEW

One paints when there is nothing else to do. After everything else is done, has been "taken care of", *one can take up the brush.*
—AD REINHARDT, "ROUTINE EXTREMISM"[4]

I can swim like everyone else, only I have a better memory than them. I have not forgotten my former inability to swim. But since I have not forgotten it, my ability to swim is of no avail and in the end I cannot swim.
—FRANZ KAFKA[5]

What happens next? Of course, I don't know.
It's appropriate to pause and say that the writer is one who, embarking upon a task, does not know what to do.
—DONALD BARTHELME, "NOT-KNOWING"[6]

1. Slavoj Žižek, *Organs without Bodies: On Deleuze and Consequences* (Abingdon-on-Thames, UK: Routledge, 2015), 61.

2. David Kaiser, "Physics and Feynman's Diagrams," *American Scientist* 93, no. 2 (March–April 2005), 157. The article focuses on the role, in quantum electrodynamics, of the diagrams introduced by physicist Richard Feynman in 1948 to represent the mathematical expressions describing the interactions of subatomic particles. [Editors' note]

3. Obsolete joke! (Dating back to 2009 and the second version of the essay.) The Higgs boson was eventually "seen" at CERN in 2012. [Editors' note]

4. Ad Reinhardt, "Routine Extremism" (n.d.), in *Art-as-Art. The Selected Writings of Ad Reinhardt*, ed. Barbara Rose (Berkeley & Los Angeles: University of California Press, 1991; first edition, New York: Viking Press, 1975), 127.

5. Franz Kafka, *Dearest Father: Stories and Other Writings*, trans. Ernst David Kaiser and Eithne Wilkins (New York: Schocken Books, 1954), 297.

6. Donald Barthelme, *Not-Knowing: The Essays and Interviews of Donald Barthelme*, ed. Kim Herzinger (New York: Random House, 1997), 11.

In 2009, I got a grant to live in Berlin, arriving with barely any German language under my belt. An old friend, who seemed in the know, warned me: "German is a *spatial* language." I have no sense of space, so it sounded ominous. I got what she meant fast at my first German lesson, when they said that in German you can't just ask "where?"—you have to specify where *to* or where *from*. And German grammar went on from there, a thicket of specificities. And German history was a veritable morass. I was an American: I hadn't read Hegel or Schlegel! But once I got into it, I went into an accelerating state of diagram fever, going a little crazy thinking about how everything in the world is a diagram. I took a seminar on diagrams at the Freie Universität with Danish diagram expert Frederik Stjernfelt[7]; I got new diagram study-buddies, my mind stretched out with increasingly dizzying interconnectivity; everything started to make a weird kind of sense, and I got it: *everything was related to everything else*. The Enlightenment, Romanticism, Symbolism, modernism, Bad Painting, it was all locatable on one big map. I also sheepishly realized that I was probably the *last* person to figure this out—that this diagram thing had already been laboriously theorized by many others. But thinking about the diagram liberated my work. Abstraction itself suddenly seemed like one big diagram of moving time and space. The process of making something go away from "realness" to abstraction seemed like a big memory-diagram—things seen and then registered in the mind's eye undergoing a process of being stripped clean, or becoming a bit tattered and distorted as they move off into

7. Frederik Stjernfelt is notably the author of *Diagrammatology: An Investigation on the Borderlines of Phenomenology, Ontology, and Semiotics* (Berlin: Springer, 2010). [Editors' note]

your past. I was planning an art show at the time, and I also thought, if everything is everything, then why not hang things all together: satirical diagrams next to figure studies next to abstract paintings? I would just need some way to explain it all, a kind of translation device. And what is a zine if not a slapdash chance to present one's own epiphanies? And what is a diagram, but a way of holding disparate ideas together?

So I began planning my exhibition with everything in it, from abstract paintings to comical seating diagrams,[8] to figure drawings to a zine on a table. Let jokes be paintings, paintings be memories, and memories be meaning. I decided to write an essay about diagrams for my first zine (and I've been slowly adding to it ever since).

Diagrams are great because you can put anything in them. No wonder they have been so useful for generations of kooks, mystics, Cubists, ecstatic poetics, Dadaists, Futurists, and weird scientists. A diagram is a perfect visual schema for posing impossible things, invisible forces, enigmas like the future—all posed as perfectly plausible vectors. The diagram even outdid the camera as the early twentieth century's best new thing because it could depict things in the universe that exceed the eye, like particles, waves, and quarks. A diagram's scale is endless. It can indicate how dwarfed we are by the universe, or how busy the microscopic world is, all mapped out on the back of some envelope. Tides, black holes, white dwarfs, red rings around Saturn, crazy particles, the waves of the Big Bang, all teleporting around in unstable ways, all this stuff and how it interacts

8. Sillman refers to the *Seating Charts* series she started then: see "Having a Voice," page 38, and the drawings reproduced pages 155–60. [Editors' note]

can appear equally on the diagram, democratically, like the pedestrians in Times Square or the people in a Saul Steinberg cartoon all walking around together. The diagram's arms, its vectors, embrace everything at once. Parts are not distinct from wholes, and divisions between aesthetic formats don't have to exist. Diagrams aren't medium-specific: everything is a continuum; everything is relational. In this sense a diagram is utopic, showing how things *should* or *might* go, re-envisioning things expansively, not merely describing them categorically. It can include contradictory grammars, fragments, part-objects, nouns *and* verbs, acts *and* objects. As a painter, I was on solid ground, then, because I already knew that paintings are both things *and* events. And one of the first things artists learn is that scale and size are different. Scale is relational, whereas size is just measurement. Likewise, a mere page in a notebook, a flimsy joke, a drag act, can change the world. My own life was altered definitively by the aesthetic detonating charge of a confessional 16mm George Kuchar film, *Hold Me While I'm Naked* (1966) in which an erstwhile filmmaker from Queens tries in vain to complete a porn film. It affected me way more than beholding the majesty of the Pergamon Gate, or beholding the Mona Lisa. (Likewise, in Freud's famous diagram, the idea of a Baby holds the same valence as Shit!)[9] Any little thing, impure as can be, can change your life.

My favorite diagram thinking was about painting and language: Gilles Deleuze, Charles Olson, David Joselit. In Deleuze's

9. This diagram accompanied the 1917 essay, "On Transformations of Instinct as Exemplified in Anal Eroticism"; see *The Standard Edition of the Complete Psychological Works of Sigmund Freud, Volume 7*, ed. James Strachey and Anna Freud (London: Hogarth Press, 1953). [Editors' note]

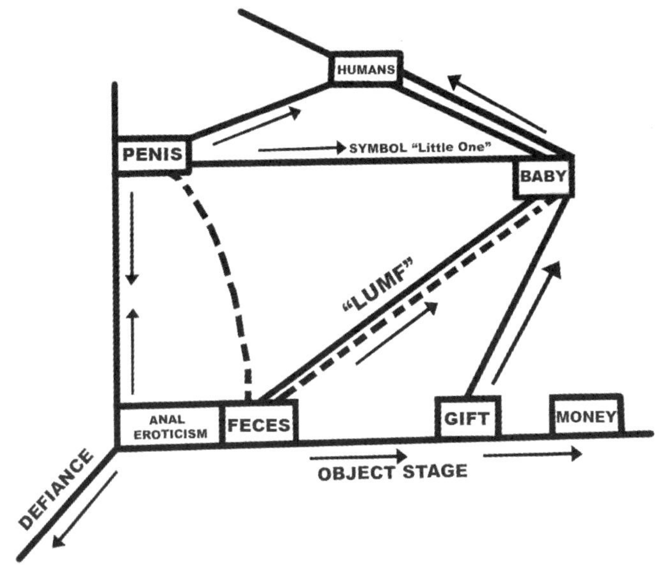

book on the painter Francis Bacon, *The Logic of Sensation*, the very concept of the diagram is an action, not a thing but a moment, a moment of transformation. Perhaps inspired by the visual portals, stages, and furniture that Bacon sets his figures against, Deleuze's "diagram" is his way to describe the action of Bacon's figures as they transform agonistically.[10] David Joselit's essay "Dada's Diagrams," describes diagrams as a kind of container, a come-one-come-all structure for representing the polymorphous perversity, the rupture, of the early twentieth century: "Far more important than [Francis] Picabia's adoption of a vocabulary drawn from industry in his 'machine

10. See Gilles Deleuze, *Francis Bacon: The Logic of Sensation* (1981), trans. Daniel W. Smith (New York & London: Continuum, 2003); in particular chapter 12, "The Diagram," 99–110. [Editors' note]

drawings' is the model of polymorphous connectivity between discrete elements that these works deploy in order to capture the uneven economic and psychological transformations and the jarring disequilibrium characteristic of modernity."[11] The poet Charles Olson's manifesto from 1950, *Projective Verse*, also describes a kind of spatial diagram of action.[12] He imagines language as a set of something like arrows—utterances as projectiles that ride out of the poet's mouth and land in the world, demarcating a sort of invisible forcefield. This kind of invisible language-force might be subtle but it's big: the relational aesthetics of language as a force.

I always felt that what made the painter Ad Reinhardt great wasn't the otherworldly clarity of his abstract paintings (I wasn't really that into the religious way that people would gasp when they finally SAW the colors); it was the fact that alongside his austere experiments with pure color and structure were his diagrams about the art world, which included puns, mockery, and sarcasm. It was the split of his greater whole, the parts mapped together, neither his solemnity nor his jokes, but the passage between such states (and, in between those two, his deadpan slide-show presentations of shape-forms). When I re-

11. See David Joselit, "Dada's Diagrams," in *The Dada Seminars*, ed. Leah Dickerman (Washington, D.C.: National Gallery of Art, 2005), 232. Joselit focuses on works by Picabia that were published in the pages of Dada journals such as *291* in 1915, and *391* in 1919. Fragments of the essay, annotated by Amy Sillman, were reproduced in *The O.-G.*, v. 1 and v. 1–2, accompanying the first and second versions of "Notes on the Diagram." [Editors' note]

12. See Charles Olson, "Projective Verse," in *Collected Prose*, ed. Donald Allen and Benjamin Friedlander (Berkeley & Los Angeles: University of California Press, 1997), 239–49; first appeared in *Poetry New York*, no. 3 (1950). Olson insists on the "kinetics" of the poem with the idea of "composition by field": led by the breath and the ear, the poet transfers energy to the reader. See also "Some Thoughts on John Chamberlain," pages 208–10. [Editors' note]

alized the larger diagram of his work, I realized that what was great was his circulation system, an economy of high and low parts given equal value. I had never been able to resolve the two coasts of my own sensibility, my love of cartoons with my love of serious-minded abstraction. But diagrams made me realize that they were related, constituted precisely by the interactions between them. All the good funny modern art (like Daumier, Guston, Reinhardt, Beckett) was tragicomic. Making art came from the same psychic pneumatics that Freud mapped out as the origin of jokes: distillation and compression. The joke work, the dream work, the art work: all of these were ways to cope. Ways for the mind to grasp what it has seen, moving it from the optic nerve to the mind's eye as it moved from the present to memory, via abstraction. Jokes were the bailiff of high art, getting it out of its cramped quarters, and providing skepticism so you didn't love it *too* much.

At first I was in this love affair with diagrams. Weren't they wonderfully inclusive models of multiplicity, contradiction, and change? Weren't they democratic? That was before I read Benjamin H. D. Buchloh's sobering essay on Eva Hesse, "Facing the Diagram."[13] In his more critical eyes, the diagram was also a manifestation of social conditions, a state of quantification, surveillance, and bureaucracy. Diagrammatic works like Duchamp's *Network of Stoppages* (1914) or Hesse's drawings from 1966–67 therefore also registered "the total subjection of the body and its representations to legal and administrative

13. Benjamin H. D. Buchloh, "Hesse's Endgame: Facing the Diagram," in *Eva Hesse: Drawing*, ed. Catherine de Zegher (New York: The Drawing Center; New Haven & London: Yale University Press, 2006), 117–51.

control."[14] This diagram was not my protagonist! Was the diagram also a form of violence? Was the flip side of the feeling of the "authentic" body always bounded by the "externally established matrix" of conditions?[15] Was the body even possible without the conditions surrounding it? Oh god, Buchloh was probably right—I had been filled with euphoria, but the diagram and painting were linked, and in the bad sense: the same problematics that I had faced in painting were back to haunt me with the diagram.

Postwar painting, which I loved, was riddled with the same problems. It was the same sentimental stuff that Ad Reinhardt was attacking with his diagrams, with his stubborn refusal to be boxed in. When I first learned about AbEx painting as a student, I had felt liberated by it, not oppressed—the way it located thinking as something you do with your body—the way that by including the body in intelligence, you were attacking something. I felt that gesture painting was done with a kind of political body, maybe akin to the poets and their projective verses. I went for the idea that gesture painting was a form of expression lying *between* language and image, an utterance that implicates the maker, along the lines of "the personal is political." I got out of the AbEx-by-genius-men problem by seeing how many women painters there were, how many great painters of color there were, and thought the problem wasn't the art but the art history. Art history was wrong. Critical theory didn't seem wrong but I got out of the commodity problem by focusing on drawing, not painting. Could I also get out of the

14. *Ibid.*, 119.
15. *Ibid.*, 117.

diagram-as-control problem by thinking about the way a diagram makes you think? Could emancipatory possibilities exist in new thinking? Could instrumentalization be defeated? Could diagram-thinking/studio practice/painting go "beyond control"? I felt intuitively that the answer *had* to be located in some way in something messy: accidents, negations, a spill, some excess found on the floor, some physical inexplicability, the idea of desire, urges, pleasure, which I thought was exactly bound up with the not-knowing part of the art-making process, the drawing process as entirely separate from value-formation. This was not utopian, it was just practical: thinking and hoping that exactly where those arrows of *Projective Verse* land, is where something like being and life can be felt. As in Emily Dickinson:

I am alive—I guess—
The Branches on my Hand
Are full of Morning Glory—
And at my finger's end—[16]

At finger's end, beyond the graph, off the chart, in the realm of not-knowing, lay the weird unformed excess, the *chora*, not *information*.[17] Thc fact that I don't know what word will come

16. Emily Dickinson, "I Am Alive—I Guess" (ca. 1863), in *Emily Dickinson's Poems: As She Preserved Them*, ed. Cristanne Miller (Cambridge, MA & London: Belknap Press of Harvard University Press, 2016), 276.

17. A concept elaborated by theoretician Julia Kristeva (who took the word from Plato's *Timaeus*) the *chora* refers to a pre-linguistic, non-expressive totality. It is maternal, instinctual, and rhythmic; it belongs to the semiotic vs. the symbolic, which is logical, naming, and castrating. For Kristeva the *chora* plays an essential role in the signifying and poetical process, as it challenges the closure of meaning. See Julia Kristeva, *Revolution in Poetic Language* (1974), trans. Margaret Waller (New York: Columbia University Press, 1984). [Editors' note]

out of my mouth next, exactly, when speaking a sentence, or what jerky motion I'll make when taking a step, or whether I'll continue living past the bus stop at all, made me turn to the idea of improvisation as a kind of conscientious reminder of how fragile everything is, how unstable and unknowable. The diagram's best form, painting's best aspect, seemed to lie in its unknowns, its silence, its way of not working out, or being at risk, a matter of fate, ruin, or possible resuscitation. Painting was dead, but it surprised me. So, isn't there an end-zone, an off-stage in the theater? The painter Charles Garabedian said making a painting is like purposefully stumbling around in a fog near a cliff.[18] It's a mess of unknowns, beyond diagrammable. So it seemed like the very idea of *knowing* was where the problem lay, maybe. The diagram only shows us the stuff arrayed in a space. The diagram doesn't consider its errors. Therefore, comedy, accident, mistake, is the corrective for the diagram, because it includes everything the diagram can't even hope to establish as a solid: spasms, screw-ups, sabotage, refusal, stupidity, the saggy droop between the vector showing "what you did" and what really resulted. Whatever is incalculable, including the feeling of a mistake. I'd like to see the diagram of that. Failure and dread. That's why I still loved abstraction, because we *knew* it didn't work, that it was a failure, a paradox, a realm of both potential *and* unchartability. David Joselit wrote

18. "It would be really dull if you just went to the studio and did great work, because it couldn't be great. . . . This is what makes it interesting to be an artist. It's the idea of testing yourself and knowing you can be 100% wrong with each decision, each brushstroke. The fun is wandering around in the fog, with the cliff nearby." *Charles Garabedian: Twenty Years of Work*, exh. cat. (Waltham, MA: Rose Art Museum, Brandeis University, 1983), 12. Charles Garabedian (1923–2016), an American painter who lived most of his life in Los Angeles, was included in the 1978 show *"Bad" Painting* (see "Shit Happens," note 3, page 164). [Editors' note]

that the "act of reconnection does not function as a return to coherence, but rather as a free play of polymorphous linkages which . . . remains a central motif of modern (and postmodern) art."[19] Diagrams are failures, paintings are failures, and life is a failure. The diagram can only do so much. The rest is as Donald Barthelme asks, "What happens next?" And then the answer is, "I don't know." That's what a good diagram indicates: that there are things beyond control. ♦

19. David Joselit, "Dada's Diagrams," *loc. cit.*

"In 2009 I had a Fellowship at the American Academy in Berlin. Each night at the Academy there were seated dinners, with seating assignments posted on a bulletin board. I began making diagrams as satirical responses to amuse my fellow Fellows. It was a project that continued, as I began thinking about chronicling the endless dinners and events in the art world."
—Amy Sillman

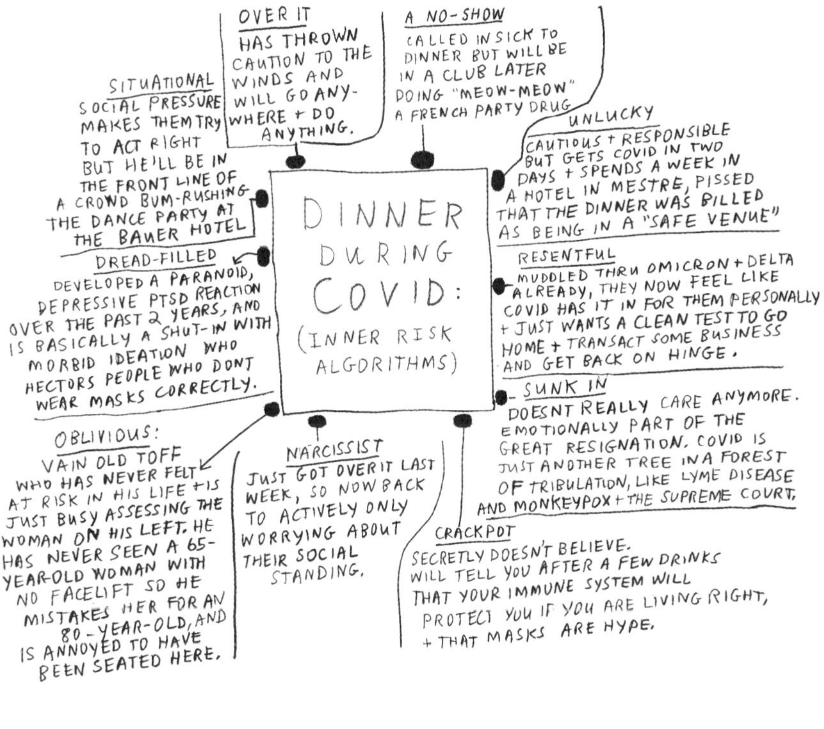

DINNER DURING COVID: (INNER RISK ALGORITHMS)

OVER IT
HAS THROWN CAUTION TO THE WINDS AND WILL GO ANYWHERE + DO ANYTHING.

A NO-SHOW
CALLED IN SICK TO DINNER BUT WILL BE IN A CLUB LATER DOING "MEOW-MEOW" A FRENCH PARTY DRUG

SITUATIONAL
SOCIAL PRESSURE MAKES THEM TRY TO ACT RIGHT BUT HE'LL BE IN THE FRONT LINE OF A CROWD BUM-RUSHING THE DANCE PARTY AT THE BAUER HOTEL

UNLUCKY
CAUTIOUS + RESPONSIBLE BUT GETS COVID IN TWO DAYS + SPENDS A WEEK IN A HOTEL IN MESTRE, PISSED THAT THE DINNER WAS BILLED AS BEING IN A "SAFE VENUE"

DREAD-FILLED
DEVELOPED A PARANOID, DEPRESSIVE PTSD REACTION OVER THE PAST 2 YEARS, AND IS BASICALLY A SHUT-IN WITH MORBID IDEATION WHO HECTORS PEOPLE WHO DONT WEAR MASKS CORRECTLY.

RESENTFUL
MUDDLED THRU OMICRON + DELTA ALREADY, THEY NOW FEEL LIKE COVID HAS IT IN FOR THEM PERSONALLY + JUST WANTS A CLEAN TEST TO GO HOME + TRANSACT SOME BUSINESS AND GET BACK ON HINGE.

SUNK IN
DOESNT REALLY CARE ANYMORE. EMOTIONALLY PART OF THE GREAT RESIGNATION. COVID IS JUST ANOTHER TREE IN A FOREST OF TRIBULATION, LIKE LYME DISEASE AND MONKEYPOX + THE SUPREME COURT.

OBLIVIOUS:
VAIN OLD TOFF WHO HAS NEVER FELT AT RISK IN HIS LIFE + IS JUST BUSY ASSESSING THE WOMAN ON HIS LEFT. HE HAS NEVER SEEN A 65-YEAR-OLD WOMAN WITH NO FACELIFT SO HE MISTAKES HER FOR AN 80-YEAR-OLD, AND IS ANNOYED TO HAVE BEEN SEATED HERE.

NARCISSIST
JUST GOT OVER IT LAST WEEK, SO NOW BACK TO ACTIVELY ONLY WORRYING ABOUT THEIR SOCIAL STANDING.

CRACKPOT
SECRETLY DOESN'T BELIEVE. WILL TELL YOU AFTER A FEW DRINKS THAT YOUR IMMUNE SYSTEM WILL PROTECT YOU IF YOU ARE LIVING RIGHT, + THAT MASKS ARE HYPE.

BIRTHDAY DINNER

THE TWINKLY HALF OF A FASHION/POWER COUPLE, WEARING AN ALL-BLONDE WARDROBE AND ATTITUDE, INCLUDING AN ANNOYINGLY SUPERFICIAL-SOUNDING LAUGH.

HANDSOME, BUT WORRIED, SICILIAN BOYFRIEND OF THE AUTHOR, WHO HAS A DETACHED MANNER DUE TO HIS INNER PANIC AT HIS OWN PERSONAL LOOMING DEBT CRISIS. HE IS JUST NOT LISTENING.

SLEEK-HAIRED IVY-LEAGUE ASST PROF. CARRYING AN "IT-BAG" AND WEARING A BACKLESS DRESS. SHE CONSIDERS HERSELF FECKLESS AND WITTY, BUT HER DINNER COMPANIONS ARE INCREASINGLY IRRITATED BY HER INANE QUESTIONS.

FRAGILE NEW WIFE OF A FAMOUS PERSON, WHO SUFFERS FREQUENT MIGRAINES AND INFREQUENT PANIC ATTACKS. CURLY HAIR, DIMPLES, CUTE AS A BUTTON, BUT MAYBE NOT AS GOOD AS ORIGINALLY CRACKED UP TO BE.

PROFOUNDLY AMBIVALENT LITERARY AGENT, A DEBONAIR MAN-ABOUT-TOWN, WITH AN INWARDLY DARK, DEPRESSIVE STREAK. SECRETLY IN LOVE WITH SOMEONE IN A BAD MARRIAGE, A HARPIST WITH A DRINKING PROBLEM.

FILMMAKER HUSBAND WHO WILL SOON GET DRUNK AND DISPLAY HIS MORE RUTHLESS EGOMANIA. HE GETS MORE MONOMANIACAL AS THE NIGHT WEARS ON, 'TIL FINALLY HE PASSES OUT ON THE BED, SNORING, BUT WILL BE IN HIS EDITING ROOM AT 8 AM THE NEXT MORNING IN AN OBLIVIOUS BOUT OF WORKAHOLIC DISPLACEMENT.

THE OTHER HALF OF THE FASHION/POWER COUPLE, THE MORE RESERVED AND RICHER ONE, WEARING AN ABSURD BLACK OPERA CAPE. LOOKS LIKE A GIANT STUFFED ANIMAL IN GLASSES. CAN'T WAIT TO LEAVE.

AUTHOR, HOST, WITH EXPLOSIVE LAUGH AND INWARDLY-EXPLODING SENSE OF OUTRAGE THAT HIS 2ND NOVEL SEEMS UNPUBLISHABLE. WEARS A SUIT AND TIE, INEXPLICABLY.

SCHOLAR OF THE QUATTROCENTO WITH A SQUARE JAW AND NOTHING MUCH ON HIS MIND.

QUIETLY INTENSE ABSTRACT PAINTER, WHO USED TO BE AFFABLE AND HAS GROWN INCREASINGLY WITHDRAWN LATELY. IN BLACK VELVET.

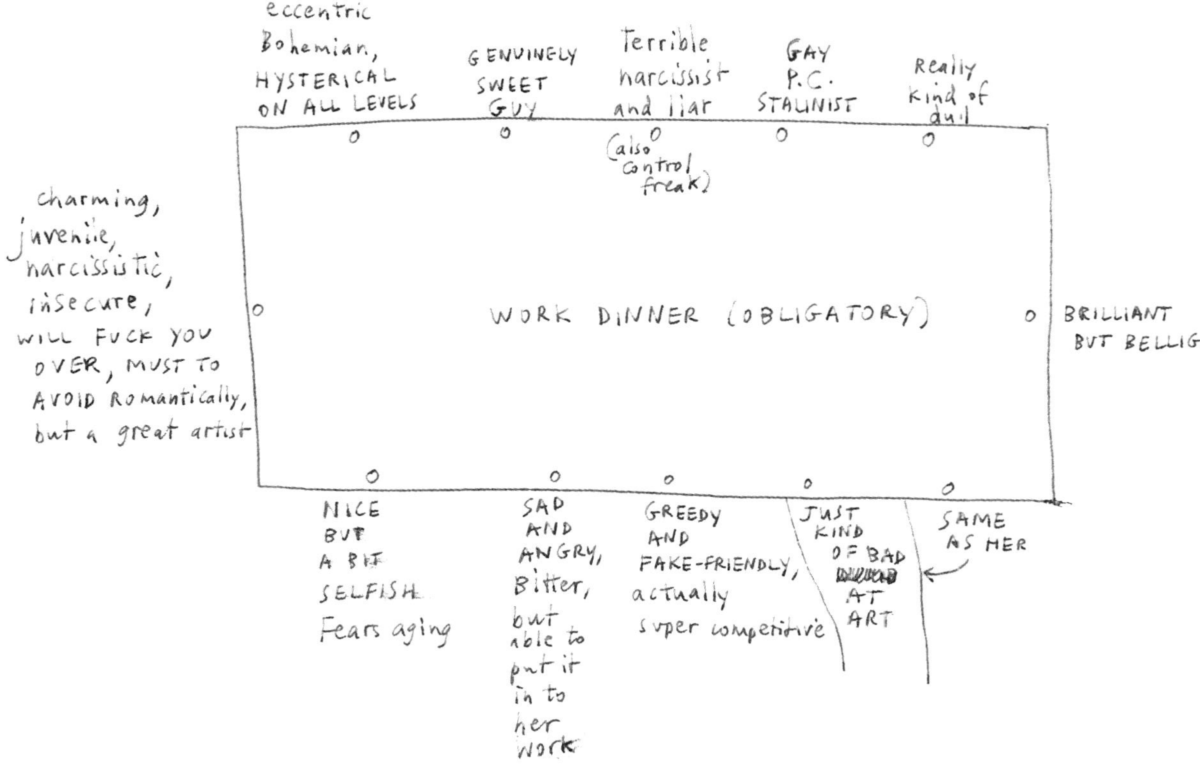
eccentric Bohemian, HYSTERICAL ON ALL LEVELS
GENUINELY SWEET GUY
Terrible narcissist and liar (also control freak)
GAY P.C. STALINIST
Really kind of dull
charming, juvenile, narcissistic, insecure, WILL FUCK YOU OVER, MUST TO AVOID ROMANTICALLY, but a great artist
WORK DINNER (OBLIGATORY)
BRILLIANT BUT BELLIGERENT
NICE BUT A BIT SELFISH Fears aging
SAD AND ANGRY, Bitter, but able to put it in to her work
GREEDY AND FAKE-FRIENDLY, actually super competitive
JUST KIND OF BAD AT ART
SAME AS HER

FRUSTRATED ARTIST
WHO STILL HAS HER
BEAUTIFUL LOOKS
BUT WHO ALSO HAS
FINANCIAL PROBLEMS
THAT KEEP HER UP
AT NIGHT. SHE CAN'T
RECONCILE HER BEAUTY
WITH HER DIFFICULT
ROW TO HOE.

ARTIST
FRUSTRATED
BY HOW
STUPID
EVERYONE ELSE
IS, AND THE NAGGING
PROBLEM OF, WHERE'S
MY DADDY?

ARTIST,
FRUSTRATED BY
BOTH ENCROACHING
OLD AGE AND TOTAL
OBSCURITY, BUT
REMAINS OUTWARDLY
CHEERFUL. WEARS LOUD NECKLACE.

DRUNK
CURATOR
WHO KEEPS
SHOUTING
QUESTIONS THAT
MAKE NO SENSE.
HE IS FRUSTRATED
THAT NO ONE
ANSWERS.

FRUSTRATED PEOPLE
AT DINNER

GUY WHO'S REALLY
A FRAUD AND JUST
THERE TO SUCK UP
TO THE CURATOR
AT THE NEXT TABLE.
(KEEPS LOOKING OVER...)

FRUSTRATED
ARTIST WHOSE SURVEY
SHOW HAS JUST
CLOSED. HE IS ON
THE VERGE OF
GOING ON A MAJOR
BENDER AND WILL
SUBLIMATE HIS POST-SHOW
DEPRESSION IN OBSCURE
THEORY BOOKS THAT
FRUSTRATE UNDERSTANDING
BY NORMAL HUMAN
BEINGS. HIS WORK
IS BASED ON THESE
READINGS, MAKING THE
SURVEY SHOW ITSELF SLIGHTLY
UNREADABLE.

FRUSTRATED BY
LONELINESS AND
ARTHRITIS IN HER
FOOT, THIS
MIDDLE AGED ARTIST
SEEMS FRIENDLY
BUT IS WRACKED
BY ANXIETY
ABOUT MORTALITY
AND ISOLATION.

FRUSTRATED ART HISTORIAN
WHO WONDERS IF SHE
SHOULD QUIT THE FIELD,
MOVE TO AN ASHRAM,
TAKE UP VEDANTIC PHILOSOPHY
AND HINDU SINGING.
IN OTHER WORDS, FRUSTRATED
BY HER OWN CAREER CHOICE,
SHE MAY OPT FOR DOXOLOGY.

BENEFIT DINNER

BON VIVANT IN A BOW TIE – really knows how to work the room, – BUBBLY CHEF

PULITZER-PRIZE-WINNING SPOUSE –

WHO WILL LEAVE BEFORE DESSERT – WITH mental problems

QUIET DOWAGER, WITH BANGS AND A BROOCH

Terse CHIEF CURATOR, IN A twill houndstooth SUIT

COMPLEX FLORAL Arrangement

ANXIOUS, WORRIED EARNEST, CHUBBY, ADMINISTRATOR. whose Boss will meet Pres Obama in the morning. tryin to keep it together

STRANGE RICH WOMAN WITH SNAZZY WARDROBE AND FRIZZY HAIR –

FINANCIAL WIZARD IN A PINK SILK TIE; NO SPARK WHATSOEVER, BUT HAS A SECRET. Looks like the undead.

Sleeveless leather shirt and frizzy bangs – Looks surprisingly like Joey Ramone

MONEY GUY – CAN'T WAIT TO LEAVE – Keeps checking time – cant remember if he fed the dog –

PLUS-ONE, ONLY here by accident

MISS DAGMAR C. POPP

OUT-OF-SORTS SOUND ARTIST WHO USED TO BE QUITE A GAMIN BEFORE THE PERI-MENOPAUSE MADE ~~HER~~ SLEEP ~~PATTERNS~~. IMPOSSIBLE. IN HER NEW GROUCHY STATE, SHE CASTS SILENT ASPERSIONS ON ALL THE OTHER WOMEN IN THE ROOM, BUT THEN FEELS PANGS OF FEMINIST REGRET, WHICH RESULT IN AN INWARD SHAME SPIRAL AND SET OF CONFLICTS THAT ~~IS~~ MAKES IT QUITE ~~COMPLEX~~ DIFFICULT FOR (HER) TO TALK TO (ANYONE).

MS. WANDA DIBBELSCHAFT

THE QUEEN OF MEAN FROM STUTTGART. A CRUEL MOUTH, NOT A HAIR OUT OF PLACE, ~~WITH A~~ GUCCI ~~BIG GOLD~~ BELT AND A TRUST FUND. WORKED BRIEFLY AS AN ASSISTANT FOR HORKHEIMER AND LIKES NOW TO GLORIFY THIS ASSOCIATION. ~~WENT~~ ~~THE~~ ... ~~CURATOR~~, AND IS ANGLING TO BECOME EDITOR OF "MOTE" MAGAZINE.

MR. JEAN-PHILIPPE OBU-STEVENSON Herving

TINY BUT ~~UBIQUITOUS~~ MAN-ABOUT-TOWN — THE GET-TO-KNOW-ME AND BON VIVANT WHOSE NEW PROJECT, "ELEVATION THROUGH ASSOCIATION" SEEKS TO ~~PLACE~~

WHO LOOKS A LITTLE LIKE ~~PEEWEE~~ HERMAN IN A MONKEY SUIT.

MR. PANCRETIUS FLORSCHEIM

SNOOTY, WELL-EDUCATED, LONELY ARCHITECTURAL HISTORIAN WHO IS ON THE LOOKOUT FOR SOME NEW ARM CANDY, PREFERABLY AN ASIAN MAN. HIS FATHER HAS A VAST COLLECTION OF PORCELAIN HIPPO FIGURINES.

MISS FLOSSIE KLEMPERER

A MESOMORPH TRYING TO DIET HER WAY DOWN TO AN ECTOMORPH, BUT CURRENTLY LOOKS LIKE A SAUSAGE STUFFED INTO SOME MARGIELA. HOPING TO MEET A CHUBBY CHASER. A SWEET HEART, BUT WITH A ONE TRACK MIND.

MRS. INEZ ALPENFLATTERER

A DUTCH-WEST-INDIAN DIVA OF A STRUCTURALIST, WHOSE 90 MINUTE FILMS TRACK THE MOVEMENT OF TRAFFIC IN A PARKING STRUCTURE. HER FRIENDS CALL HER "THE BODY" BECAUSE SHE IS TALL AND CLUMSY. SHE HAS ABSOLUTELY NO SENSE OF HUMOR WHATSOEVER.

MR. CHESTER "BINGO" HORDINATE.

NOVELIST AND BELLE-LETTRIST WITH A COLOSSAL AMOUNT OF RAGE IN HIM THAT EMERGES ONLY WHEN HE DRINKS TOO MUCH (LIKE, EVERY NIGHT AT 8.) HIS MOST RECENT BOOK "THE STRENUOUS LIFE" WAS OPTIONED TWICE BUT THE FILM FAILED TO MATERIALIZE, LEADING TO EVEN GREATER RAGE AND THE SECRET AFTERNOONS SPENT WATCHING ANGER MANAGEMENT LECTURE VIDEOS ON SHOWTIME.

MR. ADALBERT BEETLEBROX: A LACANIAN FROM LUXEMBOURG WITH A NEED TO CONTROL EVERY ~~THING BY MEANS~~ OF AN EXTRAORDINARILY WHISPERY VOICE THAT FORCES YOU TO LEAN IN, AT WHICH TIME YOU ENCOUNTER HIS DANDRUFF.

MISS AUDRINA ZUMWINKEL

TALL, ~~AUD~~ ~~WILLOW~~ DEMANDING, ~~OATY~~ OATMEAL-~~FACED~~ COMPLEXIONED PHOTOGRAPHER WHO ~~DOESN'T~~ KNOW HOW ~~NOT~~ TO GET ALL UP IN EVERYONE'S GRILL. A CLOSE TALKER, TOO. YOU JUST WANT TO TELL HER TO BACK THE FUCK UP. HER MODEL IS PATTI SMITH BUT SHE COMES OFF MORE LIKE ETHEL MERMAN.

MR. PHOENIX BENEDRILLO

PULLED ~~UP~~ A CHAIR THOUGH HE WASN'T INVITED — ANNOYING, VAPID CULTURAL STUDIES GUY — A.K.A. CUB REPORTER AND GOSSIP COLUMNIST MOTIVATED PRIMARILY BY A RELENTLESS NEED FOR APPROVAL THAT FAILS TO MASK A TRULY FLIMSY THEORETICAL GRASP.

MR. HERVING ROTUNDI-LAMMERBUTZ

LEFTIST FILMMAKER FROM SOUTH AMERICA, TWICE NOMINATED FOR AN OSCAR IN SHORT SUBJECTS, WHO HAS FALLEN ON HARD TIMES IN THE CRISIS AND IS NOW DOING CORPORATE BRANDING TO MAKE A LIVING. HE FEELS ~~ASHAMED~~ ASHAMED ashamed ABOUT IT BUT JUST DESIGNED THE NEW TRUMP LOGO WHICH WILL PAY FOR HIS ENTIRE 6-PART SERIES ON THE HISTORY OF THE ~~CHINESE SPACE PROGRAM FOR~~ ITALIAN SQUATTER MOVEMENT WHICH WILL EARN HIM A PULITZER BUT FOR WHICH HE WILL BE SLAMMED BY FEMINIST CRITICS FOR SEXISM.

MR. WOLFGANG MOULE-RASKO

CONSIDERED A CATCH — MOVIE-STAR GOOD LOOKS AND A BROKEN HEART BECAUSE HIS WIFE RAN OFF WITH THE HEAD OF THE "STREIFF" FOUNDATION, A MACARTHUR-WINNING BLONDE WOMAN. MOULE-RASKO IS TRANSLATING FOUCAULT'S LAST DIARY, AND IN HIS SPARE TIME HAS BUILT A SUSTAINABLE HOUSE MADE OF BAMBOO IN SUBURBAN ANTWERP.

This essay was originally published in Frieze d/e, *no. 22 (December 2015–February 2016).*

Shit Happens: Notes on Awkwardness

... but what do such large, loose, baggy monsters, with their queer elements of the accidental and the arbitrary, artistically mean?
—HENRY JAMES, PREFACE TO *THE TRAGIC MUSE*[1]

The first question confronting artists is: "What should I do?" And the next question is: "What would make it better?" Is this "aesthetics?" I don't know—but I do know that we are no longer making things for the Beaux Arts, for truth, beauty, elevation, or virtuosity. Yet the familiar forms of what could be called "negative aesthetics"[2] also fail to adequately describe what a lot of artists are doing in their studios. Dada, the readymade, Bad

1. The "monsters" James has in mind are actually three great nineteenth-century novels; as he discusses the role of "composition" in writing, he notes that: "There may in its absence be life, incontestably, as [William Thackeray's] *The Newcomes* has life, as [Alexandre Dumas'] *Les Trois Mousquetaires*, as [Leon] Tolstoy's *Peace and War*, have it; but what do such large, loose, baggy monsters, with their queer elements of the accidental and the arbitrary, artistically mean?" Beyond that quote, it is worth noting that James' preface echoes the present essay's concerns, as it deals with creation as a complex, if not erratic, process. See *The Novels and Tales of Henry James, New York Edition, Volume 7* (New York: Charles Scribner's Sons, 1907–09). [Editors' note]

2. See Theodor W. Adorno's writings on aesthetics, in particular the posthumous *Aesthetic Theory*, ed. Gretel Adorno and Rolf Tiedemann, trans. Robert Hullot-Kentor (Minneapolis: University of Minnesota Press, 1997). To put it quickly, according to Adorno, art can't represent the possibility of emancipation but "negatively," in order not to be assimilated by the culture industry; art has truth when it doesn't smooth the ugliness and inauthenticity of today's world and society under beauty or satisfactory emotions, but when its forms reveal the breaks and the contradictions of our damaged lives. One shouldn't forget, though, that Adorno "really missed the boat with jazz" (see the drawing *Some Problems in Philosophy*, page 300). [Editors' note]

Painting,[3] the dandy, "provisional" painting,[4] deskilling,[5] etc.—none of these ring quite right in accounting for something I would call negativity-at-work, the arduous search for form, the feelings of dissatisfaction, the endless decisions and changes that constitute the work of various artists. How to discuss this, without resorting to a cliché of artistic work? What is everyone doing, and how do they decide to make it "better"?

We are trying to surprise ourselves and that is hard to do. I think it is a kind of metabolism that drives me to change and change and change my forms, searching rather earnestly for something I don't quite know already, a kind of questioning machine, endlessly discontent. I would say that form is the shape of my discontent, and that what interests me is how form can match that feeling or condition—of funny, homely, lonely,

3. The highly influential 1978 exhibition, *"Bad" Painting*, curated by Marcia Tucker at the New Museum—a place she had founded—included artists such as Joan Brow, William Copley, Neil Jenney, and William Wegman. In her catalogue essay, Tucker defined Bad Painting as "figurative work that defies, either deliberately or by virtue of disinterest, the classic canons of good taste, draftsmanship, acceptable source material, rendering, or illusionistic representation. In other words, this is work that avoids the conventions of high art, either in terms of traditional art history or very recent taste or fashion. Nevertheless, 'bad' painting emerges from a tradition of iconoclasm, and its romantic and expressionistic sensibility links it with diverse past periods of culture and art history." Tucker, "'Bad' Painting," in *"Bad" Painting*, exh. cat. (New York: New Museum, 1978), 5–6. [Editors' note]

4. The term "provisional painting" was coined by New York-based art critic Raphael Rubinstein in a 2009 essay: mentioning artists such as Raoul De Keyser, Jacqueline Humphries, Mary Heilmann, and Michael Krebber, he insisted that their paintings looked "casual, dashed-off, tentative, unfinished or self-cancelling." "Provisional Painting," *Art in America* 97, no. 5 (May 2009), 123. [Editors' note]

5. The term "deskilling" was first introduced in art discourse by Ian Burn in 1981: as he pointed out how practices such as Pop Art, Post-Painterly Abstraction, and Minimal Art were "marked by a tendency to shift significant decision-making away from the process of production to the conception, planning design and form of presentation," he noted that "this mode of production encourage[d] artists to devalue not just traditional skills but the acquisition of any skills demanding a disciplined period of training." See Burn, "The 'Sixties: Crisis and Aftermath (Or the Memoirs of an Ex-Conceptual Artist)," *Art & Text*, no. 1 (Autumn 1981). Deskilling has further been discussed in relation to notions of artistic labor as well as taste, alienation, or the readymade. [Editors' note]

ill-fitting, strange, clumsy things that feel right. In other words, a form that tries to find itself outside of what is already okay. Awkwardness is the name I would give this quality, this thing that is both familiar and unfamiliar.

The internet tells me that "awkward" comes from an Old Norse word, *afugr*, meaning "turned the wrong way." In Middle English, *awk* is "backwards," "clumsy." Art school used to be where you learned how to make things well, but most people (outside of some academies) nowadays are masters-of-none. On the other hand, the "deskilling" discourse just doesn't account for what I'm talking about. There's this diligence, this nerdiness to the search; it is a demanding job to attempt Samuel Beckett's fail-better.[6] Paintings can look good just after one stroke. What urge makes you want to do something that pushes further, on toward contingency, clumsiness, strangeness, or even brutality? Awkwardness is that thing, which is fleshy, funny, downward-facing, uncontrollable; it is an emotional or even philosophical state of being, against the great and noble, and also against the cynical. It is both positive and negative, with its own dialect and dialectic.

There was a time in the '90s when, as a younger artist, I started to be invited to panels about "beauty" and "visual pleasure."[7] People were trying to reclaim some idea about pleasure for po-

6. See Samuel Beckett, *Worstward Ho* (New York: Grove Press, 1983). [Editors' note]

7. On this notion and the context, see Johanna Drucker's "Visual Pleasure: A Feminist Perspective," *M/E/A/N/I/N/G*, no. 11 (May 1992); reproduced in *M/E/A/N/I/N/G: An Anthology of Artists' Writings, Theory, and Criticism*, ed. Susan Bee and Mira Schor (Durham, NC: Duke University Press, 2000), 163–74. In this essay Drucker reclaimed the very notion of visual pleasure, and insisted on its importance in women artists' work—focusing on women painters, amongst whom Joan Mitchell, June Leaf, and Pat Steir—as a quality likely to "generate theoretical discussion, on a par with that generated by male artists" (*ibid.*, 168). Drucker added: "Pleasure of production is one of the most fundamental elements of most painters' work" (*ibid.*, 169). [Editors' note]

litical purposes, sometimes with a feminist agenda. People assumed that as a painter and feminist, I would be interested in these discussions, but instead I would find myself quiet, sullen, usually blurting out at some point that I couldn't give a shit about beauty. They would look at me: what, then, was I looking for? I came up with the idea of hatred—a shortcut for sure, but I didn't really know how else to say it. I just knew that attractiveness was the enemy. I recently heard Franco "Bifo" Berardi give a talk about not working (something that doesn't make a lot of sense if you actually like "working" in your studio).[8] Finally he made a distinction between work and art, saying that to make art is to make something beautiful, meaningful, erotic, empathic—and as usual, when this is the language used to describe what we're doing, I wanted to barf. We're not making sexy beasts. If anything, call it libido instead of erotics—but we want an art also animated by ugliness, destruction, hatred, struggle. Punk seems as close as one can get to describe it, but what could be less punk than staying up late in a studio trying hard to make a "better" oil painting? That's so earnest, so caring—with a smock, and our tongue between our teeth, paintbrush poised, trying so hard—like the artists in a Jerry Lewis movie.[9] So what are we

8. That lecture, given at the Städelschule, Frankfurt-am-Main, on May 10, 2011, was part of the project *Time/Bank* at Portikus, initiated by artists Julieta Aranda and Anton Vidokle. The notion of the "refusal to work" was instrumental in the Autonomia movement, in the context of political struggles in the 1970s in Italy, in which Franco "Bifo" Berardi played an active part; it started to be used in contemporary art in the early 2000s, with reference to radical practices as well as to dandyistic attitudes, in the context of a broader discussion on the relations between late capitalism and art. [Editors' note]

9. In Frank Tashlin's *Artists and Models* (1955), Dean Martin is a struggling painter who, thanks to his roommate Jerry Lewis' dreams, becomes a successful comic book artist—like his love interest in the movie, Dorothy Malone. When Martin and Lewis dress as painters to perform the movie's title song at the "Artists and Models Ball," Lewis wears a silver smock, Martin a black tuxedo with a cravat. [Editors' note]

doing? I can still only call it looking for this fragile thing that is awkwardness. This is not alienated labor, nor a commodity precisely, but a need, a way of churning the world, as your digestive system churns food.

I spent last year reading Ovid, and was excited to learn about a Roman poetry meter called choliambic, or "lame iambic," in which the stress at the end of the line purposefully comes down on the "wrong" foot, giving the line an unexpected little thud or sonic punch: da-dum, da-dum, da-dum, da-dum—DUM. The offbeat turns around and questions the whole rest of the line, and is therefore a signal of the poet's aggression or satire. The idea of an ignoble form, named for limping, put me in mind of the way Mr. Hulot walks in Jacques Tati's *Mr. Hulot's Holiday* (1953). Mr. Hulot's funny walk is a running gag throughout the film, a symptom marking his difference from the rest of the bourgeois holiday-goers. He skitters along like a sand crab, and ends up alone, even though he gets a dance with the pretty girl at the costume ball. Tati's movies deftly portray the comic mechanics of modern living, almost as illustrations of Henri Bergson's quotient for the comic, the starting point for which is "something mechanical encrusted upon the living."[10] In the digital age, this relationship also goes the other way around: the living weight of the body is encrusted like a barnacle upon the perfection of the algorithm. Just *having* a body is a daily comedy. From the control tower of the head, one gazes downward, always downward, upon this "loose, baggy monster" that

10. Henri Bergson, *Laughter: An Essay on the Meaning of the Comic* (1900), trans. Cloudesley Brereton and Fred Rothwell (New York: Macmillan, 1928), 39. In that section titled, "Expansive Force of Comic," Bergson also remarks how "a person embarrassed by his [*sic*] body" provokes laughter. [Editors' note]

we find ourselves in, this laughable casement that is the body below, as ankles swell, farts are emitted, rolls of fat jut out, the penis does its own thing. Shit happens and then you die.

It's not an accident that people use "awkward!" after a *faux pas*, a moment of tension between the ideal and the real, where what's supposed to happen goes awry. The real, like the body, is embarrassing: your hand is too moist, your fly is open, there turns out to be something on your nostril, somebody blurts out something that I wasn't supposed to know, your ex-partner shows up with their new lover (and your work is uncool). But you're stuck there. That tension is what abstraction is partly about: the subject no longer entirely in control of the plot, representation peeled away from realness.

This ambivalent state is precisely the state of mind for making a painting, being stuck with the uncertain future of the loveable, but fallible, body that is the artwork. Oil painters work with a substance that's low anyway: putty, shit, dirt, mud that is scraped, pushed, smeared, scumbled into form. After a while, your body is the partner to the materials, you are the medium as well as the tool, the boundaries between you and your object become unclear, mirroring or antagonizing each other. The art-making process is a recording of these restless interactions between subject and object on a par with one another, locked together. In fact, really, improvisation is about working between subject and object; the object is merely a place through which questions are addressed. Perhaps this is particular to abstract painting, where you often don't really "know" what you're doing, and so you are doomed to work in between hoping and groping. In abstraction, time goes by in fits and starts, with resistance of materials being part of that time. Like the body, you look down at your creation and think, "My god, you are ugly."

I know of no artist who is attempting to make something more beautiful, but I do know many artists who are looking for a form that "feels right" without knowing why. Maybe it's just satisfying to see something productive come of feeling like an idiot and the accompanying feeling of embarrassment. Isn't embarrassment what Kafka's *Metamorphosis* is partly about? The book matter-of-factly narrates Gregor Samsa's miserable discovery that he is a bug, while the real drama is the Samsa family's embarrassment to be *living with* a bug, and their relief when Gregor finally dies. He literally dies of embarrassment, because the family no longer knows how to take care of him.

Kafka's bug, a good example of making do with what you're stuck with when you've got a body, is a contrast to the much-cited Bartleby position of "I'd prefer not to," an aesthetic *style* of negation. The awkwardness I'm trying to describe is not a style, but could be one result of a dialectic. I would rather call it a metabolism: the intimate and discomforting process of things changing as they go awry, look uncomfortable, have to be confronted, repaired, or risked, i.e., the process of trying to figure something out while doing it. I don't know if that's abstraction, but I know it's awkward. Finding a form is building these feelings (in this case, dissatisfaction, embarrassment, and doubt) into a substance. This is a very fragile thing to do. ♦

This text was written for The O.-G., *v. 12 (Winter 2018), a zine Amy Sillman published in conjunction with the exhibition,* Mostly Drawing *at Gladstone Gallery, New York, January 26–March 3, 2018.*

The previous summer, Sillman had taken part in the writing workshop, "All Inseparable Now," with poet Sara Jane Stoner, at Wendy's Subway, in Brooklyn: "I did all the reading and participated in the discussions every week. It was really great—but I couldn't write anything. I was frozen. I couldn't do the assignments. I wrote 'Rejective Verse' in fifteen minutes two months after the class, because I was forcing myself to write something. That was my homework."

Rejective Verse

Rejective verse.[1] Unbecoming language. Painting that is writing that is gesture and shape; image that is word that is sound. What comes out of the mouth and goes back in; food in reverse. A gesture made from between the legs and discharged from the gullet. The drawings that result lie on the floor like abandoned arrows from a quiver, dejected and excited. Gesture of rejection, impulse, object and action. Energetic inscription. Indifference {or actually, hostility} to the laws of representation: who cares, really. The process of figuration is boring when you care more about the energetic moment when the mark comes out of the body as expulsion, in-digestion, constrained only by the urge and the shape of the hole it comes out of. The shape of memory, the imprint of social structures on marks, marks as drives, psychical marks, the *chora*,[2] that molten place, a totality, a forge, the womb. The pleasure of refusal. The law of skepticism. (I can't go on, I will go on.)[3] The brick of no thrown from the mouth. A step, un *pas*, which is also a *NOT*, *pas*. Rejection

1. The expression is an echo of Charles Olson's "Projective Verse": see "Notes on the Diagram," page 148, and "Some Thoughts on John Chamberlain," pages 208–10. [Editors' note]

2. On this notion, see "Notes on the Diagram," note 17, page 151. [Editors' note]

3. A borrowing from Samuel Beckett, *The Unnamable* (1953), in *Three Novels* (New York: Grove Press, 1958), 418. [Editors' note]

for digestion—expulsion, revulsion, expression—the negative feeling within oneself, an interiorized negativity that comes out as a quasi-friendly gesture pointing to a threshold, inviting the other to accompany one to a boundary. The process is tricky. Can't always do it. Can't write a poem. (Can't or won't? Refusal to refuse?) The feeling of an icicle in the womb. Destruction as a double-edged sword. Nothing to say except not. (I do not have a mama or papa. I do not take a step. A not knot. Paw in mouth. Footstep in the snow, an animal who passed. She has a past.) Only the voice is seen. There is nothing to paint and nothing to paint with.[4] There is nothing that can be said. Erase it anyway. Negating the absurd suggestion that painting is inexpressive with drawings that begin and end on the ground. Standing above the paper like a midwife, it lying flat below [flatter it]: moving upward fast, bring out the utterance—staccato, blasting, insisting, gagging, swiping, griping: wanting to see a signifier and not know it. A proliferating language of dissatisfaction and rage: disagreement in decals, dashes, emojis, cartoons, drop shadows, bubble type, outlines, scripts, bad handwriting, bad grammar, punctuationless chunks. An other appears. Wanting to eat and touch it at the same time. Eating: saying: hand: mouth. Rejecting a ghost. Can a trace argue? Can a shadow disobey? Tick. Tick. Tick. The situation is a little helpless if one cannot paint, since one is obliged to paint.[5] The best question is, what is your basic unit—the swipe? What does the gesture weigh? Too much? But can a slender thread

4. Another borrowing from Beckett, this time from "Three Dialogues" (1949), in *Disjecta: Miscellaneous Writings and a Dramatic Fragment*, ed. Ruby Cohn (London: John Calder, 1983), 142. The sentence is in the third dialogue, that deals with the work of painter Bram van Velde. [Editors' note]

5. See also Beckett's "Three Dialogues," *id.* [Editors' note]

destroy? "Plato said that the art or technique of writing was a *pharmakon* (drug or tincture, salutary or maleficent.) And the disquieting part of writing had already been experienced in its resemblance to painting."[6] {Derrida} Can destruction build? Can a letter get past its meaning? Can a language be illegible? If so, is it bad language? If it passes the boundary of meaning, and lies on the ground of pure affect, then can it be reincorporated into the body for more energy? Will the wound heal? Isn't the wound a collective act? Is the skin shared? Don't have a mark. Expression. Impression. Enigma. Flatter. Extend. Substract. ♦

6. Jacques Derrida, *Of Grammatalogy*, trans. Gayatri Chakravorty Spivak (Baltimore, MD: Johns Hopkins University Press, 1976), 292.

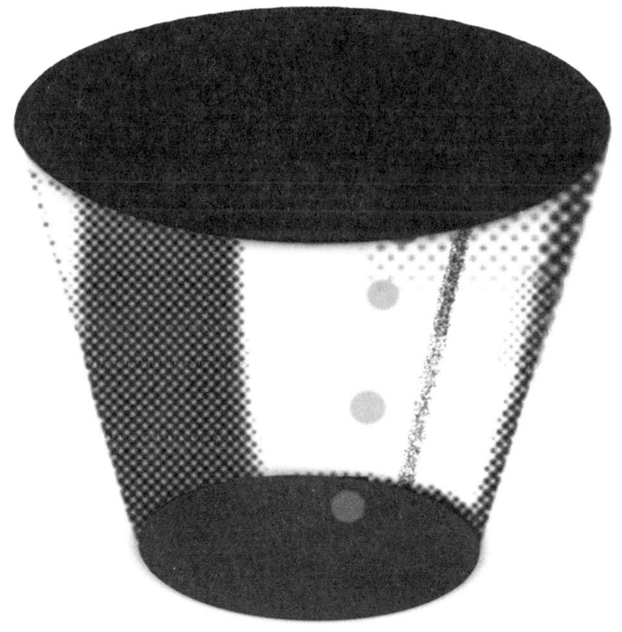

This text was written as a response to the question, "What is the current state of abstraction?" that artist Jackie Saccoccio posed to several painters (Cheryl Donegan, Dan Walsh, and Carroll Dunham among others) for a series of short articles on bombmagazine.org in the winter of 2009–10.

Breakup Letter

Dear Jackie,

I guess you didn't know this but me and Abstraction broke up!!!!! Last summer!!!! Well, I mean, I've been feeling like kind of confused for a long time, like years. I'm friends with all of A's friends and stuff, and I think A's really cool and I totally learned a LOT from A—but you know what? I don't want to say anything bad about A, but I have to TOTALLY MOVE ON with my LIFE. I started to really feel like A's been holding me back and even like kind of manipulative. I mean, when I moved to NYC it was kind of incredible to get to know A . . . but you know what? I am super worried that when you get really to the core of things, A is just super conceited and can't talk to me. I feel really bad saying this but I KIND OF WONDER sometimes if A is just DEAD INSIDE. I don't know, maybe A is like a meal ticket for me. I mean, I get invited to a lot of shows and things because of A, but when I'm there, A just kind of talks to other people. Like I don't feel A can really concentrate on one person at a time—A always addresses the whole room, if you know what I mean. I mean, it's not like Representation even knows

I exist either. I feel like when I come into the room, R is like all glassy and actually really conservative; it's a weird feeling, too. But anyway I just started to feel like I can't be tied down and I have to play the field. I guess all of you know that I was always like that and totally non-monogamous, but that's why you didn't hear from me all winter. I totally learned a lot from A, and I even got to be friends w/ Cézanne who I didn't even LIKE before and now I like totally, like, LOVE, and I super love Cubism. (I am so mad at my friend Kerstin in Berlin because she doesn't even LIKE Cubism but I feel like Cubism is like so amazing.[1] It's basically a diagram, if you know what I mean.) OH, and also, I never would have understood Process without A but I just feel like A's really old friends are just WEIRD. And kind of pompous? Or something? Well, anyway, I feel really bad telling you this, like you'll be pissed, but I hope you know this has nothing to do with you and I really love you and the part of A's friends that are really open like you are AMAZING and everything. But basically I kicked A out of my studio this summer, and afterwards I felt really good. I had this amazing fling, don't tell anyone, but I had this fling with this face, and I don't know, that was the straw that tipped the iceberg and I just went with it. I feel like me and A can be good friends after a while, though, and I am super hoping that all of A's friends will still be friends with me, but, sometimes I almost kind of wish, you know, I was sleeping ALONE. You know what I mean????

Love,
Amy

1. Art theoretician Kerstin Stakemeier, currently professor at the Akademie der Bildenden Künste Nürnberg. See also "Having a Voice," pages 38–39. [Editors' note]

TRAIN OF THOUGHT

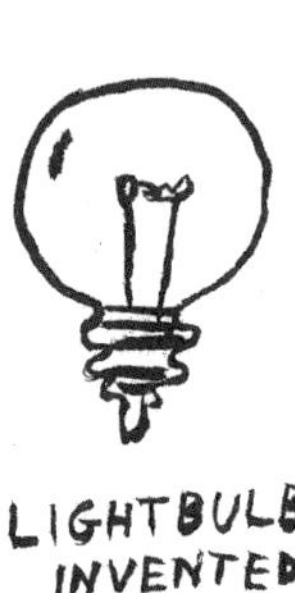

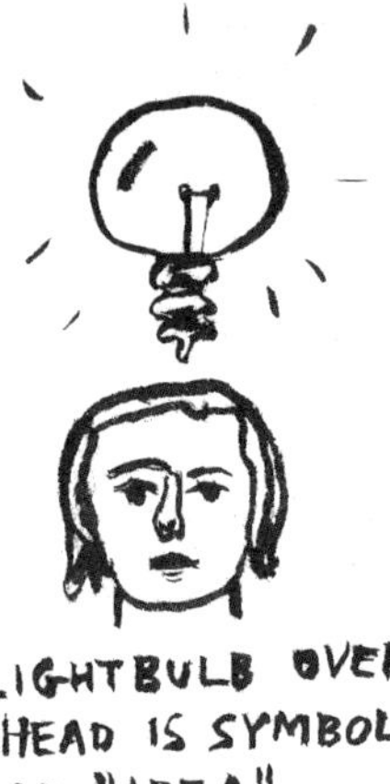

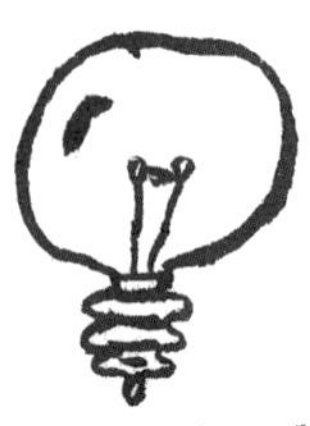

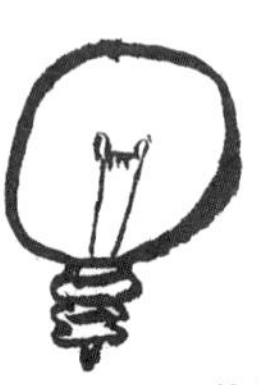

From The O.-G., *v. 3 (Spring 2010), published for Amy Sillman's solo show* Transformer (. . . or, how many lightbulbs does it take to change a painting?) *at Sikkema Jenkins Gallery, New York, April 15–May 15, 2010.*

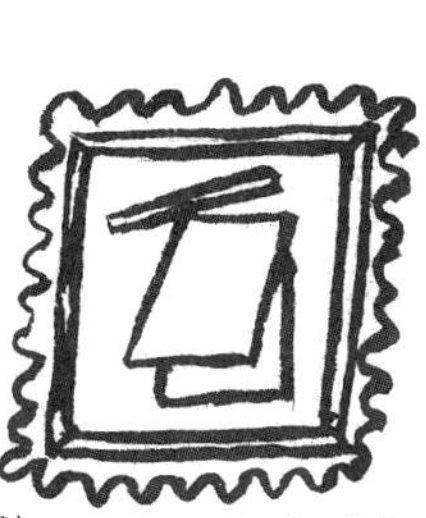

"PAINTING IS DEAD" THING IS A PHENOMENON OF THE 20TH C.

"PAINTING IS DEAD" ERA SAME AS "CONCEPTUAL ART" ERA

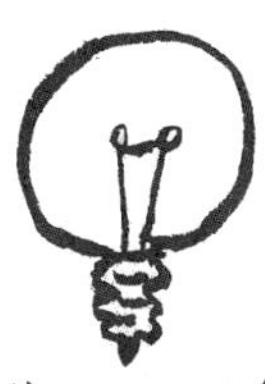

"IDEAS" SIMILAR TO "CONCEPTS"

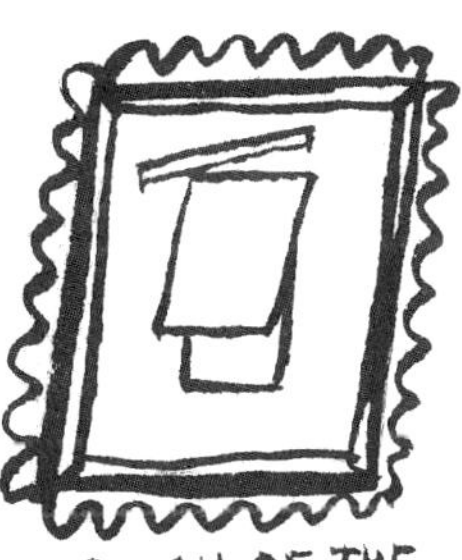

MUCH OF THE PAINTING I LOVE MOST OCCURS AFTER "PAINTING IS DEAD"

ARE PRECEPTS, CONSTRUCTS, PERCEPTIONS SIMILAR TO IDEAS?

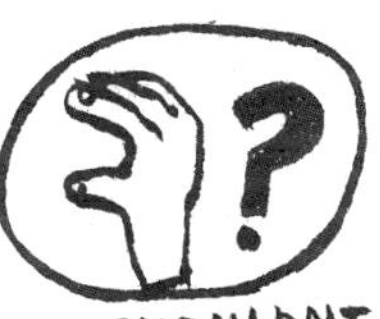

SHOULDNT THERE BE A SYMBOL FOR HAVING A FEELING IF THERE IS A SYMBOL FOR HAVING AN IDEA?

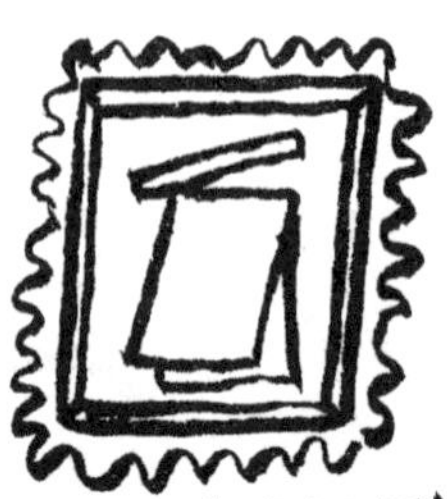

20TH C. PAINTINGS PAINTED MOSTLY UNDER ELECTRIC LIGHTBULB LIGHTS

CONCEPTUAL ART ALSO MADE (OR CONCEIVED OF) MOSTLY IN LIGHTBULB LIGHTING

GOOD PAINTING ALSO HAS GOOD IDEAS

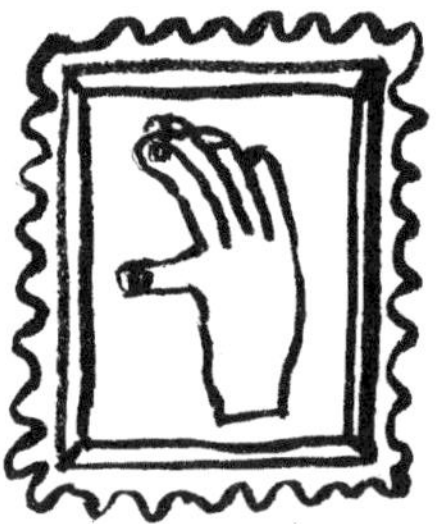

PAINTING OFFERS UNIQUE ENGAGEMENT WITH THE PHYSICAL

PAINTING WAS IMPROVED AFTER CHALLENGES AND CRITIQUES OF 20TH C. CONCEPTUAL ART

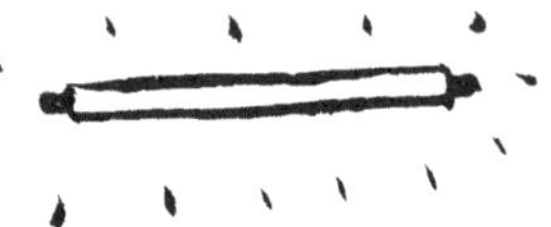

WILL CONCEPTUAL ART IMPROVE? HAS IT IMPROVED?

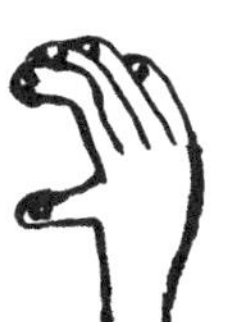

SHOULD THE HAND SYMBOLIZE "FEELING"?

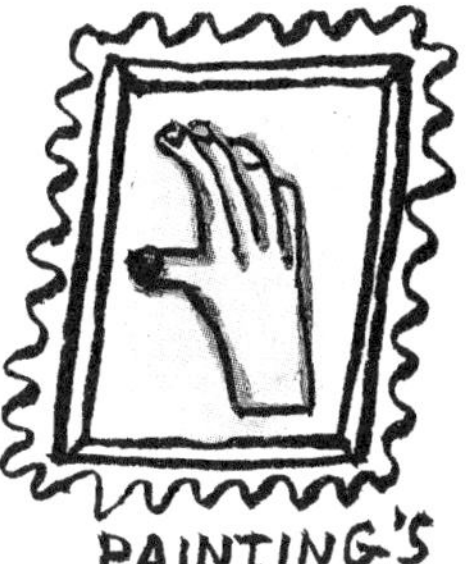

PAINTING'S TACTILITY IS ONE THING I LOVE ABOUT IT.

SOME ART SHOWN + MADE UNDER FLOURESCENT LIGHT, ESPECIALLY IN GERMANY (I NOTICED) LOOKS UGLY

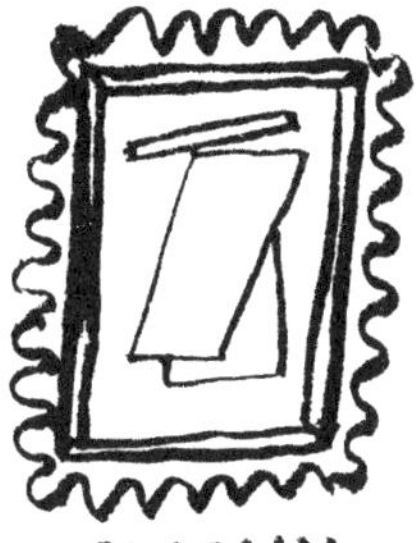

GERMAN 20TH C. PAINTING RATHER IMPORTANT

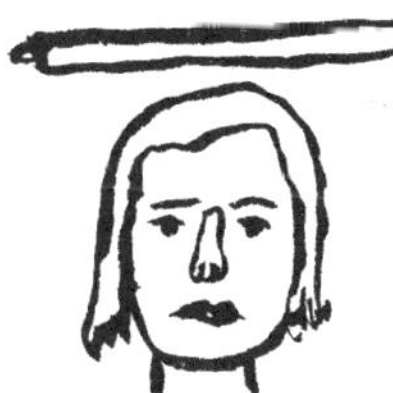

PEOPLE DON'T LOOK NICE UNDER FLOURESCENTS

FUTURE ART WILL ALL BE MADE UNDER FLOURESCENT LIGHT (OR HALOGEN?) UNLESS THEY INVENT SOMETHING ELSE

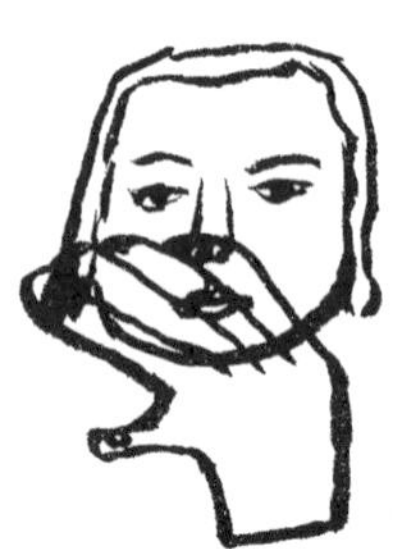

WHERE DO
WE PLACE
THE PICTURE
OF THE HAND
IN THE SYMBOL
OF "FEELINGS"?
CAN'T PUT IT OVER
THE HEAD OR YOU
RISK PRIVILEGING
MIND OVER BODY...

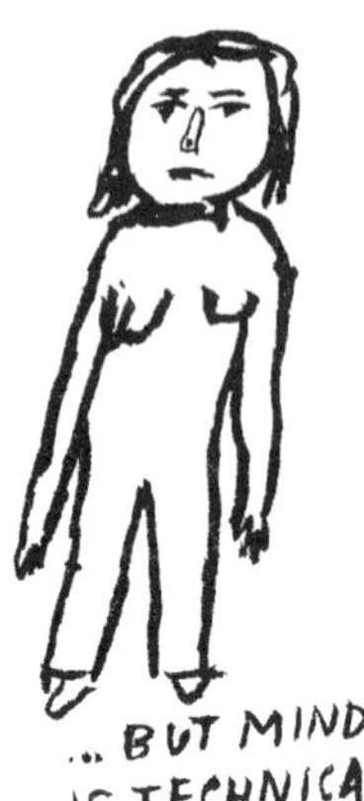

... BUT MIND
_IS_ TECHNICALLY
ABOVE BODY
ANATOMICALLY...

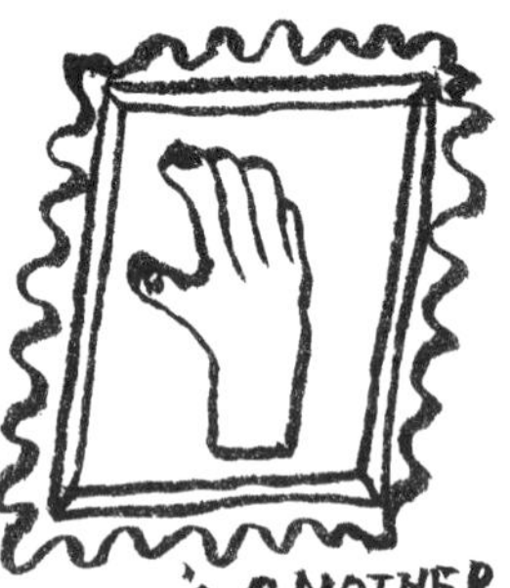

THAT'S ANOTHER
GREAT THING
ABOUT PAINTINGS-
HAND/BODY OVER
MIND AS REVERSAL
OF RATIONAL ORDER
OF THINGS

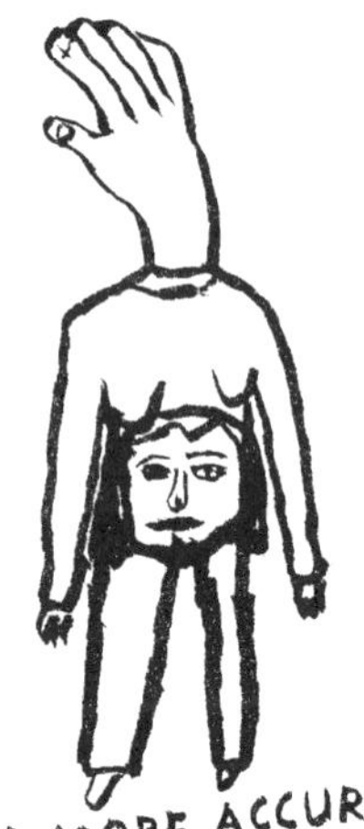

A MORE ACCURATE
PORTRAYAL OF ME
AS AN ARTIST

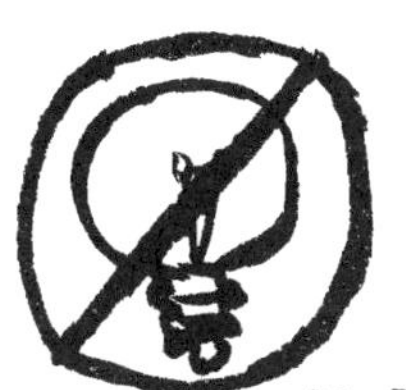

NOTHING MORE IRKSOME THAN IDIOTIC CURATORS WHO DON'T UNDERSTAND THE CONCEPTUAL + EMANCIPATORY POSSIBILITIES OF PAINTING...

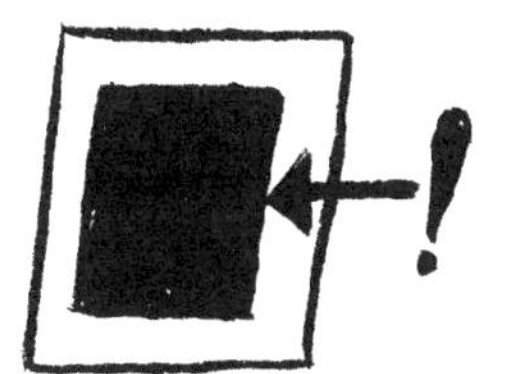

...OR ABSTRACTION'S ENGAGEMENT W/ THE POLITICAL... (HELLO!? HAVE YOU EVER HEARD OF THE RUSSIAN REVOLUTION OR VISITED SOUTH AMERICA?!)

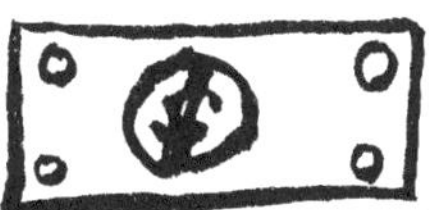

(....WELL PERHAPS THE MORE IRKSOME PHENOMENON IS PAINTINGS MADE JUST TO SELL... BUT ANYWAY....)

LONG LIVE "DIFFICULT" ART, "DIFFICUT WOMEN, & ART THAT'S NOT JUST MADE TO SELL!

LONG LIVE THE RADICAL MERGING OF MIND AND BODY!

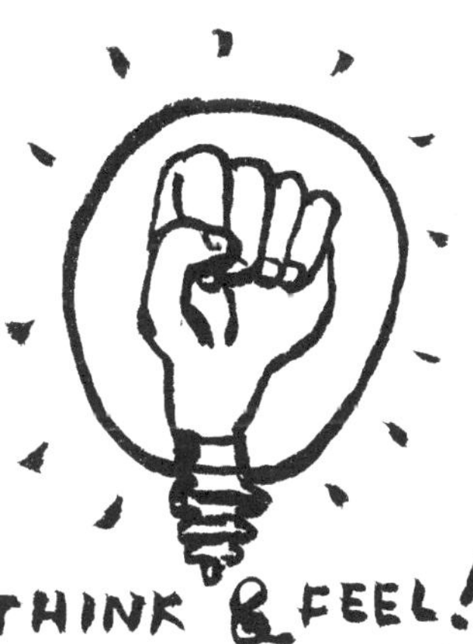

THINK & FEEL! SPEAK & ACT!

This essay was originally published in the monograph Rachel Harrison: Museum With Walls, *ed. Eric Banks (Annandale-on-Hudson, NY: Center for Curatorial Studies, Bard College; London: Whitechapel & Frankfurt-am-Main: Portikus, 2010).*

That monograph followed several solo shows by Harrison, notably Consider the Lobster, *at the Hessel Museum of Art, Bard College, Annandale-on-Hudson, June 27–December 20, 2009. The title of that exhibition was taken from the 2005 book by David Foster Wallace,* Consider the Lobster and Other Essays. *(Harrison's solo show was actually complemented by an exhibition titled,* And Other Essays, *wherein she had invited other artists to re-install works from the Hessel permanent collection.)*

A Few Remarks on Rachel Harrison's Use of Color

A naked color . . . is not a chunk of absolutely hard,
indivisible being . . . ever gaping open . . . less a color or a thing,
therefore, than a difference between things and colors . . .
not a thing but a possibility, a latency, a flesh of things.
—MAURICE MERLEAU-PONTY[1]

The lobster is pugnacious.
His manners are thoroughly unpleasant.
He is always prepared to have a row.
—VOICE-OVER FROM LÁSZLÓ MOHOLY-NAGY'S *LOBSTERS*[2]

1. Color plays a forceful character in Rachel Harrison's farcical situations. Absurdity generally prevails over gravitas: yellow trumps green and lady-shape mugs man-form. A phallic green sculpture is goofed up by a blond wig. A bunch of dumb, dark-green trash bags hunker down lugubriously on the floor, concealing something ominous, but their weight is cheerfully rigged up to a pulley system made of canary yellow ropes. And the only words you could really use to describe the shape loitering over in the Sheetrock corner would be hot orange or boobs.

1. Maurice Merleau-Ponty, "The Intertwining—The Chiasm" (1964/1968), trans. Alphonso Lingis, in *The Visible and the Invisible* (Evanston, IL: Northwestern University Press, 1969), 130–31.

2. *Lobsters* (16mm black and white film, 16 min, 1936) is an unorthodox film about Sussex crustaceans and fishermen, that László Moholy-Nagy was commissioned to co-direct, with John Mathias, while he was working as a commercial artist in London, after fleeing Nazi Germany in 1935. In case you haven't read the introduction on the opposite page, Rachel Harrison did a show in 2009 titled, *Consider the Lobster*. [Editors' note]

2. Harrison sets in motion a pugnacious and almost mechanical dynamic between three forces: the concealed, the sensate, and the discombobulating absurd. As components in this system, her colors are roughly equivalent to shapes. These colors are forms-in-the-shape-of-colors, or colors-in-the-form-of-shapes. She throws in merchandise, manufactured surfaces, and jokes to further scrapple with the proceedings.

3. It strikes me that Harrison's colors strike me. Little jabs and punches.

4. The Greek word *pharmakon* means remedy, poison, substance, charm, artificial color, and paint—all of these. Harrison's colors are jabs, spells, fast-acting drugs that kick in briefly and then are over. They are little hand grenades that detonate meaning.

5. Shapes are things whose outlines hit you in the eye. Color and shape are bright tools for perception and contradiction, and Harrison uses them as you would the white keys on the piano, to set the dominant pitch. Then she adds black keys, undertones, the minor emotions, like neurotic concealment, lowered expectations, disappointment, giggling, snide laughter, estrangement, or annoyance. The result is not thoroughly unpleasant. As Gertrude Stein notes, "Merchandise is always a pleasure."[3]

6. Harrison deploys colors with the scale and force of bodies. Her colors do things: they loom up, they come at you in big corporeal patches, as blobs and facades and silhouettes that confront you like an encounter with another person or their shadow. These colors constitute shapes and are constituted by

3. Gertrude Stein, *Lucy Church Amiably* (Paris: the Plain Edition / Imprimerie Union, 1930; reprinted by New York: Something Else Press, 1969), 63.

shapes. Rarely in Harrison's work is a color used in a way altogether different from how a shape is used.

7. Bodies, shapes, colors, and sizes therefore achieve equivalent objecthood in Harrison's work.

8. Is there such a thing as a subjective semiotician?

9. Traditionally in sculpture, color took a subordinate role because color is surface, the literally "superficial" coating for the more important function of form. But since Harrison deploys manufactured objects to mean (or represent) everything in the world that is really superficial (or perhaps, artificial), then color is free (as it is in painting) to be a formal player and to engage in the formal relations that are the very visual "flesh" of the world. We can therefore take note very specifically of how Harrison works as colorist. First of all, she seems purposefully to avoid tonal shading and to make her colors legible always as individual shapes. Second, though she continues to develop her color vocabulary, she consistently uses color to delineate specific edges and to indicate relations between those edges and the shapes that lie near them. Third, she uses color very specifically to play with the idea of depths—sometimes as the traditional thin coating of a form, and sometimes colors that seem to soak in, stain, imbue themselves, instantiate themselves into or as a form. Fourth, her specific choices of color are often strident or aggressive, almost to the point of being vulgar.

10. Harrison uses color in both a narrative and non-narrative way. In her earlier work, colors were symbols—for example, her symbol for "the divine" was iridescence. Gleam equaled god, a kind of straightforward symbolic system in which shine is a symbol for something holy. But later on, Harrison seems to have become enchanted by the appearance of the iridescence

itself—it went from standing for something to visually being something. This is an important shift: it's when Harrison comes to fully believe in the visual itself, without the support of a simplistic "explanation" or text. Being = appearing.

11. Brown light vs. iridescence. Ludwig Wittgenstein: "'Brown light.' Suppose someone were to suggest that a traffic light be *brown*."[4]

12. Suppose someone were to suggest a world made of cardboard, a world with a monochromatic dun color and with only two dimensions. What could be revealed in this flat, matte world? Few events would be able to pierce its surfaces, to jab or cut past its folded edges.

13. Harrison sets up such a world made of cardboard, with pictures of iridescent windows hung around its periphery.[5] It is like a medieval diagram, where the world is reduced to the stark duality of brown vs. shiny. But paradoxically, the simplicity of this boiling down into a mere two-ness, the dun world versus the radiant one, offers us a way to sense more palpably the possibility of contact between two worlds, two entities, or to imagine more powerfully the possibility of their conflation or collapse.

14. Inside the folds of the cardboard world are little visual jokes, little punch lines in the form of figurines. Some of the figurines are brightly colored.

4. Ludwig Wittgenstein, *Remarks on Colour*, ed. G.E.M. Anscombe, trans. Linda M. McAlister and Margarete Schättle (Berkeley & Los Angeles: University of California Press, 1978), 25e.

5. Throughout these lines Sillman alludes to Rachel Harrison's installation *Perth Amboy* (2001): a cardboard labyrinth, where small assemblage works are dispersed, and that is surrounded by photographs of windows. (Perth Amboy is a New Jersey town where in 2000, people saw the Virgin Mary appearing, in the window of a two-storey apartment.) [Editors' note]

15. Harrison names three ways to cut through a two-part world: 1) color; 2) hole; and 3) joke.

16. In this world, then, colors and holes and jokes are one and the same. They have the same valence. What is there, what is visible, what is lacking, what is repressed, what has been removed, what is invisible, what is tactile, all render themselves in outline form.

17. *Indigenous Parts.*[6] Cut-up white shapes interact with a punch list of color swatches that hit the eye: first pink, then orange, purple, green, lemon-lime, rabbit gray, raspberry, and aqua. When Harrison breaks from narrative color, she turns first (like a good modernist) to categories.

18. White, or no-color, attains equal status with color or material, and therefore the act of removal attains equal status with coloring in. To cut or to color, both are to delineate pugnacious little patches that punch you in the eye. In Harrison's hands, colors and cuts stay as shapes. All colors are treated equally as holes and cuts, and all the removals are treated as shapes. What isn't seen is equal to what is seen. Is this female?

19. Comedy. Jewish comedy? Carl Andre's famous line, "a hole is a thing in a thing it is not,"[7] could be paraphrased into the following Borscht Belt formulation: a hole is a joke in a thing it is not. How much more pugnaciously slapstick can you get than cutting a hole out of a room?

6. *Indigenous Parts* is the title of an installation by Rachel Harrison; first exhibited in 1995, it has been evolving since then with each new presentation. [Editors' note]

7. Andre's aphorism actually is: "A thing is a hole in a thing it is not." Carl Andre, in conversation with Robert Barry and Lawrence Weiner, during a symposium organized by Seth Siegelaub at Bradford Junior College, on February 8, 1968; quoted in Lucy R. Lippard, *Six Years: The Dematerialization of the Art Object from 1966 to 1972* (New York: Praeger Publishers, Inc., 1973), 40. [Editors' note]

20. What if you withdraw from sensation? What if you cut out a hole? Is the removal of a hole an obstacle? Is a failed obstacle a way through? Can you remove the world?

21. I recall that Gertrude Stein is Jewish and also female.

22. We must also consider iridescence and patterns.

23. When used with irony, iridescence tends toward the profane. Ineffable shine is replaced by vulgar fluorescence. Grace becomes secretion, and the color narrative goes dystopic, almost cynical. Harrison is not above irony: she has honed her use of it chromatically. When Harrison uses iridescence this way, it comes in the form of an irradiated purplish-green body blow: the color of bruises, depravity, bad sorcery, and death. This purple is like merch and its soundtrack is the sub-satanic sounds of an old, used LP of a KISS concert.[8]

24. Harrison's narrative can go dark and it can go light. In some of the rooms of her solo show *Consider the Lobster* at Bard in 2009, it gives way to cleaner refreshments, patterns, flavors, health, sports, competition. Patterns conceal and reveal surface. A grandstand is marked by ochre and violet patches. A room is marked by a lumpen mash of pearl and chocolate. A dotted pattern gives a sustained tickling or itching sensation to the eye that confuses irritation with pleasure, that collapses surface and interior.

25. We have not yet fully considered the meaning of surfaces concealed and revealed by patterns but we'll get to that later. ♦

8. The rock band KISS features in a video that is part of Harrison's installation, *Car Stereo Parkway* (2005). [Editors' note]

This essay is a condensed and revised version of a talk, first given at Dia:Chelsea, New York, on April 28, 2008, as part of Dia's "Artists on Artists Lecture Series," on the invitation of Lynne Cooke; then at the Solomon R. Guggenheim Museum, New York, on May 8, 2012, as part of the "Eye to Eye" series of artist-led tours of the exhibition John Chamberlain: Choices, *February 24–May 13, 2012. A different version appears in* Chinati Foundation newsletter *17 (October 2012).*

Some Thoughts on John Chamberlain

With illustrations by Michael Smith

The Couches, and Taste

I didn't think too much about John Chamberlain's work until a visit to Chinati in 2002 when I saw one of his couches.[1] I actually wasn't sure WHAT this huge foam thing was, but you could climb on top of it, and it was flanked by two video monitors playing a Jack Smith-esque hippie sex movie (which turned out to be Chamberlain's 1968 film, *The Secret Life of Hernando Cortez*). On a little shelf nearby there was a printed statement by Chamberlain partly about laziness: "In what I do, constant hard work is not necessary; my drive is based on laziness. I don't mind admitting that I'm lazy because laziness is, for me, an attribute."[2]

All this was an eye opener to say the least. I thought Chamberlain was the car crash guy, a relic from the age of expressionist machismo. What was he even *doing* at Marfa, the home of

1. The Chinati Foundation / La Fundación Chinati is a contemporary art museum that was founded by artist Donald Judd in Marfa, Texas, in 1986. Twenty-two sculptures by John Chamberlain are part of its permanent exhibition, presented as originally installed by Chamberlain and Judd. [Editors' note]

2. This quote comes from a statement originally published on the occasion of the exhibition, *John Chamberlain*, at the Dia Art Foundation, then located at 67 Vestry Street in New York, in late 1982; reprinted under the title, "John Chamberlain on John Chamberlain," *Chinati Foundation newsletter* 11 (2006), 34–35. [Editors' note]

Protestant Judd boxes? And why was he at über-classy Dia, by the way? Until the scales fell from my eyes in Marfa, all I knew was that he was a denizen of the '50s who came from Beat poetry and welded junk sculpture. I did not know much else about him. I had no idea that his work actually extended from crushed steel to delicately layered paintings, from underground movies to conceptual writing and process photography; I hadn't a clue about his work in foam, plastic, foil, film, video, nor about his many unrealized and funny ideas for installation and other social projects. Only after seriously reading up did I find out that his fans included Donald Judd but also Dan Graham and Lawrence Weiner, Donna DeSalvo, Brian O'Doherty, Klaus Kertess, Christopher Williams, and other smart, non-vulgar people. And it was hard not to notice that some of his chromatic and formal moves practically predicted work seen in galleries now. So I started marveling that Chamberlain could have remained hidden in plain sight; that an artist could become a cliché *and* remain simultaneously under-known. Not that Chamberlain's situation hasn't been duly noted; O'Doherty wrote that Chamberlain suffers from "category trouble": he's always "out of joint."[3] I would say that because his production runs restlessly down the middle of various genres, adhering to none as doggedly as it would seem, so his work actually ends up being predictive of later hybrid forms. As Judd said, the work is "simultaneously turbulent, passionate, cool and hard."[4]

3. Brian O'Doherty, "Chamberlain: Projective Sculpture" (1990), in *Brian O'Doherty: Collected Essays*, ed. Liam Kelly (Berkeley & Los Angeles: University of California Press, 2018), 298.

4. Donald Judd, "Chamberlain: Another View," *Art International*, December 1963; reproduced in *Donald Judd: Complete Writings 1959–1975* (Halifax: Press of the Nova Scotia College of Art and Design & New York: New York University Press, 1975), 110.

Chamberlain is a collagist, jamming shards and pieces together, not only pieces of steel, but ill-fitting pieces of culture, making jokes that fit with monuments, making fluff go with glare, an oeuvre that is in fact a patchwork of the culture around him.

Chamberlain's 1971 retrospective at the Guggenheim, curated by Diane Waldman, featured a range of many of the materials that Chamberlain had used up to that date, including early welded pieces and foams, paper bags and plexis. In the lobby of the museum was an enormous installation of one of his couches—he called them "barges"—which invited viewers to lounge around on its soft surfaces. That piece was installed with monitors on either side playing some homemade country-western music being performed by Chamberlain's friends in a loft. Chamberlain was totally ahead of his time with the 1967 foam couches: by now they seem like a kind of proto-relational aesthetics. Their scale alone marks them as a form of social art, because there's no way to put them anywhere except in public, the lobby of a museum or some other institutional space—they are gargantuan slabs, up to 25 feet long. Then there is the impropriety of their method and use: Chamberlain cut and carved them roughly and crudely by hand and with saws and knives—there's a film of Chamberlain on YouTube making one on these couches, hacking at the foam with giant kitchen knives, wearing suspenders, a T-shirt and a hat, though eventually the T-shirt comes off and he's just in suspenders and a hat, with just his hairy chest and moustache and a little pair of khaki shorts, while pretty girls and other guys hang around drinking and smoking on and around the foam slabs.[5] The couches

5. The video, titled *The Chamberlain Couch*, dated 1976, and shot at writer John Hersey's apartment in The Dakota, was uploaded by its maker Anton Perich, https://

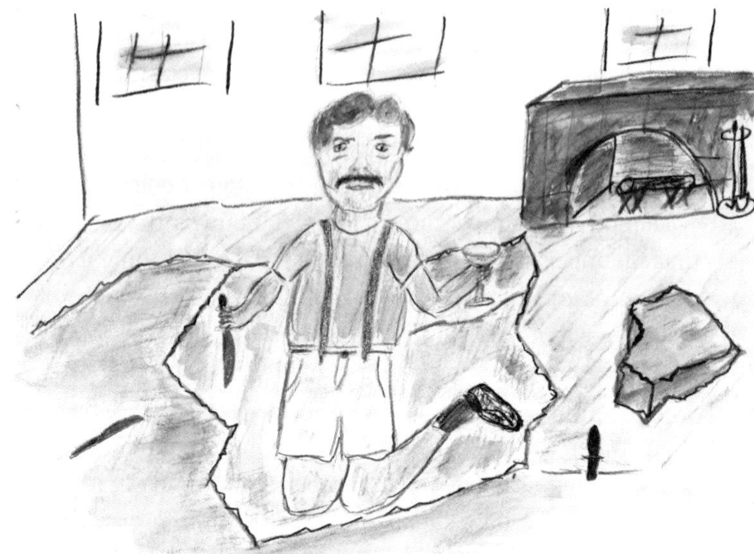

always defy propriety. They are soft ridiculous stations covered with silky fabric that invite people to lie down, to flop on. As the writer Gary Indiana put it: "Consider the eroticism of the massive foam couches: . . . carnal invitations *designed for one thing and one thing only*."[6] Or Klaus Kertess: "Furniture as sculpture as instant party."[7] Chamberlain himself describes the origin of these pieces in a more slapstick way; he says they began while he was trying to figure out how to change a mattress pad with a friend and the mattress pad foam kept getting out of whack: "Shoving the foam rubber into the mattress was

youtu.be/acJ4Fdihvjk (last accessed July 5, 2022). [Editors' note]

6. Gary Indiana, "John Chamberlain's Irregular Set," *Art in America* 71, no. 10 (November 1983), 212.

7. Klaus Kertess, "John Chamberlain: Squeeze Play" (2008), in Klaus Kertess, *Seen, Written. Selected Essays* (New York: Gregory R. Miller & Co., 2011), 70.

funny."[8] (In typical Chamberlain vernacular-speak, he also noted that the foam work makes people uncomfortable because it is made from urethane foam that deteriorates at a rate faster than that of human cell tissue.)

Dan Graham wrote praisefully of Chamberlain's couches in *Rock My Religion*, saying that they were important in offering a charged sensate experience not unlike sex or drugs, one that confuses subject and object in social space, and noting the presence of a "cultural and aesthetic irony in Chamberlain's questioning of the effect of mass consumption" and of a "social irony concerning the economics . . . of built-in obsolescence."[9]

Meanwhile, the *New York Times* critic Hilton Kramer reviewed the 1971 show dismissively. In a column titled "Serving a Period Taste," while crediting Chamberlain with adapting welded steel sculpture to the pictorial syntax of the New York School (AbEx) painting, he still chided the artist for doing nothing else of interest, for leaving sculpture "as he found it." Chamberlain's genre was pronounced a thing of the past, "of interest now primarily to researchers gathering data on the wayward tastes of another era." (Ouch.) And the review snarked: "There is something stupid in treating a minor artist as if he were a major figure."[10]

Actually the review is interesting because it shows the old, conservative Kramer oddly in alignment with a part of the left/critical art world of the time, with both parts struggling to distance themselves from a then-totally-commodified

8. Phyllis Tuchman, "An Interview with John Chamberlain," *Artforum* 10, no. 6 (February 1972), 41.

9. Dan Graham, "Art as Design" (1986), in *Rock My Religion: Writings and Projects 1965–1990* (Cambridge, MA: MIT Press, 1993), 214–15.

10. Hilton Kramer, "Serving a Period Taste," *New York Times*, January 2, 1972, 17.

expressionism. Kramer wrote: "When Abstract Expressionism was enjoying for the first time a widespread influence . . . [the] ideal artistic statement would have consisted in a pair of paint-spattered blue jeans and an unironed blue work shirt, somehow elevated into a saleable commodity."[11] Apparently whether from the right or the left, Chamberlain was just too gauchely celebratory of the capitalized gesture of intuition; from either side gesture itself was now at least suspicious, if not completely bankrupt. But what this bad review points its finger at are the very characteristics that we might find great about Chamberlain's work now: his work's identifying a specific (bad) taste. One of his work's formal functions is precisely its superficiality: literally, how things appear, are formed by their surfaces, deal with surface. With a historical turn of the screw, this quality is somehow redeemed in a post-Warhol time when surface itself is of supreme importance and self-critically reveals what is suppressed by what lays on top. By fully deploying tactility, in all its expressionistic vulgarity, Chamberlain literally provokes the issue of taste, the limits of taste, the dictates of taste. His delivery system of surfaces and facades, all done up in a fleshily audacious array of color, are all part of what I love about this work now. His work may be a commodity, but it is a meeting of flesh and commodity.

When Chamberlain's couches were originally shown, they were often flanked by those video monitors broadcasting looped programs of various kinds, (organized by Chamberlain), in some cases his own movies, like *The Secret Life of Hernando Cortez*, and in another case (an installation in

11. *Id.*

1981 in Germany)[12] an ultra-modern looped program of ridiculous American TV commercials, such as fake commercials from *Saturday Night Live*. Chamberlain actually spent much of the year 1968 involved in film: he made 16mm films, *Wedding Night*, *The Secret Life of Hernando Cortez*, and *Wide Point*, as much parodying underground film as they ARE underground films, and featuring downtown superstars Taylor Mead and Ultra Violet. Chamberlain himself hung around the set of Andy Warhol's *Lonesome Cowboys* (1968) and was asked to *be* in the film, though he declined, when its original star Ondine failed to show up. Chamberlain's own films are ambient, distracted, Dionysian extravaganzas where the characters exist in various exotic, dreamy, strange places amid meandering scripts and voluptuous goings-on. *Wide Point* was a proto-installation project, supposed to be projected on seven screens simultaneously. Chamberlain had lots of other never-realized film projects, including a Navajo creation myth vehicle for superstar Viva, and a film based on the "secret life" of William Shakespeare.

In these film projects you find the same basic entanglement of sex and a sense of humor that are evident in his giant couches. Chamberlain said many times, "I deal with material as I see fit . . . which has to do primarily with sexual and intuitive thinking."[13] His films mock and imitate underground films simultaneously, as the couches *are* both sculptures and a

12. *American Barge* (1979), now in the collection of the Dia Art Foundation, was shown, with TV monitors on its armrests, in the entrance of *Westkunst*, Messehalle, Cologne; curated by Kaspar König and Laszlo Glozer, this exhibition ambitioned to survey art from the Western world since 1939. Dan Graham has mentioned seeing this work as an important influence, notably in the aforementioned "Art as Design." [Editors' note]

13. Statement from 1982, reprinted in *Chinati Foundation newsletter*, *art. cit.*

brazen parody of themselves. This dual consciousness of making something and being something is neither parody nor cynicism, and is perhaps similar to the early work of another Pop expressionist, Claes Oldenburg. Barbara Rose could have been writing about Chamberlain when she wrote about Oldenburg's *Store* in 1969: "It was 'a place of 'quick love,' as well as a museum' . . . With its brilliant color, sensuous surfaces, and abundance of goods, *The Store* hinted at the joys and pleasures that industrial civilization *might* bring . . . It was also both a celebration of the vitality of American culture, and a satire on the American obsession to consume . . ."[14] Chamberlain's work is also carnal and comical in its base enjoyment of low-ness. His work both establishes and mocks the language of formalism. The couches are an example of this duality, and so are his many famously punning and lewd titles, which read like a parade of burlesque acts: *Pardon My Breeze*, *One Stop Smut Shop*, *Toasted Hitlers*, *Mrs Swayed Schwooz*, *Lord Suckfist*, *Infected Eucharist*, *Wandering Bliss Meets Fruit of the Loom*.

Process, Color, and Surface

Though Chamberlain's work is usually described simply as a kind of Pop expressionism, the adjectives you might assign to it are baroque, hybrid, anthropomorphic, performative, relational, wrecked, collapsed, and camp. This sculptural vocabulary makes clear the connection between his work and a whole generation of newer artists, artists who themselves make a broad spectrum of work with both form and satire. Chamberlain's excessive shininess, delighted fakeness and assertive exteriority

14. Barbara Rose, *Claes Oldenburg* (New York: Museum of Modern Art, 1970), 175.

evince jokey forms of postmodern desire. His work also shares with contemporary artists a defiant rejection of the clean-cut medium specificity. His sculptures *are* arguably paintings, or collages. One of the formal ways that Chamberlain blurs the line between painting and sculpture is that the work often seems to have no structural armature, like a good modernist thing does. Chamberlains are centrifugal; their underlying structures are suppressed or not there at all. They are formed like cabbages or roses, sheaths of concentric surfaces bent around mysterious cores, which we cannot know because we never see them, though we can peek in between the ply of the work and see that there is nothing in there but more of the same. In fact, Chamberlain proposes different options for volumes of space inside the work, in some cases to have NO space inside—as I've been describing—and in others to *start* with a strongly declared inner space and then to crumple or crush it away in a single gesture. The oil cans and the galvanized steel works from '67, '68, and '69 are examples of this latter way of dealing with interior space—the work almost contains the loud pop as the air inside is crushed like a cigarette package, which was in fact what he based the proportions of these boxes on—at that time, he was going to nightclubs like Max's Kansas City,[15] and was famous for sitting around drinking and crushing cigarette packs. It was said that no one could crush a pack of Gauloises like Chamberlain could. The galvanized steel works were begun by working on some discarded Judd boxes that had been rejected for having slight irregularities; then other galvanized steel boxes were fabricated especially for him to crush. His *Penthouse* pieces

15. See "Dear Maria Lassnig," note 4, page 234. [Editors' note]

from the late 1960s, made of paper bags with paint and resin thrown on them, were expressly made to capture the energy of blowing up and popping a paper bag. Chamberlains are more de-compositional than constructional. These forms are arrived at through a series of gestural decisions, made with swatches of metal, but the question of *how* they were made or *where* they were torn from to begin with, is oblique. There are little hints that they were once cars or appliances, found or chosen from scrap metal yards, but mostly in the end they are rendered as strokes or patches of color, just like in a painting, strokes that register time and change and motion and flux as a painterly painting does. They're sculptures that overtly perform their own process, materiality, and trajectories. The raw torn edges are held together with a little tack bolt here or there, but are seemingly always on the verge of falling apart. Clearly if there is such a thing as minimalism, this is its opposite, and Judd called it "snazzy, elegant in the wrong way, immoderate."[16]

All his work is somewhat anthropomorphic, though it is notable for omitting a sense of head or face, and concentrating instead on suggestive bodies. The bodies are absorbed into the materiality of the sculpture itself, but a sense of a figure always seems to be fundamentally present. Chamberlain said, "The definition of sculpture for me is stance and attitude."[17] About the sculpture *Miss Lucy Pink* from 1963, Chamberlain said, "[it] has a sort of a front and a back . . . it reminds me of somebody who's putting on a good front, but you take a look around

16. Donald Judd, "John Chamberlain," in *7 Sculptors*, exh. cat. (Philadelphia: ICA Philadelphia, 1965); reproduced in *Complete Writings*, *op. cit.*, 190.

17. Statement from 1982, reprinted in *Chinati Foundation newsletter*, *art. cit.*

the back and her ass is hanging out."[18] As his work progresses chronologically, the figures multiply, swell, accumulate into masses or assemblies of figure. Perhaps this formally connects to Chamberlain's interest in the 1950s as an art student in Chicago in the orgiastic architecture of Hindu temples like Khujaraho, for example, which features a roof with thousands of copulating gods and goddesses, an orgiastic crowd scene that rivals some of Chamberlain's film productions.

Painting and Color

By the 1960s Chamberlain had moved away from the language of the scrap metal yard, and started to engage specifically with saturated, painterly color combinations, used not just as a surface treatment, but as the palpable material that you mold and crush. This assertion of color as a primary force rather than a secondary one is what makes Chamberlain a painter as much as anything. Chamberlain's color is second to none: neither second to volume, nor form, nor drawing, nor structure, nor part of a semiotic system in which the color merely signifies. He is one of the only sculptors to really use color, except Judd and George Sugarman (though in their sculptures, various parts or shapes are painted a different color, whereas in a Chamberlain, thousands of colors prevail over recognizable objects, even if there is sometimes a fan blade or a car fender visible). The colors in Chamberlains ooze and spread across parts, and do all the things that color does in painting, like smear, tint, stain, scumble, feather, layer, veil, glaze, harmonize, contradict. It's

18. Julie Sylvester, "Auto/Bio. Conversations with John Chamberlain," in *John Chamberlain: A Catalogue Raisonné of the Sculpture, 1954–1985*, ed. Julie Sylvester (New York: Hudson Hills Press, 1986), 15.

an extravagant and promiscuous polychromatic experience, matched by these sexy-sounding color functions as described by Klaus Kertess, writing in Chamberlain's catalogue raisonné: "The inhaling swell is anchored by a multisectioned diagonal of off-whites that occasionally secretes a pale, shiny blue and drips with a cascade of yellow-orange. Broad, irregular rectangular blades of red push out from underneath . . ."[19] Or: "A pale silver-lilac boxlike container capped with a peaked golden umbel shape . . . until it bursts open to reveal a flatulent gable sheltering a wrinkled blue cone with an orifice enveloping red folds."[20]

Chamberlain's use of color therefore follows the logic of his production of surfaces: colors as well as surfaces are literally ripped from somewhere else, picked from piles, torn from parts, and then pressed, smashed, crushed, bent and collaged into fractured accumulative masses in which color relations change as you move around them. Chamberlain's *Kiss* pieces from 1979, which Judd called his "hard, sweet, pastel enamels,"[21] were exceptions to his usual process. These were crushed-up oil cans which were painted both before *and* after being crushed; paint was applied to the various facets of the cans first, *then* they were crushed, afterwards various surfaces were painted on top.

1969–70 and the Odd Text Pieces

In 1969 and 1970 Chamberlain was in the middle of a seven-year-long hiatus from most of his painted steel work, but this

19. Klaus Kertess, "Color in the Round and Then Some: John Chamberlain's Work, 1954–1985," in *A Catalogue Raisonné, op. cit.*, 33.

20. *Ibid.*, 34.

21. Donald Judd, "In the galleries," *Arts Magazine*, March 1962; reproduced in *Complete Writings, op. cit.*, 46.

was a productive time for him: a time during which he produced innovative sculpture made from scrap appliances, as well as plexiglass works and his paper bag *Penthouse* pieces. In 1969 he made one of his two sets of elegant white scrap-appliance material, in which he did not disguise the sources and left handles and bits of the appliances themselves showing. In 1970, back in East Los Angeles again, Chamberlain made a body of West-Coast-looking work made of melted sheets of plexiglass, then a new material. These works were made by heating the plexiglass in a giant walk-in oven, forming it into folded or collapsed shapes, and then annealing it with lustrous translucent glazes made of quartz and aluminum in his friend Larry Bell's vacuum-coating machine. Chamberlain himself has said that he moved on—to the paper-and-resin *Penthouse* pieces—before he really perfected the use of these new and exotic materials.

In the 1960s, all of Chamberlain's paintings were named after popular singing groups: *The Righteous Brothers*, *DeeDee Sharp* (whose song "The Mashed Potato" ushered in the popular dance of that same name), *Ray Charles*, *The Supremes*. (A painting that he actually sold to Diana Ross. There is a wonderful picture of Chamberlain with Diana Ross and the Supremes; they really were hanging out.)[22] Also from 1969–70 he worked on several somewhat vexed language and text projects, first through the Art and Technology program at LACMA, run by Maurice Tuchman, who paired artists and corporations to work together collaboratively. Chamberlain was paired first with Dart Industries, where he tried to realize a video-mapping project, suggested to him by the artist Douglas Huebler,

22. This 1964 photograph is in *A Catalogue Raisonné*, *op. cit.*, 228. [Editor's note]

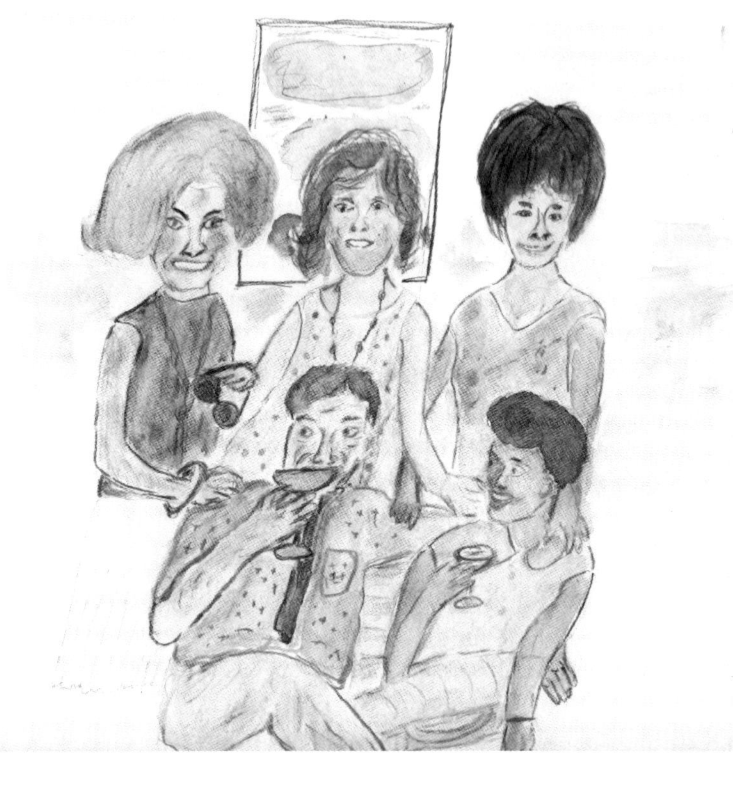

to be shown simultaneously on fourteen screens. That didn't pan out. Next he came up with a smell environment project called SniFFter, a presentation of more than a hundred odors indexed into a kind of parodical poetics categories including mother's milk, German Shepherd, wrestling arena, moonshot at Cape Kennedy, Hostess cupcakes, Larry Bell's studio, and Charlie McCarthy. The SniFFter project didn't work either, and Chamberlain moved on rather inexplicably to the RAND

Corporation, a conservative think-tank partially responsible for the development of the internet and war policymaking, and specializing in the development and study of gaming structures, and war games. (RAND Corp. was where Daniel Ellsberg worked, from which he stole the Pentagon Papers.) However, in this highly charged politicized time at the height of the Vietnam War, Chamberlain did NO political activist work, but rather trafficked in the absurd. He worked at RAND Corp. for six rather disastrous weeks on illegible poetic texts. The RAND people mostly didn't like him and he didn't like them back. He complained to a friend at the time about how uptight the people there were, saying, "I can't get into any of their circuits, . . . like the girls wear too much underwear."[23] He tried arranging screenings of his *Secret Life of Hernando Cortez* film, which most of the RAND people hated, and the film was shut down. He sent the RAND workers questionnaires in which respondents were to make up their own answers, rather than to answer questions, and asked that these answers be sent to his office in room 1138. The workers mostly refused and sent him antagonistic notes like "the answer is to terminate Chamberlain," or, in one case, merely "fuck you." He ended up writing his own answers, and publishing a tortuous 34-page long poetry-text formulation, which is divided into two parts: "What are the circumstances to these responses?" and "What is the response to these circumstances?"[24]

23. *A Report on the Art and Technology Program of the Los Angeles County Museum of Art, 1967–1971*, ed. Maurice Tuchman (New York: Viking Press, 1971), 72.

24. *Ibid.*, 74–76; the section of the *Report* focusing on Chamberlain's projects, written by Jane Livingston, is a hilarious read. About the LACMA program, see Catherine Wagley, "Closed Circuits," *East of Borneo*, May 11, 2015, https://eastofborneo.org/articles/closed-circuits-a-look-back-at-lacmas-first-art-and-technology-initiative. [Editors' note]

In the 1970s Chamberlain worked on other never-finished text pieces, including a project to collect hundreds of clichés set into grids, as the artist said, "washed" with different "informational fields"—whatever that means. In the mid-1950s, Chamberlain had studied with the poet Robert Creeley at Black Mountain College, and they had sustained a lasting friendship. By the 1970s he was also friendly with Lawrence Weiner, who interviewed him for his Dia catalogue in 1991.[25] These associations and projects underline his interest and use of language as a structure and a material, not unlike his use of tactile materials. Yet his language projects, which are in line with the work of contemporary artists of his time, remain the most obscure part of his work.

Surface and Words

Black Mountain was arguably one of the most radical and generative art schools in the history of America. From 1933, Josef and Anni Albers were influential teachers there, coming straight from the Bauhaus and the rise of the Nazis in Germany. In 1955–56, when Chamberlain was a student at Black Mountain, its director was the poet Charles Olson, and Creeley was a teacher. Under these mentors, Chamberlain developed his procedures of word games and lists, and generally treating language as just another material. In the Dia catalogue interview, Chamberlain told Weiner: "My teachers were Kline, De Kooning, Charles Olson. Kline gave me the structure. De Kooning gave me the color."[26] Though Chamberlain did not elaborate

25. See *John Chamberlain: Gondolas and Dooms Day Flotilla* (New York: Dia Center for the Arts, 1991).

26. *Ibid.*, 9.

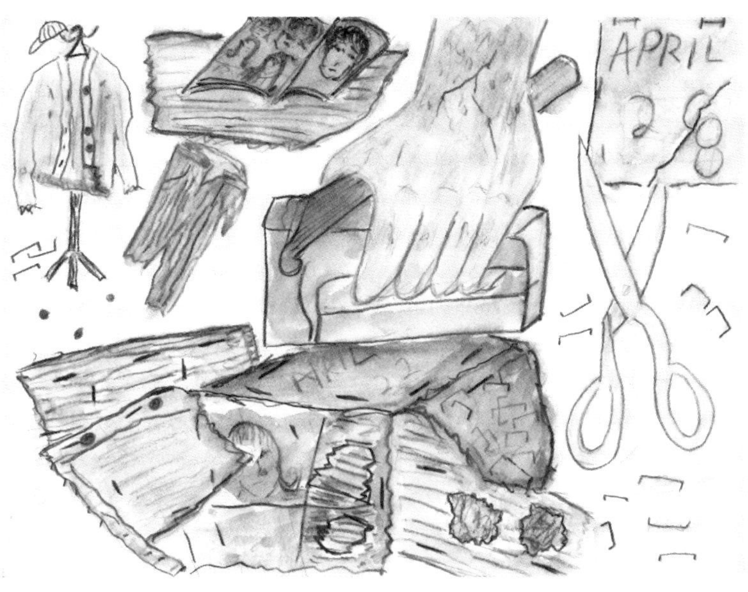

exactly what he got from Olson, you can intuit what it was by reading Olson's 1950 manifesto *Projective Verse* about the kinetics of American-type poetry: Olson gave Chamberlain both a method and a speed. *Projective Verse* describes poetry as a physical form of language discharging energy as it moves out of the poet's mouth, on the breath, the poem conceived as something like an imaginary polyhedron that connects the speaker, the hearer, and the world itself at various points—indeed, like one of Chamberlain's own complexly wrought forms. And Olson insisted that "if you also set up as a poet, USE USE USE the process . . . always one perception must must must MOVE, INSTANTER, ON ANOTHER!"; "keep it moving as fast as you can, citizen"—and the word "citizen" is important here, because this is a social engagement, a social concept of expression, a form of radical expression, as opposed to "expressionism."[27] As Creeley wrote later in a poem about Chamberlain: "There is a handle to the world that is looked for, a way of taking it in hand."[28] In a literal sense, these action-based procedures coincide with a change in Chamberlain's process at Black Mountain: working there he stopped using glue to make his collages in the old slow way, and started to use a stapler, an immediate and faster way to attach things, a way to move "instanter," as Olson says. "You just throw on the materials and the paper and staple them down."[29] Perhaps a more precise way to describe it is with a Chamberlain-type of list: grab, assemble, cut up, throw down, scramble, rearrange, staple, all in a swift, kinetic dialectical chain of actions.

Hairdressing, History, Restlessness, Foam

By 1962 Chamberlain was a respected and established artist; he had been included in a group show at MoMA in New York and had had a solo show at Leo Castelli Gallery. Yet, as Kertess writes, "his acceptance was primarily among fellow artists and the immediate inner circle of the artworld. Deserved critical and commercial success still eluded him."[30] By the middle of the 1960s he had already begun branching out of the crushed cars he was famous for, and was working with the diverse materials I've been describing. He moved back and forth between

27. See Charles Olson, "Projective Verse," in *Collected Prose*, ed. Donald Allen and Benjamin Friedlander (Berkeley & Los Angeles: University of California Press, 1997), 240. See also "Notes on the Diagram," page 148. [Editors' note]

28. Robert Creeley, "John Chamberlain," in *Recent American Sculpture* (New York: Jewish Museum, 1964); reproduced in *The Collected Essays of Robert Creeley* (Berkeley & Los Angeles: University of California Press, 1989), 392–93.

29. Phyllis Tuchman, "An Interview with John Chamberlain," *art. cit.*, 39.

30. See Kertess, "Color in the Round," *op. cit.*, 35.

LA and NY at least eleven times. He made numerous large bodies of paintings and innumerable works on paper. He began to show his work in Europe. During this restive time, he removed himself from his own cliché of production by quitting the painted scrap steel in 1967, largely not to return to it for seven years. Chamberlain's practice was restless and irregular, often stopping doing one thing well before he became known for it. His staunchest support came from the stalwart art world figures of Donald Judd and Barbara Rose, but as Kertess puts it, Chamberlain "remain[ed] the pagan friend of the monastic order."[31] Here is how Chamberlain describes the period of '67: "I was tired of using automobile material, because the only response I ever got was that I was making automobile crashes and that I used the automobile as some symbolic bullshit about our society. . . . The fact that all this material had color had made it very interesting to me. But the more interested I got, the more everyone kept insisting it was car crashes. Since nobody got it, I grew bored with the whole idea and thought I would do something with no color in it."[32] So, in the mid-1960s he explored other avenues, culminating in his large body of foam rubber work from 1966 to 1972. These amazing, raw and swift foam sculptures and couches began with a set of thirty or so small works made quickly from kitchen sponges, which became the basis for larger sculptures made with urethane foam, all cinched and tied with lassos and ropes, some bare and some with paint dripped on them. They are remarkable, vigorous works that speak a common language with Process Art or performance art, yet

31. *Ibid.*, 34.
32. Julie Sylvester, "Auto/Bio," *op. cit.*, 21.

at the time they were largely overlooked and not commercially successful. Chamberlain showed this body of foam works at Virginia Dwan Gallery in Los Angeles as early as 1966 and then in Cologne and Munich in 1967, but none were sold. All were returned, and Chamberlain sold a few for pocket money to anyone who asked, including Walter Hopps who came knocking on his studio door and walked away with one for twenty bucks. Chamberlain gave the rest away.

Michael Kimmelman wrote in the *New York Times* in 2003: "The connection between his sculptures and bouffant hairdos is an unexplored avenue of art historical inquiry."[33] In the 1950s, Chamberlain had been a hairdresser and makeup man, teaching at a hairdressing and makeup school. He said, "I was sort of ahead of my time , in a sense. Like, if we had a *Vogue* magazine lying around and somebody saw a hairdo in it, I was the one who could figure out how to do it."[34] A collector recalled Chamberlain this way: "I think he was somewhat embarrassed by his salon days and presented himself as a very gruff and hairy character, looking more like a North woodsman than a sculptor. He would come to the very sedate law firm where I was working and bring new work to show me. The receptionist would call me saying, 'A person is here to see you.' They wouldn't let him sit in the client's waiting room, but rather they would put him in the messenger's delivery room. They said that he didn't go with the décor."[35]

Though his foam work asserts some of the specific goals and attitudes of Process Art of the early 1970s, and though this work

33. Michael Kimmelman, "John Chamberlain: 'Early Works,'" *New York Times*, November 14, 2003, Section E, 35.

34. Julie Sylvester, "Auto/Bio," *op. cit.*, 10.

35. *John Chamberlain. Early Works*, exh. cat. (New York: Allan Stone Gallery, 2003).

began before Robert Morris made his felt pieces, the Chamberlains were never valued at anything like the Morris pieces. In 1969, Chamberlain was included in the exhibition *New Media, New Methods* at MoMA, curated by Kynaston McShine, along with Warhol, Richard Serra, Eva Hesse, and others—an important show, though there was no catalogue. One of Chamberlain's 1967 foam pieces was in the show, listed in the museum's records as being worth $900. A 1968 Morris felt piece that was included, with a recorded value of $5000. Subsequently, Chamberlain was left out of several big surveys of the new art from 1969 on at the Whitney Museum in New York and other venues in Europe. Morris, who virtually wrote the textbook on the art of the 1970s, never wrote a word on Chamberlain, though he was clearly familiar with the work as they both showed at Castelli and had been in the MoMA show together.

Vulgarity

When I was first thinking about Chamberlain, a few years ago, the persona of the dandy was in vogue in the art world. In the face of the dandy's disdainful refusal to get his hands dirty, I wondered what you could call the artistic persona that Chamberlain seemed to embody. There was that statement about laziness, and he certainly seemed like a *refined* flâneur or bricoleur, but he still seemed to throw himself into the world with a big fat expressionistic embrace. I started to wonder if on the flip side of the dandy there was a counter-dandy, someone I would call a *vulgarian*. As I understand it, a dandy is a figure that arose partly in relation to the class distinctions of late nineteenth- / early twentieth-century French society—a sort of ironic self-assignation of class, an imitation aristocrat who is actually from the middle class. It seems that such a persona can only arise when the classes aren't exactly fixed, when there are upper-middle classes and lower-middle classes and the possibility of class movement. The dandy classically expresses a posture of disdain for work as a form of critique of the bourgeoisie—the lower or middle bourgeoisie striking a farcical pose of the upper bourgeoisie. I was thinking that a vulgarian is just the reverse: a person whose work revels in effort. Vulgarians *do things* rather than keeping themselves at an ironic remove; they exalt in the corporeal goings-on of the body. Dandies don't care; vulgarians care. A vulgarian transgresses refinement by going downward into carnality and buffoonery instead of upward into the haughtier aesthetics of the ironic. By contrast, in the 1950s and later in the 1970s, downwardly-mobile bohemians achieved a kind of class self-re-assignment by seeming like *all* they were doing was working. Work, and the worker, was a position, was sexy, as were jeans and work boots and workers' caps. Workers were another romantic figure, the highest form of low. So Chamberlain, in a kind of urban poet / rag-picker-*maudit* gleaner persona, delved into the baseness of the city and its refuse, an anti-dandy archiving scrap and garbage, sorting things judiciously, finding treasures in urban junk, willfully embracing the vulgar.

Of course both of these positions are constructs. T. J. Clark's famous 1994 article "In Defense of Abstract Expressionism," limns the inescapable framework of such taste in art and aesthetics, linking the handmade and expressionist with the vulgar, and the vulgarly middle-class. In the essay, Clark says, "I think we might come to describe Abstract Expressionist paintings better if we took them above all to be *vulgar*. . . . To call an art work vulgar is . . . to do something more transgressive than to call it low or *informe*."[36] The term vulgar, he adds, "points two ways—to the object itself, . . . some atrociously visual quality that the object will never stop betraying however hard it tries; and to the object's existence in a particular social world, for a set of tastes and styles of individuality . . ."[37] Saddling AbEx with lyricism, and inexorably with the ludicrous, Clark concludes, "lyric in our time is deeply ludicrous. The deep ludicrousness of lyric is Abstract Expressionism's subject, to which it returns like a tongue to a loosening tooth."[38] Clark's reading, in which all expression is lumped together under the heading expression*ism*, involves an embarrassed (or faux-embarrassed) grappling with his own squeamish feelings about expressions at all. (What, after all, are they really expressing?) Nevertheless, by pointing to these connections between class and taste, Clark gets to something often suppressed in the literature of New York School art, and which remains unclassifiable in Chamberlain's work, which is its own paradoxical sense of bad/good taste. As Chamberlain's work contains both bad taste and self-reflexive enjoyment in just how bad he's being, he therefore points two ways—having his excess and eating it too. The writer and painter Sidney Tillim wrote in 1989: "Much of modernism's taste is rooted in a form of 'bad' taste. A too-generalized taste has debilitated most of modern art. Taste as I define it is not just about itself but an index of contact with feeling."[39]

36. T. J. Clark, "In Defense of Abstract Expressionism," *October* 69 (Summer 1994), 26. See also "AbEx and Disco Balls," page 129. [Editors' note]

37. *Ibid.*, 28.

38. *Ibid.*, 48.

39. See Sidney Tillim, "Ideology and Difference," *Arts Magazine* 63, no. 7 (March 1989), 141–43. Tillim discusses Jeff Koons' and Jules Olitski's works. [Editors' note]

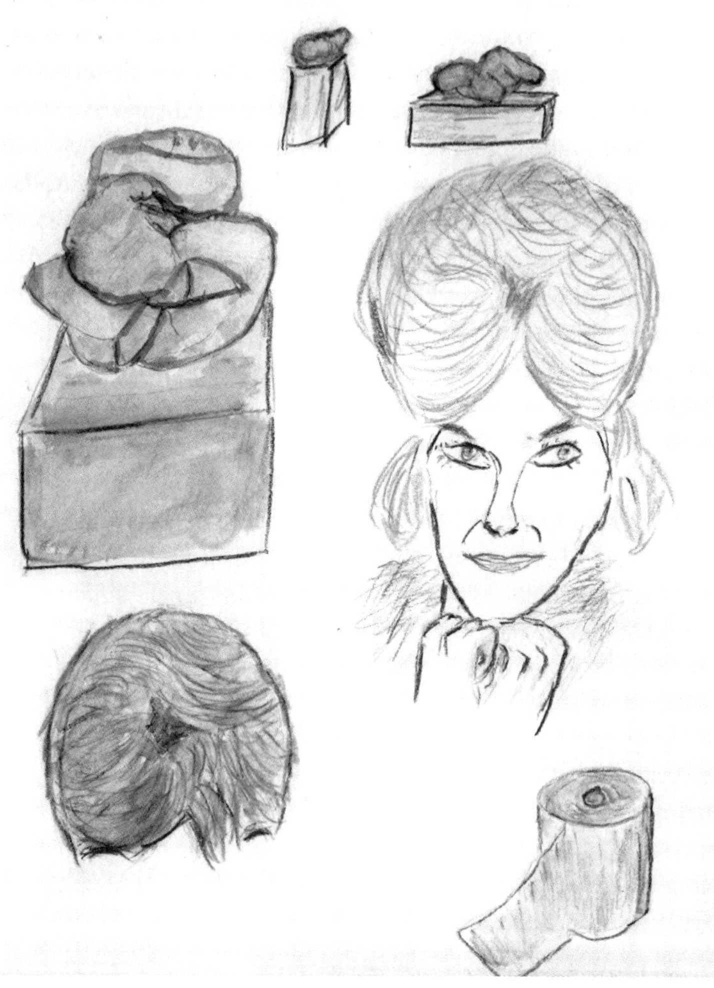

So I am interested in thinking about John Chamberlain in terms that I call vulgar, *because* of the specific drive in his work toward the sexual and brazen and showy, and *because* Chamberlain makes a slapstick of the idea of progress. He consciously repeats himself when it seems that things should be ended: his jokey titles, his crushed forms, the whole idiom of AbEx. At the same time, he insists on the lyrical and almost radically "female" associations of care, touch, attachment, repeating the verbs of his process consistently: wadding, squeezing, hugging, bunching, and scrunching. For Chamberlain, everything is making and feeling and doing, handsy and by hand. In his characteristically provocateur's way of describing things, he likened his process to the way people bunch toilet paper up: "... the wadding—the only time [people] can do it is instinctive, with toilet paper. They get this long line of material and they do something with it, very personal."[40] Chamberlain's method is an insistently tactile, sexualized, and instinctual form of making, and hands are the tools for knowing and for producing objects that are as much sentient bodies as corporeal objects. I think for Chamberlain the hand is analogous to the breath in Olson's *Projective Verse*: in other words, the vehicle upon which thought intrudes on and receives information from the world. When Chamberlain says "sex," it is really a shorthand for a phenomenological, experiential way of knowing. ♦

40. Edward Leffingwell, "The Irregular Set: An Interview with John Chamberlain," in *John Chamberlain: Sculpture and Work on Paper* (Youngstown, OH: Butler Institute of American Art, 1983), 18.

This essay was originally published in the monograph Amelie von Wulffen. Bilder 1998–2016, *ed. Isabel Podeschwa, Bernhart Schwenk, Joe Scotland, Amelie von Wulffen (London: Koenig Books, 2017).*

Why Amelie von Wulffen Is Funny

> The individual does actually carry on a twofold existence: one designed to serve his own purposes and another as a link in a chain . . .
> —SIGMUND FREUD[1]

> A joke is a double-dealing rascal . . .
> —SIGMUND FREUD[2]

AvW's comic drawings are really funny. I mean, how can you *not* laugh at a sausage smoking a cigarette, or a screw singing Schubert? But that's not exactly what's funny about them. What's *funny* is how vW invites the comic into the room with painting, and how the very presence of the comic skews the usual relations between paintings and their context, and vice versa. She enacts what Freud calls the "joke-work"[3] partly by a consistent sense of doubling—pairing, mirroring, transposing,

1. Sigmund Freud, "On Narcissism: an Introduction" (1914), trans. James Strachey, in *The Standard Edition of the Complete Psychological Works of Sigmund Freud, Volume 14*, ed. James Strachey and Anna Freud (London: Hogarth Press, 1957), 78.

2. Freud, "Jokes and Their Relation to the Unconscious" (1905), trans. James Strachey, *The Standard Edition of the Complete Psychological Works of Sigmund Freud, Volume 8*, ed. James Strachey and Anna Freud (London: Hogarth Press, 1960), 155.

3. *Ibid.*, 54 sq.

and displacing. Added to this is her keen instinct for narrative, for turning stories into pictures and back again. This Möbius strip of dual relations, which could also be called a comic strip, is vW's own expanded field in painting.

I was struck by this state of affairs when I saw her two, simultaneous gallery shows in New York City in 2011. The one at Greene Naftali downtown consisted of oil paintings and pencil-drawn pages from the ego comic (as she calls them) *November*. Uptown, at Alex Zachary, were aquarelles from the series *This is how it happened* (2011), depicting anthropomorphized fruits, vegetables, and tools. The very presence of flat-out humor in the domain of painting brought with it a conundrum: it walked and talked like art—the ego comics at Greene Naftali were hung alongside paintings, and the aquarelles at Alex Zachary were nicely framed and hung in a proper manner—but was it a joke? And if it was a joke, who was it a joke *on*? The comics proposed a state of fight or flight, an *otherness* from painting. What if something from a desk drawer, like a diary, or from another room, maybe the bedroom, staggers into the gallery? Can painting survive the crack-up of *the personal*?

Ordinary painting on canvas involves a form of stately compression: its layers, its decisions, and the time that went into the painting are all packed underneath the top layer. vW's drawings and some of her aquarelles, by contrast, are mobile, horizontal: they slide out sideways from painting; they go high and low. Their motility is psychic as well as physical. She installs them all over the room, even on furniture or architectural structures built especially for shows, sometimes using drawings as ladders, descending *downward* from painting to baser narratives below, other times using them as bridges, extending *outward* from painting to pages, comic strips, storyboards, animations, and slideshows. By referencing various literary formats, from the intimacy of a girl's diary to the broad social satire of *la comédie humaine*, vW gets at matters that a painting often just doesn't touch. The narrative itself can be funny, obscene, confessional, and sometimes brutal or aggressive, a little too personal, too anecdotal, and too entertaining. In her 2015 show at the Pinakothek der Moderne in Munich, the installation included a built-in architectural structure painted girly pink, complete with its own doorway and light fixture, further convoluting a fixed sense of interior/exterior or formal/informal. vW thus created a visual *situation*, rather than a painting *show*, in which the viewer was surrounded by a condition of narrativity—both de*pict*ion and de*script*ion—a situation of looking at and reading the entire room. This is clearly a move that doubles painting's usual square footage.

Even the title of the show at Alex Zachary, *This is how it happened*, proposed a type of doubling, not only letting the viewer know *what* happened, but *how* it happened. Many of vW's viewers recognize (or will find themselves in) the scenarios depicted in her work, literally or figuratively. They mirror our lives, including both our mediated lives (John Travolta, as in some of her earlier works) and our personal lives, revealing the gossipy *how* to the paintings' *what*, disclosing, dishing, divulging who was there, what they said, what they wore, what they daydreamed, how much things cost, what they did in the bathroom, etc. The comic strip is a slice of life—a form generally more cinematic or literary than painterly. Or maybe if not "literary," just textual: I am reminded of how comic strips come in the newspaper—if so, what "news" does vW's work bring?

I believe it brings us news of a painter's life, and that this is the prerogative of fiction, that it can be built upon a detailed description of an individual's life. This is not usually the wager of painting. To take it on means that vW has risked a new condition for painting. She pries painting open, letting some of its contents spill out from the back, flipping the back and the front, the high and the low. And once you've been behind the scenes, the front of the painting will never be the same again.

AvW's aquarelles from the series *This is how it happened* work on a different front, flipping subjects into objects, and objects into subjects. Our little human dramas are being played by *things*: it is a pear getting a blowjob, a paintbrush that pauses in a moment of pre-exhibition anxiety, a pretzel and a *Weißwurst* in the middle of a breakup, and a tomato experiencing *Schadenfreude*. These narratives, illustrated with a kind of relentless cheerfulness, punt away the straight face we could maintain with painting. Anything that might have been called art's "autonomy" is flooded by the contamination of the joke. vW implies that this surplus is a necessary condition of looking at the art, part of its materiality, and that just as comics come with the newspaper, that it must be part of the show. The pages from the ego comic *November* pinned to the wall at Greene Naftali opposite large-scale paintings created a kind of circulation, not just around the room but inside and around the paintings themselves, generating irresolvable möbial relations between serious/funny, high/low, comic/abstract, staged in the deceptively simple form of a comic strip or a children's book illustration. Walter Benjamin noted that children's books are "not without an ironic-satanic streak. The craftsmanship in these books [is] fully committed to the everyday life of the petty bourgeoisie."[4] And vW's too include a lampoon of all our failings—shame, pride, *Schadenfreude*, irritation, boredom, and other *petit bourgeois* emotions and feelings that constitute the inescapably embarrassing *how* of being alive.

Pointing to the issue of narrative in vW's work in a 2005 essay, Josef Strau wrote that her mechanism is the "invocation of a story linked in the imagination of the viewer with the object portrayed."[5] Indeed, vW's comic portrayals begin with our familiars, whether they are animal, vegetable, or mineral. In *November*, the enervated main character is shown making her way through a wearying succession of art events, openings, dinners, and studio visits, and spending an inordinate amount of time in bed or in the bathroom. Drawn with both an impatient scrum of pencil marks and an eye for detailed gray tones, the narrator's attention moves fluidly from the petty to the tragic and back again. Meanwhile the main character, the artist's alter ego, is struggling to get her work shown and then lying in bed, thinking of the terrifying gates of Auschwitz and its slogan "*Arbeit macht frei*." The main character encounters similarly changeable psychic swings in a later ego comic, called *Am kühlen Tisch (At the cool table)* (2013), which vW also showed alongside paintings, notably at her exhibition of the same name at Portikus in 2013.[6] *At the cool table* is a psychoanalyst's field day, chronicling a veritable minefield of anxieties ranging from

4. Walter Benjamin, "A Glimpse into the World of Children's Books" (1926), trans. Rodney Livingstone, in *The Work of Art in the Age of its Technological Reproducibility, and Other Writings on Media*, ed. Michael W. Jennings, Brigid Doherty, and Thomas Y. Levin (Cambridge, MA: Belknap Press of Harvard University Press, 2008), 233.

5. Josef Strau, "The Invocation," in *Amelie von Wulffen*, ed. Rita Kersting and Philipp Kaiser, exh. cat. (Ostfildern: Hatje Cantz, 2005), 156.

6. Amelie von Wulffen, *At the cool table*, ed. Bart van der Heide and Sophie von Olfers, exh. cat. (London: Koenig Books, 2014).

death to taxes, and along the way such gendered details as the fatness of one's ass or what it'd be like to be co-dependent with Goya.

The aquarelles shown uptown back in 2011 were like moments from a little Woody Allen movie, set somewhere between Charlottenburg in Berlin and the Upper West Side, but with fruits, vegetables, and tools as the main characters who are enduring the same tedium, tribulations, and occasional triumphs that we do—smoking, jogging, exercising, moping, applying for jobs, performing, worrying, fucking, breaking up, and attending meetings. The aquarelles are caption-less, but we still feel the characters' pain—these objects are at key moments of yearning, ridicule, or annoyance. If AvW's work links image to narrative, it is wed not to a saga or an epic, but to a cheap novella. And to a critique of bourgeois subjectivity, these cartoons would answer: *What else is there?* Aren't all the days of our lives built of the parade of minor details that populate such subjectivity? (Even Kant left a note in his drawer, found after his death, reminding himself to forget about Lampe, the old servant with whom he had a falling out before he died. If even he had a secret personal problem in his top desk drawer, you know it's universal.)[7] You just have to laugh at this maneuver of vW's, not only to stretch painting and drawing out horizontally, but to send it down the rabbit hole of the everyday.

As I've been trying to argue here, vW employs a consistent form of *linkage* or doubling in her work. But we might view

7. The tragicomic account of Kant's relations with Lampe can be found in Thomas de Quincey's *Last Days of Immanuel Kant* (1827) (Seattle: Sublunary Editions, 2021). [Editors' note]

this situation another way: does the presence of linkage also indicate the possibility of *breakage*, or of something that is essentially *split*? Might one then ask, in addition to how vW doubles things, how she *splits* them, how breakage—or breakdown—figures into her work? In painting, she hobbles linearity with collage, overlay, interruption, fragmentation, glitch, and omission or just by letting the picture fade away. She cuts up architectures, people, and places, and reconstructs memories into a series of collisions. Within this painterly fracture, drawing appears as if it were glue, a form of recuperation, a way to hold things together. Skeins and thickets of line extend across the cuts in her paintings, rebuilding connections with repetitious strokes, lines, hatch marks, tones, patterns, curlicues, and various natural and decorative motifs. vW seems to relish the arrested time of a carefully redrawn or repainted photograph from an art history book or a family album, or the slowed-down response time of answering a story with a picture or vice versa. Time itself is recuperative, not just reviving the image, but reinstating sentiment itself to its original function. To paraphrase Benjamin, sentimentality can be restored to health.[8] The process of drawing is what gives rise to affect in vW's work, whether it's sorrow or satire.

In fact, I think all the modern "funny" painters are drawers at heart—think of Francis Picabia, Philip Guston, Florine Stettheimer, Sigmar Polke, Martin Kippenberger, Nicole Eisenman. Part of what makes them funny is how they factor themselves as personae in a painterly drama. Guston, the tragi-comic hero of painting, always lying in bed balefully, smoking

8. Benjamin, "These Surfaces for Rent" (1923–26), trans. Edmund Jephcott, in *The Work of Art*, *op. cit.*, 173–74.

and doubting, with a plate of French fries on his belly; Kippenberger, in his white underpants, ridiculously inserted as an anti-hero onto the very platform of Romantic expression, the raft of the Medusa. (Ad Reinhardt's funniness is kept more like a secret: cordoned off and consigned to the other room.) A friend once asked me if new paintings could have new feelings? I said I thought that irony *was* the new feeling. vW's work seems to propose that to find new feelings, we have to seek them in new places, or come at them from a different angle: from underneath, from outside—in the desk drawer, in confessionals, novellas, or magazines.

Where *have* we seen these kinds of walking and talking fruits and vegetables before, anyway? Either in children's books, comics, or advertisements. AvW's work is neither juvenilia, nor comedy, nor Pop, though it *does* share mass media's sense of humor and its formats: graphics, periodicals, television, and spaces made familiar in these media. The aquarelles *This is how it happened* resemble *The New Yorker* magazine covers; her ego comics read like an HBO series about an artist. In fact, vW's comics are set in the same site-specific places as TV shows, or comedy in general: the office, the beach, the stage, the doctor's office, the therapist's couch, the bedroom, the art gallery, the smoking lounge, etc. Even to draw attention to such banal places is funny, and allows us to laugh about the suppressed anxiety that they carry. In fact, this is also the standard opening for stand-up comedy. Think of Seinfeld grabbing the mic and asking, "So what's the deal with X?" Transposition is a classic comic technique in both art and comedy, like in Robert Smithson's 1967 essay "A Tour of the Monuments of Passaic," which is fundamentally funny because it supplants the architecture of classical antiquity with infrastructural buildings in New Jersey. Or Preston Sturges' classic 1941 screwball comedy *Sullivan's Travels* (itself a twist on a satire by Jonathan Swift), funny because it tells the story of a rich guy who lives life as a hobo. These are textbook examples of what Freud calls "the technical methods of the joke-work"[9]—to allay anxiety with jokes about things being in the wrong place, mix-ups, and switches that highlight boundaries, what is "here" versus what lies beyond; in other words, pointing to the off-site, the off-limits, the off-stage, the off-modern, the off-color.

And vW's cartoons and comics *are* off-color. Not only are there blowjobs, coke parties, and S/M dungeons, but also all the dismaying feelings that go along with them: regret, anxiety, boredom, excruciation, embarrassment, dismay . . . the high lows and the low highs. Isn't it rather embarrassing anyway, somewhat forbidden, to say what you're *really* thinking in the art world, that country club of manners? To rephrase something T. J. Clark wrote about Abstract Expressionism, vW's comics blurt out the vulgar secrets that paintings usually conspire to keep.[10] Not really so secret, actually: it is the struggle between art and everyday life. AvW has aggressively found form in the connections between painting and its affects, that material usually X'ed out of the picture: not only the minutiae of daily life, its gripes and moods, but an actual depiction of how the so called "network" *works*. She uncloaks material from the "wrong" place or the "wrong" time, inserts notebooks, financial

9. Freud, "Jokes and Their Relation to the Unconscious," *op. cit.*, 96.

10. T. J. Clark, "In Defense of Abstract Expressionism," *October* 69 (Summer 1994), 26. See also "AbEx and Disco Balls," page 129, and "Some Notes on John Chamberlain," pages 214–15. [Editors' note]

ledgers, family albums, and illustration in general into painting and reveals the social and economic conditions that churn endlessly in its background, as well as the ordinarily unexamined conditions that go with these social conditions: self-hatred, hatred of others, jealousy, embarrassment, anxiety, competition. In doing so, vW's ego comics and her aquarelle series *This is how it happened* deliver another duality, the possibility that they are both funny and not at all funny. As Alex Zachary wrote in the catalogue to her 2011 show: "Von Wulffen's series is an illustrated compendium of our worst nightmares."[11] This is the pleasure/discomfort metric of her work, which is also the metric of the comic—and this is partly what makes AvW's work essentially very funny, and yet not a joke at all. ♦

11. Alex Zachary, "Dreams Errors Symptoms Jokes," in *This is how it happened*, exh. cat. (Berlin: Distanz Verlag, 2011), 5.

This essay was originally published in the catalogue Maria Lassnig: The Future is Invented with Fragments from the Past, *ed. Hans Ulrich Obrist, Peter Pakesch, and Denys Zacharopoulos (Cologne: Verlag der Buchhandlung Walther König, 2017), issued in the aftermath of the exhibition by the same name at the Municipal Gallery of Athens, April 7–July 16, 2016.*

Dear Maria Lassnig

February 14, 2017

Dear Maria Lassnig,

I can't believe I didn't get to hang out with you when you lived in NYC. I was shocked when I found out that you lived here for twelve years. Twelve years??? If we passed on the street, I didn't know it. But for six of your twelve years here, I lived around the corner from you. And I went to the same school (SVA)[1] and wore the same outfit I've seen you wear in pictures, a sweatshirt and sneakers, and like you, I smoked cigarettes while painting. I even know people who live in your old studio building on Avenue B, and went to some crazy parties there after you'd left. Like you, in the '70s I hung out with a lot of women and experimental filmmakers. But I am sorry to say that in the '70s I didn't even know your work, though we were in so many of the same rooms and streets. What boggles my mind is that this is even possible. You lived and worked around the corner from me, and I assume that means you also ate soup at Odessa, walked by the dog park in Tompkins Square Park,

1. Maria Lassnig studied animation at the School of Visual Arts (SVA) between 1970 and 1972 (NB: she was born in 1919), while Amy Sillman earned her BFA from the same school in 1979. [Editors' note]

and saw that old Russian guy with the giant newspaper hat who lived in a doorway on 7th Street? You must have done all that, because we all did. Did you have lovers? Or drink at that old wooden bar on the corner of 7th and B? Though I recognize your style in the pictures, I don't recognize you. Would I have even had the nerve to talk to you if I'd met you, or to invite myself to your studio? I doubt it. I would have been intimidated; New Yorkers can be surprisingly shy, and though you are often smiling in photos, you look a little forbidding, with your thin mouth and your rimmed glasses. Once, much later in Vienna, at a fancy dinner to celebrate a Cy Twombly show, I sat on a couch with you. You were very old, and I knew exactly who you were, but I did not say hello. I just stared at your gigantic white sneakers, which looked exactly like the clump-ish forms in your paintings. You were on one side of the couch and Franz West was on the other. I was on a seesaw of artistic greatness, balanced between you two. I was such an idiot not to address you, but you both looked pretty creaky, and each of you had canes and a helper. Right after that you both died, and I was so frustrated that I had failed to blurt out, with stupid eagerness, how much I love your work and how it sustains me. But you were absorbed in your own stuff that night, and I knew better than to bother a lady genius with giant white sneakers. So I said nothing, when I could have said, hey, you lived around the corner from me in NYC for six years, how the hell did we not meet!?

It was completely easy to be private back then, unknown and anonymous, walking the streets of the East Village, which were either very noisy (at night) or very peaceful (during the day). I know that Hélio Oiticica was also walking around down there, and I saw Jack Smith at the movies, and gave money to Valerie Solanas who was homeless and lived on my corner then. I knew people who lived in Allen Ginsberg's apartment, and knew people who knew Richard Hell, and I was friends with Eileen Myles and knew Yvonne Rainer, and went to Ken Jacobs' shows and saw Amiri Baraka in Tompkins Square Park, and ate at Gordon Matta-Clark's restaurant. Tommy Lanigan-Schmidt's East Village apartment was filled with gold foil goblets and he called it *The Summer Palace of the Czarina Tatlina*. These people were all walking around there, in their own thoughts and in their own scenes, and you were there too, but it's entirely possible that a New Yorker could walk among them but never meet any of them.

Like you, I was at Millennium Film Workshop a lot of nights, watching weird, beautiful, or boring non-narrative films on uncomfortable wooden benches.[2] You must have strolled over to East 4th Street from your Ave B studio, descending the staircase to the funereal light of Millennium, passing by Howard, who sat at the desk looking like a melancholy version of the devil. There were dirty bins on wheels all around, with strips of film morbidly hanging into them, and a still palpable odor. I remember that film scene intimately, though my crew was a little younger than yours: we were art students, we stayed up late, listened to punk music, danced to hip-hop, and went to the Pyramid Club.[3] I guess your age group went to Max's Kansas City, but

2. Founded in 1965, the Millennium Film Workshop is a non-profit space dedicated to avant-garde and experimental cinema—and today also busy with media and motion image technologies. From 1974 to 2013, it was located at 66 East 4th Street; its director was then Howard Guttenplan, a filmmaker, who is mentioned further. [Editors' note]

3. The Pyramid Club opened in 1979, at 101 Avenue A. It contributed to defining the East Village gay scene of the 1980s, and played a crucial role in the development of drag culture. [Editors' note]

did you go there?[4] Or have the slightest interest in Andy Warhol? I have no idea. You were too young for the Cedar Tavern,[5] that I know: it was mostly for old men and their arm candy—so where did you go? Ave B was super druggie: you must have been up all night painting with the sound of sirens and people shouting outside. I know that your loft was spartan, and that your furnishings were simple. Did you have a crush on anyone? Who fueled your images of naked women, animals, and men, entangled? I think you mostly hung out socially with the women in Women/Artists/Filmmakers, Inc., a group of fierce, pragmatic female filmmakers, working mostly against the grain.[6] Women whose work I didn't know, like Martie Edelheit, Rosalind Schneider, Silvianna Goldsmith, and Susan Brockman, and someone I do know, Carolee Schneemann, were your comrades, tough poetic ladies making films that extended the medium of painting into film-time. I know that working with the figure in an imaginative/expressive way and being female back then made it really hard to get a show at all. You showed at Gloria Cortella and Green Mountain galleries, but they don't exist anymore. Where did their archives go? I know that in the '70s it was hard to be famous if you were a female. Of course that

4. Max's Kansas City was a nightclub and restaurant located at 213 Park Avenue South. Opened in 1965 it quickly became a gathering place for musicians, writers, and artists as well—perhaps because Leo Castelli and David Whitney galleries were across the street. The Velvet Underground played there many times; in the '70s Max's Kansas City became a base for the glam rock scene, and then the punk scene. It closed in 1981. [Editors' note]

5. See "AbEx and Disco Balls," note 4, page 131. [Editors' note]

6. Women/Artists/Filmmakers, Inc. was a cooperative founded in 1974 by Susan Brockman, Doris Chase, Martha Edelheit, Silvianna Goldsmith, Nancy Kendall, Maria Lassnig, Carolee Schneemann, Rosalind Schneider, Olga Spiegel, and Alida Walsh. They would collaborate on each other's film projects, and support each other's practices; Lassnig made in that context several animated films. [Editors' note]

changed in the '80s—Cindy, Jenny, Barbara, Sherrie, etc.—but you were working before that, and in any case, eccentric figuration and wonky animation were sidelined and angst was being replaced with something hard-edged or cool. I can just imagine your animation set-up, made on the cheap, and we art students loved that kind of stuff. We looked for it, were thrilled with the *"Bad" Painting* show,[7] and artists whose "site" was their apartment, anything not found in official "art history," whatever that is. History is obviously less than it's cracked up to be. In any case, somehow your work flew beneath my radar—you, a serious lady thinking about time, and no one's arm candy.

I've been thinking lately about the word "undocumented." (You left America right at the moment of Reagan. I wonder what you thought of Guston's bitter cartoons of Nixon's phlebitis and scrotal nose!?)[8] When I spoke to some of your old friends on the phone, it struck me that so much about the female artists before the '80s is simply unknown, left out. All unsung artists are a kind of "undocumented." There must be a mountain of 35mm slides and reels of movies somewhere, along with the archives of galleries that have closed and the notebooks of artists whose work was not sustained financially, and fell out of memory. Or let's say it this way: you were the tip of an iceberg, and seem to have passed through NYC like a shadow. Yet paradoxically your own work is a scrupulous documentation—not of yourself, but of the nature of thought. I read your diary, I know you were examining the structure of knowing, discovering that

7. See "Shit Happens," note 3, page 164. [Editors' note]

8. An allusion to Philip Guston's *Poor Richard*, a suite of 72 drawings on the life of Richard Nixon: made in 1971 the series wasn't shown to the public before 2001. [Editors' note]

"knowledge" cannot be recognized as an image, working on the fugitive moments between thought and image, capturing how they draw together and split up again, making notes in your diary about how the mind flickers from moment to moment. Your work is a meticulous study of what/how a body thinks and feels, a lived body as a compression machine of the imaginary, the symbolic, and the real. In those years in NYC, you and your comrades in W/A/F, Inc. lived in your bodies' wits, carrying the wealth of history and the fumes of paint in your glands and your nervous systems. The life of an obscure artist is painful to contemplate: so much energy that remains undocumented. How amazing that you were here, living like that, in your giant sneakers, courageously inventing an iconography of your own and wrestling time with your bare hands.

Love,
Amy

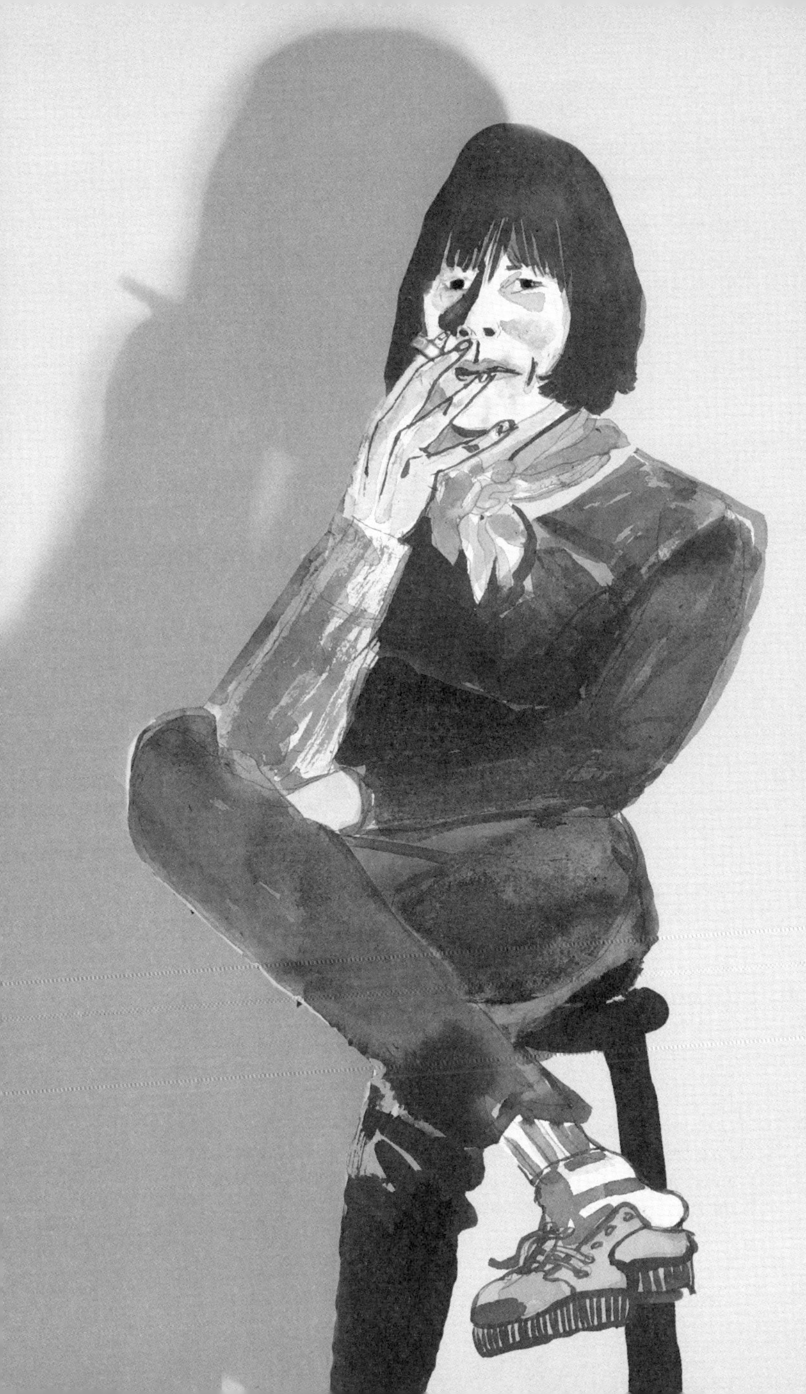

The following text is an edited version of a talk originally given by Amy Sillman as part of a program of lectures honoring Carolee Schneemann, in the artist's presence, at the conclusion of the retrospective, Carolee Schneemann: Kinetic Painting *at MoMA PS1 in March 2018. The text of the talk was edited for publication in* Carolee Schneemann: Body Politics, *ed. Lotte Johnson and Chris Bayley (New Haven & London: Yale University Press, 2022), a monograph accompanying the eponymous show at the Barbican, London, September 8, 2022–January 8, 2023.*

Carolee Schneemann: Always a Painter

> I'm a painter, working with my body and ways of thinking . . . that come out of the discipline of having painted for six or eight hours a day for years. That's got to be the root of my language in any medium. I'm not a filmmaker. I'm not a photographer. I'm a painter.
>
> —CAROLEE SCHNEEMANN[1]

Carolee Schneemann always proclaimed her love and loyalty to painting as a primary force in her work. In every book and interview, she declared painting as fundamental to her project, and wanted her work to be understood in that light. But what exactly did she mean when she said "painting"? Or for that matter, "love"?

To understand that, you have to remember that Schneemann's sense of painting, and history with it, is what we would now think of as somewhat old-fashioned. From the mid-1950s to the early '60s she toiled at the study of easel-painting techniques and genres, working with models, self-portraiture and landscapes. The art historian Leo Steinberg paid her a studio visit, in which he encouraged her to pursue her exploration of the figure in landscape. In the back of her mind was the figure of Paul Cézanne—however, it was not the "grandfather of abstract painting" so much as the cranky old man who went

1. Carolee Schneemann in Scott MacDonald, "Film and Performance: An Interview with Carolee Schneemann," *Millennium Film Journal* 7/8/9 (Fall/Winter 1980–81), 105.

out alone every day to abandon himself to the chaos of sensation and to invent a new system of notation. As he himself said: "The landscape thinks itself in me and I am its consciousness."[2] Talk about intersubjectivity: when Cézanne went to paint Montagne Sainte-Victoire, he went out to have a relationship with a mountain, to practically lick it with his eyeballs. In his paintings, people and things exist in equally molten form: paintings are a recording of a haptic seeing, an endless flickering thatch of paint strokes that aspire to capture the flux of sensation itself. This radically embodied Cézanne is the painter to whom Schneemann is referring, and who helped her to forge her intimate and passionate love affair with painting as the performance of a visionary activity, one in which form remakes itself continuously, charged with an intense compression that is seeing, feeling, and doubting all at once. It is the task of both building and destroying.

To this, Schneemann added another radical component, herself: a specifically female subject position, a female who dares to name herself and to paint from her own subjectivity and her own objectivity; a female who is keenly aware that she has been left out of the canon, and who speaks openly about gender, but not in a sentimental or easy way, and not only about sex or gender, but about non-reproductive sex and a love that is defiantly not maternal.

So when Schneemann writes about loving painting, you should first of all think of Cézanne-the-ecstatic, and then per-

2. Maurice Merleau-Ponty, *Sense and Non-Sense*, trans. Hubert L. Dreyfus and Patricia Allen Dreyfus (Evanston, IL: Northwestern University Press, 1964), 17. Merleau-Ponty seems to be paraphrasing Cézanne's words as recounted by Gasquet; see "What he told me—I. The motif," in Joachim Gasquet's *Cézanne: a Memoir with Conversations* (1921), trans. Christopher Pemberton, (London: Thames and Hudson, 1991). [Editors' note]

haps think of the predictions for painting made by her painter-friend Allan Kaprow. In 1958 Kaprow envisioned in the most prescient manner the way in which painting would develop: he diagnosed painting post-Pollock as blurring into everyday life: "Objects of every sort are the materials for the new art: paint, chairs, food, electric and neon lights, smoke, water, old socks, a dog, movies, a thousand other things . . . entirely unheard-of happenings and events, found in garbage cans, police files, hotel lobbies; seen in store windows and on the streets; and sensed in dreams . . . An odor of crushed strawberries, a letter from a friend, or a billboard selling Drano; three taps on the front door, a scratch, a sigh, or a voice lecturing endlessly, a blinding staccato flash, a bowler hat—all will become materials for this new concrete art."[3]

Schneemann made all of this come true. But Kaprow's prediction was off in one way for Schneemann, because his text ends: "Young artists of today need no longer say, 'I am a painter' or 'a poet' or 'a dancer.' They are simply 'artists.'"[4] But Schneemann went on calling herself a painter. She embraced painting like a lover, and didn't want to abandon it.

Her work is premised upon the creation of roiling, endless, intense surfaces, of touching and attachment, precisely the same kind of surfaces that she actualized later in films, performances, and every other medium in which she worked. Her art doesn't so much change from one thing to the next as it rolls on in a kind of rhapsodic endlessness. If there's a teleology at play

3. Allan Kaprow, "The Legacy of Jackson Pollock" (1958), in Kaprow, *Essays on the Blurring of Art and Life*, ed. Jeff Kelley (Berkeley & Los Angeles: University of California Press, 1993/2003), 7–9.

4. *Ibid.*, 9.

in Schneemann's work, it's the teenage sexual one, where you have to round the bases before you go all the way, and Schneemann's done it. She flirted with painting, made out with it, got to second and third base with it, and went all the way. You could say she got knocked up early by painting, and then made a lifetime commitment, even sticking around when the relationship went through rough patches, when she was seeing other media, because she really loved it. And love relationships are not teleological: they're paradoxes.

Schneemann puts painting in the position of a lover, she does things to it, within it, inside it. She gets all up on painting, and lets it get all up on her. All this feeling, stroking, and touching is staged against the limitations of the rectangle; the rectangle becomes a kind of "straight man" against which her own forces of flux come pouring out, around and through. She cuts into it, empties it, teases it into other rectangles like the film frame, or the TV screen, or the page.

Now let's talk about love. Love means joining things together. At her show *Kinetic Painting* at MoMA PS1, Schneemann's tactics of coupling, or hinging, were made completely clear in the design of the exhibition itself. As you entered the show, Schneemann's early paintings led you down a long hallway that dumped you into a room with her film *Meat Joy* (1964), with its turbulent painterly excesses projected large on a wall. This physical passage allowed viewers to grasp the connection between her paintings bursting out of their stretchers and transitioning into their kinetic film format. As you continued into the next rooms, you noted how her paintings were literally hinged to other objects, to bodies, to other media; how everything, subject and object, was coupled, hooked, bound, attached, merged,

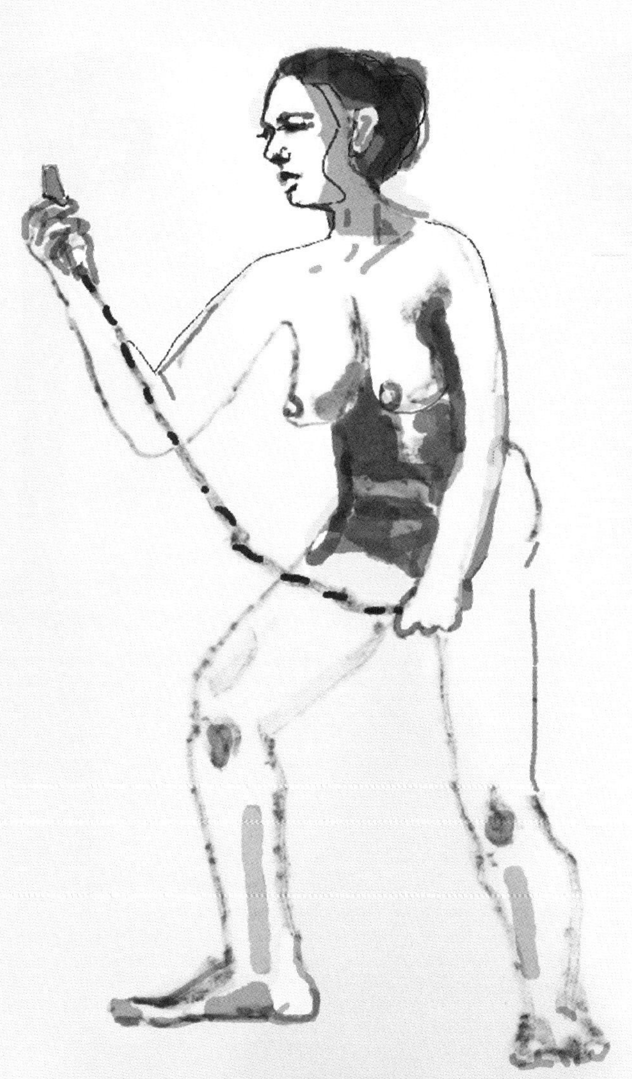

and fused in her work, and how all these fusions pointed back to the drama of painterly production and its primary quality of bodily sensation.

Besides being a painter, Schneemann is also a realist. She proclaims it almost as often as she says she's a painter. "[My work] is not psychodrama or fantasy." "I'm pleased when audience response to *Meat Joy* is: 'Yes!—life is really like that . . .' For me it is. I'm not interested in 'fantasy.'"[5] Schneemann's love of painting can be taken literally: for her, painting is sensational, an embrace, a lover. She has said she's anti-fantasy. Allan Kaprow wrote this on painting: "Truth does not exist. Painting does. That is why I love to paint."[6] Likewise, think of Schneemann's paintings as an actual, obdurate recording of the real. Take her statement of love at face value, because for her, painting is real. It is not frivolous pleasure, it is not fiction and it is not re-presentation.

5. Schneemann, "Meat Joy Notes," in *Carolee Schneemann: Uncollected Texts*, ed. Branden W. Joseph (New York: Primary Information, 2018), 53.

6. This statement was uncovered on the stretcher bars of the 1955 painting *Standing Nude Against Red and Yellow Stripes* (1955) when it was reframed by a restorer in 2017, and quoted in the press release for the exhibition, *Allan Kaprow. Paintings New York* at Hauser & Wirth, New York, February 1st–April 7, 2018. See https://www.hauserwirth.com/hauser-wirth-exhibitions/6234-allan-kaprow-paintings-new-york (last accessed June 5, 2022).

One loves only form
and form only comes
into existence when
the thing is born.
—Charles Olson[7]

Schneemann's work is a literal hinging of painting to real places and real words. She intends to give birth to a new and radical form; a form that comes out swinging, refusing and subverting. When she says "painting," she also means an actualized form of struggle. Her kind of painting is done in *spite* of capitalism, not because of it, and hers is the kind of praxis that a Marxist might appreciate, one that is neither modeled on factory production nor outsourced to alienated laborers, but done entirely by her own hand and her own devising. Her paintings track how she got increasingly out of the studio and into the world, into the crux of things. Though keeping the logic of painting at their core, her works move outward from the hidden reserve of the studio into a world where they can confront the best and most precious things in life—eros, romance, care, continuity, curiosity, imagination, vision, nature, creatureliness, generosity—even as they are harnessed to the worst: brutality, war, police violence, sexism, cruelty, ownership, enslavement, murder, and fascism. Schneemann's paintings shirk neither the task of addressing this kind of coupling, nor the aggression or hostility of love.

Schneemann spent a lifetime working on fundamentally painterly questions of touch, time, pulse, color, sensation,

7. Charles Olson, "I, Maximus of Gloucester, to You," in *The Maximus Poems* (Berkeley & Los Angeles: University of California Press, 1987), 7.

rhythm, erasure, scale, figure/ground, the all-over, collage, line, negative space—but she also worked calculatedly against things. As a painter, she chose not to work on flatness, geometricism, reduction, minimalism, iconicity, objectivity, or the laws of perspective. Arguably she didn't work on composition or pictorial arrangement either. In fact, the text of *Interior Scroll* (1975) is a refusal of a refusal: in it, she caustically rejects the values of an unnamed antagonist, who complains about qualities that she holds dear as a painter: "The personal clutter—the persistence of feelings—the hand-touch sensibility—the diaristic indulgence—the painterly mess—the dense gestalt—the primitive techniques."[8]

All the things that the antagonist of the scroll text is proud to have gotten rid of—emotion, intuition, inspiration, those unclear tendencies—are aspects of painting that Schneemann flaunts. She upholds qualities that one might find championed in a kind of Romanticism: overwhelmingness, the sacred, nostalgia, circularity, inexhaustibility, pulsations of the spirit, the search for the blue flower.

To illustrate my points, here's a little game I came up with. If you take a short paragraph of Schneemann's writing about love, and in each case replace the word "man," "lover," or "love-object" with "painter"/"painting," it discloses exactly the principles with which she approaches painting: "What do women want of PAINTING? . . . They want to be surprised, taken unawares; they are moved by intensity. She does not want to tell a PAINTING she wants flowers . . . her fantasy is that,

8. Schneemann, "Interior Scroll," in *More Than Meat Joy. Complete Performance Works and Selected Writings*, ed. Bruce McPherson (New Paltz, NY: Documentext, 1979), 238.

moved by PAINTING's feeling for her PAINTING will gather up flowers to give her . . . that she is, herself, the material for love expressions. Rather than say to her PAINTING "let's make love" she . . . expects action from the PAINTING . . . Her motion is constantly moving forward . . . For her the motion of PAINTING is enveloping inward. PAINTING reveals her to herself. PAINTING is excited by her; she is excited by what PAINTING does to her . . . her capacity for sensation seems infinite. She is not afraid to "go mad with desire"—to lose consciousness of Self, to flow outward, to become pure, dense energy exchange and encounter, to become sensation itself. Reason IS energy. Love is character." "Capacity for expressive love and for love are insolubly linked." "Sweet love, beautiful PAINTING, my joy."[9] ♦

9. Schneemann, "Notations (1958–1966)" (1969), in *Uncollected Texts*, *op. cit.*, 86, 84, and 78.

This review of the book Into Words: The Selected Writings of Carroll Dunham, *ed. Paul Chan (New York: Badlands Unlimited, 2017) was originally published in* Bookforum *24, no. 4 (December 2017–January 2018).*

The Writings of Carroll Dunham

Carroll Dunham is weird. (It's a good thing.) *Weird* is the most used adjective in his new book of essays, *Into Words*, followed by *perverse*. To Dunham, a renowned painter and frequent essayist on art, these are credentials for interesting, indicating that you might crack the nut, push the envelope, make a break for it, or run the ball out onto the fields of the crazy. Takes one to know one: he guides you to his own end zone of painting with texts from 1994 through 2016, waxing eloquent, or sometimes cranky, about the work and contexts of twenty-five or so far-flung artists, living and dead, canonical and outlier, mostly painters. The texts are presented chronologically, helpful for tracking Dunham's deeper intentions as his rig drills down into the bituminous depths. As he gets older and wiser, his prose blooms in complexity, containing wild list-accumulations ("Dada, V-2 rockets, and the discovery of LSD"[1]; "Food, farts, reincarnation, semiotics"[2]) or punctum-like moments, like the opener of his Picasso essay: "Pablo Picasso can be exhausting to

1. "Max Ernst" (2005), in *Into Words: The Selected Writings of Carroll Dunham*, ed. Paul Chan (New York: Badlands Unlimited, 2017), 76.

2. "Rawhide: On Albert Oehlen" (2015), in *Into Words*, *op. cit.*, 223.

think about."[3] Or this, on some aspect of a Jasper Johns: "This sounds like such a bad idea."[4] Or, when fed up with doxa: "The entire Greenbergian paradigm seems . . . vaguely irresponsible."[5] In two forensic interviews with artists Peter Saul and Jim Nutt, Dunham reveals these subjects as rogue nerds from the plains who refuse the usual New York cultural politesse. Pushed to make the admission, Saul finally blurts out, "When I go to the Museum of Modern Art . . . I am simply not interested."[6] Nutt spits, "I read no Greenberg, or who's the other guy, Rosenberg?"[7]

From funny-peculiar, Dunham expands outward exponentially (past crazy, zany, odd, nutty, awkward, eccentric, scruffy, bouncy, loopy, fuzzy, inscrutable, embarrassing, crotchety, uncomfortable, dizzying, unnerving, jarring, kinky, depraved, squirmy, and freaky). His greater purpose is not just to nail down what weirdness is but to take it on: he invokes it, caresses it, blows on it, and eventually *becomes* it, his prose reaching certain pinnacles of wiggy delirium, e.g., on late Renoir, whose "zaftig demigoddesses" he describes as "rolling, doughy estrogen bombs animating the glowing surface of their pulsating electric Eden. . . . Everything seems composed of a gassy alloy of substance and feeling, like a higher-dimensional Impressionism."[8] No one writes about art like this. At these points, Dunham's language billows like a cloud, past painting's brack-

3. "Pablo Picasso: *Mosqueteros*" (2009), in *Into Words, op. cit.*, 126.

4. "Jasper Johns: *Gray*" (2008), in *Into Words, op. cit.*, 116.

5. "After Frankenthaler: An Artist Statement" (2015), in *Into Words, op. cit.*, 215.

6. "Peter Saul: A Conversation" (2000), in *Into Words, op. cit.*, 33.

7. "Jim Nutt: A Conversation" (2004), in *Into Words, op. cit.*, 50.

8. "Late Renoir" (2010), in *Into Words, op. cit.*, 147. Dunham describes Renoir's painting, *The Bathers*, from 1918–19. [Editors' note]

eted rectangles, to consume art's biggest questions: what *is* it, anyway? Grappling with its very existence, he asks, "Could this be a painting? . . . This? . . . This? . . . This?"

This marks Dunham as a quintessential inheritor of the New York School, an enterprise I would describe as having the same conditions as archaeology and Freud. Same diff, actually: to dig shit up in the field. Stating that "a painter's body is his first and primary tool,"[9] Dunham shovels down beneath art's murky rectilinears, past the known and even the unknown, into the murkier area of the unknow*able*. His thinking is clearly structured by binaries: he paints a planet of protuberances and holes, and a population wrestling with Eros and Thanatos, and in his writing he thinks through the language and material of both canonical and outsider figures. Yet, reading his book, one also senses his drive toward a psychic singularity, a mysterious black hole located at the center of his thinking—the hole of the eye, the asshole, or the grave—and the sheer tactile craving to wrap the mesh of language around the mystery of art-making, to respond to art's forms with language's invisible force.

His process is both dirty and productive, a two-handed affair: he rubs language against art, and vice versa, to see what sticks after the frottage, and blows cross-pollinated seeds into the wrong holes. This dirty process is also a thrilling form of magic, desacralized and generative, which contaminates the teleological, fucks up a categorical imperative, and scumbles the idea of art as illustrations in an art history story. And Dunham loves to describe this mess. He writes attentively

9. *Id.* Dunham makes this statement as he links Auguste Renoir's late work with his physical condition, "wheelchair-bound for most of his final two decades." [Editors' note]

about Rauschenberg's "chromatic shitstorm"[10] and Johns' "decayed pictorial mulch"[11]; he even notes people as a mess, as in Picasso, where "when women appear . . . they are kind of a mess."[12] Opening his eloquent essay on Elizabeth Murray, Dunham writes, "Painting in New York during the second half of the 1970s was a mess."[13]

The '70s form the psychic center of his book, a derelict time and place after modernism's breakdown, with sculpture that is "squishy"[14] and painting that is already "being stripped for parts."[15] And in an essay on his own anthropomorphized paintings, he declares, "He was a mess, and so were the paintings. They came to life in a storm of garbage . . . gripped by the black hole at the dead center of the polluted field."[16] Dunham wants to get us in deeper, not provide a ladder for self-help. Writing in 2007 on Kara Walker's films, he articulates a greater ethics of mess as inevitably containing collapse, an important antimoralistic argument, which for Dunham serves to purposefully vex any easy standpoint where "our values will provide solace."[17] This is how his view is truly Freudian: the belief that art is a place where form, feeling, and fuckup churn together in a dynamic of irresolvable problems, fertilized by our collective shit.

10. "All or Nothing: Robert Rauschenberg's Combines" (2006), in *Into Words, op. cit.*, 96.

11. "Jasper Johns: *Gray*," in *Into Words, op. cit.*, 114.

12. "Pablo Picasso: *Mosqueteros*," in *Into Words, op. cit.*, 128. The essay deals with paintings of Picasso's last years. [Editors' note]

13. "Shapes of Things to Come: On Elizabeth Murray" (2005), in *Into Words, op. cit.*, 82. On Murray, see "Flashlight: The Signal of Elizabeth Murray's Paintings," pages 275-80. [Editors' note]

14. "John Newman" (2012), in *Into Words, op. cit.*, 167.

15. "Shapes of Things to Come . . .," in *Into Words, op. cit.*, 83.

16. "Dead, Yellow. Mule. Garbage, Ratio. Giant." (2007), in *Into Words, op. cit.*, 101.

17. "Film Noir: The Films of Kara Walker" (2007), in *Into Words, op. cit.*, 110.

By demanding new questions about and uses for form, his book lays down a pragmatic kind of polemic: artists (and other weirdos, witches, gumshoes, alchemists, provocateurs, and poets) must take the power of language into their own hands, with love and antagonism. This project is political, especially if you see art as more than junk bonds or tchotchkes—"a forward exit strategy," to quote Dunham on Murray.[18] Speaking of politics, I wish he had accounted for more of gender's specific struggles, given his choice of subjects and images. But, while out looking for the weird, Dunham arrives at the Brechtian *strange*, and articulates an art and ethics of multivalence, excess, contradiction, and defiance. Other artists should take the ball and run with it out into their own end zones. ♦

18. "Shapes of Things to Come . . .," in *Into Words*, *op. cit.*, 89.

This review of the exhibition Laura Owens, *presented at the Whitney Museum of American Art, New York (November 10, 2017–February 26, 2018) was originally published in* Artforum *56, no. 8 (April 2018).*

Laura Owens

Contradictions should be appreciated
for letting change emerge.
—CAROLEE SCHNEEMANN[1]

What do I know about LA, but my first reaction to the Laura Owens show was, *Wow, this is so West Coast*. Paintings made in Los Angeles always struck me as being these huge, clean things, which I figured was because they were designed to be visible from the highway. In New York City, we walk around, so our painting surfaces aspire to the condition of sidewalks—dirty, scruffy, and layered. In fact, painting history generally reflects a city's local conditions, its techniques of the body; consequently, some cities have developed more levity in their paintings, others a harsher critique. LA has both. In the catalogue for Owens' show, artist Monique Prieto recalls some of these coastal differences: "People coming out of East Coast schools were so comfortable being painters. . . . They weren't having big doubts. . . . At CalArts we'd had to sword fight through any critique we brought a painting to . . . like, 'This is all New York wants from you?'"[2] To upend old-school (i.e., East Coast)

1. Carolee Schneemann, *ABC - We Print Anything - In The Cards* (Beuningen: Brummense Uitgeverij Van Luxe Werkjes, 1977), card #73.

2. *Owens, Laura*, ed. Scott Rothkopf, exh. cat. (New York: Whitney Museum of American Art, 2017), 70. Prieto and Owens became friends as students at the California Institute of the Arts (CalArts) in the mid-1990s. [Editors' note]

formalism, ambitious painters like Owens and her peers threw humor, debasement, and self-reflexivity at it. Owens in particular took liberties with space. Her early work is about wittily reconstructing the spaces within painting, using extruded vanishing points, floors on drunken tilts, and crazy scale shifts, all in the service of literally finding new places for herself to *be*, in painting terms. In her hands, space is a *feeling*.

A loose confederation of Owens' fellow painters participated in this rethinking of painting, and, significantly, many of them were women. She and Mari Eastman, Rebecca Morris, Prieto, Ruth Root, Frances Stark, and Mary Weatherford came to painting (post-1970s/1980s) after decades of hostility between pro- and anti-painting forces, and the energy among these figures can be seen as partially a rejection of a rejection. The ground in LA was already fertilized by a heady mix of critique and feminism, with projects such as Womanhouse and the Feminist Art Program,[3] and critical teachers like Michael Asher and Charles Gaines.[4] But after years of authority figures telling everyone what *not* to do, or diagnosing painting as something that should just disappear, critique—especially feminist critique—was revitalizing to painting.

The teleological line—that painting was an all-male one-way ticket to hell—was clearly in need of reexamination. At CalArts, the presence of Mary Heilmann, a cool painter role

3. Womanhouse (1971–72) was a collective art project organized by Judy Chicago and Miriam Shapiro in an abandoned Victorian mansion in Hollywood. It included women artists and students from the Feminist Art Program, a woman-exclusive program they had co-founded at Fresno State College in 1970, and continued at CalArts. [Editors' note]

4. Conceptual artist Charles Gaines has been a faculty member at CalArts since 1989. Michael Asher taught at the same school from 1973 to 2008; his "Post Studio" class was famous for its "crits," group conversations on a single work that could extend far beyond class hours. [Editors' note]

model, brought some news, as did that of David Reed, a professor who, with his deep knowledge of painting, must have been a fountain of information. Reed has always been a vocal champion of generations of underknown painter-outliers, promoting an alternative canon that includes many females and non-Caucasians. He was the curatorial adviser for the 2006–08 show *High Times, Hard Times: New York Painting, 1967–1975*, which unearthed a decade of these vigorous practices.[5] And beyond that, as I've written about in "AbEx and Disco Balls" for *Artforum* in 2011,[6] even if painting *were* dead, it seemed to live on ad absurdum, so its tattered corpus was available for, if nothing else, scavenging, misappropriation, and camp.

So Owens and her peers flaunted chromophilia, shoplifted form from formalism, dealt in craftiness and sentimentality—things both brash *and* fussy—and cracked jokes. Drawing on the legacies of feminist art history and the prediction of (fellow painter!) Allan Kaprow about the blurring of boundaries,[7] they took up materials from everyday life: string, lightbulbs, gingham, notebooks, stickers, kitties, seashells, washcloths, etc. I wouldn't call this "female" life, because I find such essentialist divisions problematic, and it could be noted critically that the show feels very not-queer. Though its catalogue contains

5. *High Times, Hard Times* was organized and circulated by Independent Curators International, New York, and curated by Katy Siegel, with David Reed as advisor. It aimed at including painting in the narrative of the period, as an experimental practice able to echo radical politics and aesthetics—instead of pigeonholing it as conservative. Half of the artists in the show were women, and many were African-American. [Editors' note]

6. See pages 129–41 of the present volume. [Editors' note]

7. See Allan Kaprow, *Essays on the Blurring of Art and Life*, ed. Jeff Kelley (Berkeley & Los Angeles: University of California Press, 1993), notably his prophetic essay from 1958, "The Legacy of Jackson Pollock," that Amy Sillman quotes in relation to Carolee Schneemann's work in "Carolee Schneemann: Always a Painter," page 241. [Editors' note]

Simone de Beauvoir's foundational feminist assertion that femininity is psychosocially shaped, and features essays by the likes of Rozsika Parker, bell hooks, Frances Stark, and Sianne Ngai,[8] gender categories are not destabilized or taken up critically within the exhibition. The show's feminism appears more as a project of subjective empowerment than of collective political engagement. OK, it's a painting show. Painting *is* pretty subjective, and the personal *is* political, but I would note that the show leaves certain questions open, such as: how might change occur *in painting*, and *for whom*? Can painting offer a model of alterity, in either form or use?

One of the most interesting aspects of Owens' work is that photography is *not* at its center. Digital logics, yes, but the photograph, no. Instead, drawing carries out the task of mimesis—an explosion of drawing both handmade and cribbed from elsewhere, of *everything* in the world: trees, buildings, numbers, monkeys, soldiers, ladies, couples, fruit, boats, cats. The show overflowed with handwriting, outlines, cartoons, sketches, stencils, shadows, and their graphic proxies, drop shadows. The magic of drawing—and Owens is a fantastic draw-er—is that you can remake anything you see or think of with your own hands. You *take* a picture, but you *make* a drawing. Owens exploits all the alterations possible in her imaginative reinscription of the world, yet with an incredibly literal mind. The artist's literalism is especially evident in her deployment of

8. The catalogue *Owens, Laura* gathers already existing texts dealing with a wide range of topics, among which essays by the authors here mentioned. The Simone de Beauvoir quote can be found in one of these texts: "The Creation of Femininity," by feminist art historian Rozsika Parker, the first chapter of her 1984 book, *The Subversive Stitch: Embroidery and the Making of the Feminine*. [Editors' note]

painting in architecture. Her work's scale is basically 100 percent, in the sense that its size is often determined by the walls on which it is intended to hang. (This device was further emphasized at the Whitney by the curatorial decision to remake one of the rooms of the show at the same size as the original space where the work was shown.) Yet the flat-earth reality of Owens' positioning continually gives way to flights of fancy and illusion, and the show underlines this impulse toward twinned tactics: a painting is a wall; a painting has a twin; two paintings mirror each other; a mirror is a window; a painting is a world. Once you notice this motif of doubling, the real running parallel to the imaginary, you see twoness everywhere.

This struck me like a bolt of lightning early in the show while I was standing in front of *Untitled* (1999), a large painting that seemed at first like an abstract field of gestures, until it hit me: *Oh—a tableau = a table!* And then, *eureka!*, I realized: every mark in the painting could flip into its equivalent as an hors d'oeuvre. There were funny rectangular outlines that could be toasts; a thick paint blob that looks like a schmear; green strokes that might be celery sticks; red-green ones as olives and pimentos; a wine stain or the trail of a cigarette's smoke rendered in the exact colors of those same things. Everything sort of was what it was, exactly as it wasn't. Double twoness! From then on, Owens' imagery opened up to me as having a flatly direct and slightly funny reading. When I saw a ruler, it literally meant *size*. A heart was romance. A couple, a double bed, meant a relationship, consummated literally by birds and bees. Fairy tales suggested the presence of children. The personals showed loneliness, etc., etc. Is the work so literal-minded that it's without metaphor? That's a good question.

In fact, Owens' sense of humor appears neither arch nor ironic. Even the *Jonathan Livingston Seagull* drop shadows in *Untitled* (1997), evoke not snark so much as a thrifter's glee in the "so-bad-it's-good." (By the way, Owens' drop shadows evoke those of an older painter, James Havard, the poster boy for a group of '70s artists called the Abstract Illusionists, the *wrongest* painters in SoHo back in the day. Havard's work used tricks from '80s desktop publishing and strokes that look like gaudy thickets of Day-Glo cake frosting. His work wasn't Bad Painting, it was *bad* painting, like what would happen to modern art if there were no such thing as critique, ever. Owens, a literalist of high-low, peers eagerly into the bottom of the barrel to see what is usable down there.)

What is the effect of this literalist's uncanny? For one thing, it signals that the *worst* possible reading of this show is pleasure: "*Fun!* Sensuous! *Joy of Painting!*" Not at all. Once you get to paintings with phrases like "WHEN LIFE GIVES YOU LEMONS . . ." or "WHEN YOU COME TO THE END OF YOUR ROPE . . .," the literalist cues leading up to these messages say that the viewer can take these phrases at face value as signs of distress (even with their "cheerful" lemon-man character). But look at the spliced and diced figures and grounds in these works: they bristle with techniques of paradox and alienation. Once you understand Owens' operations of constant twoness, you become aware of the shadow underneath doubling, its nemesis: *aloneness*—even though, in her hands, it's a contradictory loneliness without solitude, or emptiness without loneliness. All her paintings, especially the most recent ones, sit on the cusp of such paradoxes. They are lonely but crowded, too loud to be intimate, too ridiculous ("CATS!") to be sincere, too synthetic to be earnest, yet with jokes, artifice, and illusion, they signal a body earnestly vexed, beset by difficulties. In contrast to the elegant and spectral way that photography hinges presence and absence, Owens' work alienates the body and plays tricks on the eye with impossible vanishing points and absurd repetitions; situations where the body should be reflected yet isn't, or is relentlessly mirrored; images that appear as illusions, or that disappear around corners or behind walls, down claustrophobic corridors or up way too high to be visible. By emphasizing this clumsy prehensile body of ours, and the need for a hand to draw, Owens' most recent work confronts the practical logistics of first-person perception even in a shattered digital multiverse. In their grandiose scale, her surfaces loom over us or splay out sideways or laterally and backward, and in doing so carry out painting's primary demand: that we behold IRL. ♦

This review of the exhibition Delacroix, *a joint project between Musée du Louvre and Metropolitan Museum of Art (the Met), presented at the Met, New York, September 17, 2018–January 6, 2019, was originally published on 4columns.org, December 14, 2018.*

Delacroix: The Sullied Enlightenment of the Body

In photographs, Delacroix is posed magisterially like a senator, or a fierce "tiger poised for its prey,"[1] as Baudelaire said in his study of the painter, the subject of a major retrospective at the Metropolitan Museum of Art, New York, 2018–19. But in real life Delacroix was small, frail, and sickly. This delicate man never married, had no children, no students, never even visited Italy, but he was passionate about his one true love: painting. "Painting, it's true, like the most exacting of mistresses, harasses and torments me"[2]; "Nothing else is of the least importance to me"[3]; "the very sight of my palette . . . is enough to fire my enthusiasm,"[4] he wrote in his journal, which functions as an exhaustive backstage pass to his mood swings.

Delacroix was by turns magnanimous, tender, curious, affectionate, loyal and then furious, dyspeptic, vain, melancholic,

1. Charles Baudelaire, *Eugène Delacroix, His Life and Work* (1863), trans. Joseph M. Bernstein (New York: Lear Books, 1947), 60.

2. *The Journal of Eugène Delacroix* (January 1, 1861), ed. Hubert Wellington, trans. Lucy Norton (Oxford: Phaidon Press, 1951), 408.

3. *Ibid.* (July 1, 1854), 234.

4. *Ibid.* (July 21, 1850), 128.

despotic. In the journal, he backstabs his best friend George Sand, accusing her of mediocrity[5]; he finds Balzac dull[6] and Poe incoherent.[7] He is irritated by his peers, Poussin and Courbet among them: "Sometimes I long to throw Poussin out of the window."[8] And: "The vulgarity and futility of [Courbet's] idea is what is so abominable. . . . What are the two figures supposed to mean? A fat woman, back-view, and completely naked except for a carelessly painted rag over the lower part of the buttocks, is stepping out of a little puddle. . . . It is quite unintelligible."[9] He waxes eloquent and mundane about art supplies: "Grey is the enemy."[10] "Buy watercolors in tubes."[11] He is always caustic: "Concert at the Princess's. It was unbearably hot, and there was an equally unbearable smell of dead rat"; "she was wearing a most unmanageable dress. . . . This absurd mass of material makes all women look like barrels."[12] "So far, I have only once been out into the streets of Paris; I was horrified by the faces of all those schemers and prostitutes."[13]

Delacroix was a snob, a petty aristocrat, a sexist, and a colonialist. You will likely be #notsurprised at his splayed-out women, "mysterious" imaginary Orient of Jews and Moors, or his endlessly masculinist portrayal of sex, violence, and battle. As a

5. *Ibid.* (October 17, 1853), 198.

6. "I have been reading that dull book *Eugénie Grandet.*" *Ibid.* (7 September 1854), 251.

7. ". . . the incoherence and obscurity that Poe mingles with his conceptions do not suit my ideas." *Ibid.* (May 30, 1856), 315.

8. *Ibid.* (May 29, 1853), 189.

9. *Ibid.* (April 15, 1853), 172. The work in question is Courbet's *The Bathers*, exhibited at the Paris Salon of 1853. [Editors' note]

10. *Ibid.* (undated, November 1852), 167.

11. *Ibid.* (March 1, 1860), 399.

12. *Ibid.* (April 7, 1854), 223, and (6 February 1855), 269. The Polish Princess Marcelina Czartoryska had been taught piano by Frédéric Chopin. [Editors' note]

13. *Ibid.* (September 3, 1857), 369.

young man he was dandyish; he became increasingly absorbed in his work as he aged and withdrew from the boulevards of Paris to the countryside. But his journal reveals bombastic ambitions: "Glory is no empty word to me."[14] "Neglect nothing that can make you great."[15] Painting is "verve allied to power."[16] In other words, he's full of it, and that attitude certainly became form in his work.

I don't admire Delacroix's vainglorious longing to seize women and territory, but I do love how he seized the surface of painting itself, and then twisted it into something alienated. He worked with the Romantic proposition that the artist's touch itself is a mark of intelligence, but in his hands, the very idea of knowing becomes something unhinged, discomforting, on the verge of falling apart. It's like the sullied Enlightenment of the body: Sade, not Kant. For comparison, swing by the Ingres room at the Met: Delacroix called his neoclassical paintings "stupid"[17] and "vulgar."[18] Their subjects smile out at you with a stifling self-contentment that clarifies Delacroix's bitterness, since what he was wrestling into painting was objectionable content and the decomposition of materials. To spread "good, fat paint thickly,"[19] he lets paint rip, drip, be raw liquids or solids—blood, sweat, tears; as one viewer described it: ". . . harsh, coarse, rocky, rough, scruffy. Is it paint, or is it glue or

14. *Ibid.* (April 29, 1824), 35.

15. *Ibid.* (October 4, 1855), 302. Here Delacroix quotes "the advice which Beyle gave [him] in one of his letters." Henry Beyle is the real name of Stendhal. [Editors' note.]

16. *Ibid.* (January 5, 1857), 328. Delacroix has in mind painters of the Venetian school: Titian, Veronese, Tintoretto. [Editors' note]

17. *Ibid.* (April 7, 1849), 96.

18. *Ibid.* (January 13, 1857), 334.

19. *Ibid.* (April 11, 1824), 30.

putty?"[20] Liquidity itself appears to be something life-threatening, and color a menacing force. In an early painting, *Mortally Wounded Brigand Quenches His Thirst* (ca. 1825), a dying soldier creeps toward a pond; the blood from his chest wound has mingled with the water and his final sip will be this red ooze. In *The Shipwreck of Don Juan* (1840), an apocalyptic boatload of the damned, clinging and grasping, are engulfed by the sea, a murderous deluge of green. And in *The Death of Sardanapalus* (1826–27), everyone goes down on the flaming plane of a red bedspread.

Delacroix made the picture plane something "bloody and animal and hot," to quote art historian T. J. Clark.[21] He painted in furious antagonism: against mechanization, boredom, mediocrity, gaps of memory, the conventions of neoclassicism, and the moralism of realism. ("Realism should be described as the antipodes of art . . . detestable."[22]) Delacroix's negative affect and negative spaces always excite future painters. Cézanne said it: "We all paint in him,"[23] meaning anyone who's against painting as merely something Beautiful or Good. Walking through the show for the umpteenth time, I thought about the many painters I love whose work emerges from this kind of meat and mo-

20. Jean-Marie Mély-Janin, *La Quotidienne*, September 12, 1824, quoted in *Delacroix*, ed. Sébastien Allard and Côme Fabre, exh. cat. (New York: The Metropolitan Museum of Art, 2018), 19.

21. T. J. Clark, *Picasso and Truth: From Cubism to Guernica* (Princeton: Princeton University Press, 2013), 157. Clark uses Delacroix's *Tiger Hunt* (1854) to explain the notion of the picture plane, and he insists on the paradoxical "thickened and animated" materiality of the transparency of the painting. [Editors' note]

22. *The Journal* (February 22, 1860), *op. cit.*, 396.

23. "What he told me—II. The Louvre," in *Joachim Gasquet's Cézanne: a Memoir with Conversations* (1921), trans. Christopher Pemberton (London: Thames and Hudson, 1991), 196. There Gasquet recounts a visit to the Louvre with Cézanne, and their conversations in front of different works—which he probably partially made up. [Editors' note]

tion: Turner, Kandinsky, Soutine, Kokoschka, Matta, Pollock, Guston, Mitchell, Rauschenberg, Jorn, Fontana, Schneemann, Nelson . . . (One painting was so close to a Cecily Brown that I texted her, jokingly: "I love your painting at the Met!")

Delacroix's world is one of jarring transitions and negative dialectics, where humans are indistinguishable from animals, bouquets are whirlwinds; riots, wars, and mayhem flatten into darkness, and people become miasmatic abstraction. Spatially, his paintings shirk the pictorial task of leading you from foreground to vanishing point by way of a sensible middle ground. Instead, Delacroix's painting space heaves you around in an imaginary bellows that compresses, squeezes, and then releases you. The lower sections of his canvases are literal floors cluttered with gravity-bound impediments, broken stones, fragments of limb, branch, sword, hat, cloth, dropped on the ground. The stuff coalesces in the central zones of Delacroix's paintings as a kind of clump, usually either a churning mass that writhes upward, or a wall-like blockade of people that huddle across the picture plane. Behind or above all this tumult lie patches of shimmering sky or incongruously beautiful clouds, getaway spaces from the central trouble. But there's no middle ground. The only intermediary force that touches both foreground people and background chroma is a kind of atomic state change whereby flesh becomes dust, spill, vapor, darkness. The painter's famous idea was that paintings are bridges to the souls of the spectators[24]—but I think his paintings are more like planks thrown over his own abyss.

24. "Materially speaking, painting is nothing but a bridge set up between the mind of the artist and that of the beholder." From Delacroix's notes for a Dictionary of the Fine Arts, dated January 25, 1857, quoted in *Delacroix*, exh. cat., *op. cit.*, xi. [Editors' note]

Delacroix deplored the gaps in his own memory, and wrote his journal partly just to shore it up. His paintings are likewise haunted with gaps: holes, little black wounds, sudden flatnesses, looming shadows of doorways and cabinets, reversals, scumbles into incoherence. Wherever these gaps occur, a kind of momentary breakdown is suggested, a confusion, a memory gone frighteningly blank, the mind's eye punctured. These little moments of aporia are choreographed by Delacroix as calculated lapses in the palpability of narrative. In *Young Tiger Playing with Its Mother* (1830), the outlines of a tiger's huge feet loom, irrationally large and flat, against the front of the picture plane. In the sketch for *Medea About to Kill Her Children* (ca. 1836), Medea's leg spills out of her body like a spectral X-ray in varicose red. In Delacroix's exquisite drawings, like *Faust and Mephistopheles in the Tavern* (1825/26), shadows become inky black shapes licking through the legs of the devil's drinking buddies.

In prints and drawings, and especially the astonishing room of Faust prints shown at the Met, you can most clearly see how Delacroix's ideas and things jumble up into scribbled tangles of notational no-thing, and that's where his work feels most immediate and most modern. The show gives us a view of Delacroix as an artist whose historical aspirations were constantly being dragged into an undertow of the here and now. And it lays bare drawing itself on a granular level as essentially a synesthetic act of touching-thinking-feeling all at the same time, working from not-knowing, almost like groping in the dark. It's a very modern feeling. ♦

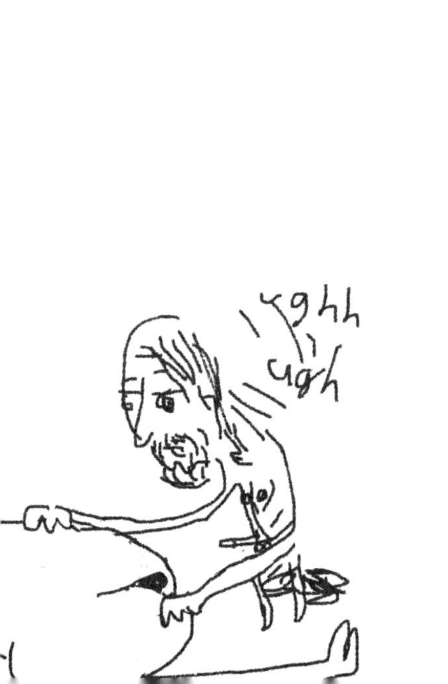
ughh
ugh

This essay was originally published in the monograph Philip Guston Now, *ed. Harry Cooper, Mark Godfrey, Alison de Lima Greene, and Kate Nesin, exh. cat. (Washington, D.C.: National Gallery of Art, 2020).*

Philip Guston: From Garbage Cans to God

I arrived in New York in 1975, when, to paraphrase the Sara Lee Pound Cake ad, nobody didn't like Philip Guston.[1] (I did meet a contrarian painter once who wasn't all in, but she was just grumpy because she said he was so easy to love.) I went to all his shows at McKee Gallery and I fell in sync immediately,[2] first as a Chicagoan, i.e., someone on the lookout for humor, and then as someone who never quite grasped the critique of subjectivity. For Guston, the subject position is a default starting point, and he occupies that position straightforwardly. I mean, what else is life made of? You plod to work, eat a sandwich, think about death, call a friend, feel dread, walk the dog, notice some stuff, get an idea, take out the trash, then go back to the painting wall. (And that's if you're *lucky*.) From garbage cans to god, pastrami to Klansmen: Guston brings the news and even

1. In 1968, advertising agency Doyle Dane Bernbach provided the Sara Lee frozen pound cakes with the long-running slogan, "Everybody doesn't like something, but nobody doesn't like Sara Lee." It was written by Mitch Leigh, who later composed the musical *Man of La Mancha*—"The Impossible Dream" . . . [Editors' note]

2. David McKee and Renee Conforte McKee opened their gallery in New York in 1974 with an exhibition of figurative paintings by Philip Guston; the gallery was then located in a former beauty salon at the Barbizon Hotel for Women, on Lexington Avenue and 63rd Street. Guston had five more solo shows at the gallery before he passed away in 1980. Until its closing in Fall 2015 the McKee Gallery represented the estate of Philip Guston. [Editors' note]

manages to include the funnies. I saw how dumb things (like flotsam, like buoys) began to appear out of the shimmering atmospheres of his earlier abstract paintings, and I loved the tragicomic appearance of these boots, books, elbows, clocks, all tangled up in the painting's very construction. Guston's crude thatch, his thicket of heavy air, was weighted by strokes of crimson, clumps of gray, patches of orange, and glowering pinks. (In Guston's work, pink often seems to indicate something menacing.)

By the way, when I say painting I really mean drawing, lines unfurling from the end of a pencil like a spider web, a stream-of-consciousness process that an artist can watch as any other spectator would. That's the magic aspect of drawing: when you're really rolling, the marks feel like they're coming equally from within and without, from some source both internal and alien. Guston's self-reflexive image of the painter painting underlines this split in consciousness, as well as the greater treachery of time itself. Time, that patient substance that the work is unraveled in, is also slowly devouring us even as our pictures unspool. The worried guy in Guston's pictures, smoking, eating, and watching, is a guy who both reveals and repudiates time; doubt regenerates him.

I can't feel this much existentialism in other painters, and not many other painters wager such ridiculousness. Guston's is the kind of unexalted comedy that museums and art history generally want to suppress. In places of high art you're supposed to see the majesty of time's arrow as it arcs across time, not the way the failed arrows fall out of the quiver between wonder and stupidness. But that's how life actually feels. So yeah, who wouldn't love Philip Guston? ♦

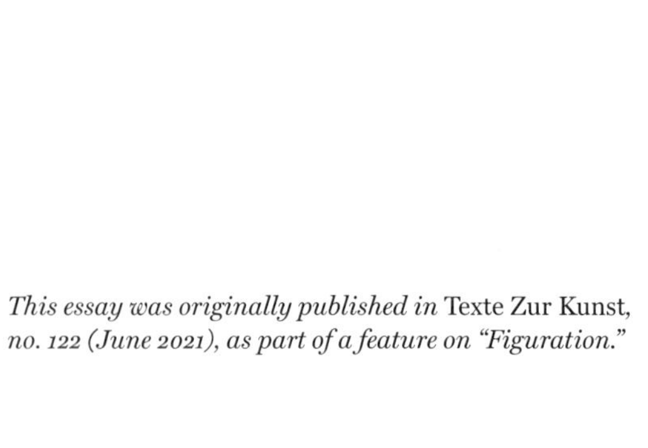

This essay was originally published in Texte Zur Kunst, *no. 122 (June 2021), as part of a feature on "Figuration."*

Flashlight: The Signal of Elizabeth Murray's Paintings

I was in Elizabeth Murray's painting class at the School of Visual Arts in NYC in the mid-1970s. She taught us, in short, to break and enter painting. Even though Murray didn't set out to create followers, as Robert Storr has noted,[1] she already had a large flank of admirers and students in her thrall back then. A lot of us were women. Those painting classes in the '70s were particularly female, both the students and the faculty, which must in part explain why later decades produced such a wave of strong women in painting, at least in the US. Female role models were already raking up painting's ground back then, and Murray was working and teaching us how to paint at a time when the ideological waters had parted into a clear binary; people arranged themselves on one side or the other side, either pro-painting or anti-painting. Art schools were made up of these partisan armies, and there was a palpable hostility between them. The anti-painting classes tended to be more male, more straight, predominantly white guys who were supposedly more hip, more critical, more into politics and theory,

1. "Murray's career did not involve positioning herself in order to create followers." Robert Storr, "Passages: Beyond the frame," *Artforum* 46, no. 3 (November 2007), 76. The article was published as part of an homage to Murray, who had just passed away; Amy Sillman also contributed a text, pages 72–76. [Editors' note]

supposedly cooler and definitely more condescending. A lot of people, including a lot of women, *did* decide to stop painting for ideological reasons and go into photography, philosophy, or punk bands, but the rest of us were mostly nerds or late bloomers, uncool people who had come to art school innocently, thinking painting was a pretty cool thing to do, realizing only after a few semesters that we'd hitched our wagons to a bad star. We *felt* the contempt coming at us, but we didn't really understand the terms of engagement, or the real mechanics of critical theory. We weren't old enough to worry about becoming commodities, and we didn't expect anything anyway. We weren't from a generation that was so thoroughly corporatized, and we had no idea that being an artist would bring us anywhere or anything, not to mention a "career strategy." There was still a counterculture, conversations about dropouts versus sellouts, the idea of an outside, an underground, of experimental form, a gestation period, being obscure, a hermit. Also, we were at least feminist enough to not just do what the boys in theory class told us to do, which was to stop painting.

So Elizabeth was exactly the mentor we sought, someone who by dint of both gender and disposition occupied an inside and an outside position. Her work was like a flashlight: a signal for navigating the highway and the off-ramps of modernism. Carroll Dunham described her approach as "a completely different way past the modernist dilemma, a forward exit strategy."[2] While Murray spoke the traditional language of painting fluently—the one that we had been taught on the painting

2. Carroll Dunham, "Shapes of Things to Come: The Art of Elizabeth Murray," *Artforum* 44, no. 3 (November 2005), 213. See also "The Writings of Carroll Dunham," pages 252–53. [Editors' note]

side of the divide—her work had a weirder, funkier quality of autobiography, silliness, slapstick. She deployed traditions of modernism for all they were worth: the big scale, concern with innovative construction, aggressively fragmented surfaces, polychromatic relations. She taught us the way that Cubism folds time and space into the body of the picture. And she counted old man Cézanne as a friend for the way he built up his paintings out of little anxious chunks of tactile brushstroke. But in her hands, none of this seemed exactly like "high" modernism, even though it wasn't postmodernism either. She just made stuff that worked across the aisle, in a both/and or a neither/nor way: too invested to be indifferent, but too irreverent to be grand; too peppy to be abject, too slapstick to be superior, too lyrical to be negational, too hard-won to be blasé, too funky to be ironic, etc. Her studio practice was partly about the pleasure of immersing yourself in your craft, a non-alienated kind of labor, a labor of love.

Speaking of labor, it's important to mention gender. Murray simply refused to submit to the position of illegitimacy that women experience in painting history. She just broke in, seemingly taking what she needed from painting and moving forward with it, like a shoplifter, or someone from inside the Trojan Horse. What she offered us was an aegis, an umbrella, under which painting was an option. If Murray had personal misgivings about the questionableness of being a painter, she did not express that to us, the students. She was busy with her project, working in a *both/and* space, both within and outside of the traditions of painting that were being critiqued in the other class. This seemed like an appealing and ambivalent position, a kick against the pricks on both sides of the binary.

I see how Murray's work made sense within the logic of '60s and '70s painting: all that cutting, pushing, moving, digging, the mashed-up references, flipped high and low, hard edges with soft reefs of color washing up against them, Pop colors and shadowy undertones, and cartoons edging forward from Cubist infrastructures. Her process made sense within the particular materialist logic of that time and place. "Making" was the über-verb of the time. (It was uttered with the same ubiquity that "studio practice" is now.) It was clear that, for people outside painting, it was hard to get the proposition, or to see her work for its achievements. For one thing, the medium *was* specific. And since a lot of people had dropped out of painting, it was a little like speaking Latin: you know there's a Classics Club out there somewhere, still putting on plays by Virgil, but there aren't as many people around to understand exactly how the Latin poets expressed their opposition to the Roman Empire within the meter of their poetry. Similarly, Murray was painting for painters, an insiders' game. But what she was doing was both essential and generous for a next generation of painting, which, as it turned out, very much continued.

Murray, working with the infra-fractures inside the medium, was legible as holding an inside/outside painting position on a number of different levels. She had many fellow travelers in the New York scene, figures like Jo Baer, Susan Rothenberg, Howardena Pindell, Mary Heilmann, Ron Gorchov, Louise Fishman, Jack Whitten, Ed Clark, Dona Nelson, etc., etc., etc., and for all of those people Murray's paintings would be perfectly clear. But still, formally she was making challenging hybrid work. Her thinking process was both analytic and Romantic. Her forms were both driven by their narratives and constructed with a materialist logic. She worked with a vast scale ranging from intimate to monumental, with manic to melancholic moods, with surfaces that were resolved variously as structural, decorative, figurative, humorous, monochromatic, and sometimes all at the same time. Like a fluid gender, all of this puts categorical people on edge.

She weaves back and forth between abstraction and a seething kind of corporeality and narrativity, between the facture of surface and the fiction of stories. Though her work juts out at you from the wall, like massive limbs, boots, containers, and bulwarks, and keeps edging toward the condition of sculpture, it never really gives up its being on the wall. Though her work is all about things spilling, toppling, leaking, they never really give in to the force of gravity. Her images, her objects, remain in the realm of the illusory and the fictional, like a folktale hanging in the air. Besides being the maker of swashbuckling planar constructions, Murray also populates her surfaces with figures and unruly carnivalesque situations that cover and define them, stories that extrude from the logic of their own construction and that are made up of specific details of personal or everyday life: menial things, kitchen details, cups, appliances, animals, tears, or "female" things like umbilical cords and belly buttons. All these things smack of elbow grease and labor, of female subjectivity and daily stuff, but they keep falling over, morphing, squeezing, swelling, and the paintings themselves involve evidence of endless remaking, tinkering, and revision. The work of these art objects is seemingly never done. And part of the story is about the housework of her production: all that scraping and shaping, pushing and heaving, tucking and unholstering. Murray's work is fraught with a sense of fussily managing the details of something massive. She had a way of working a painting almost to death while somehow keeping it looking as if she wasn't really worrying about it at all, even though you know she WAS in agony over it. A will to storytelling, embroidery, animation, and disclosure is at the core of her work, and in this way her work lies far afield from the stripped-down narrative that modernism wants us to keep.

I'm cutting to an encounter I had recently in front of her work, in early 2018. I went to a huge Chelsea gallery to see a show of Murray's giant works from the 1980s,[3] and I ran into a cool guy I know looking at the show, someone I've known since he was a student, which wasn't that long ago. He's a very good painter and a nice person, but I associated him with the kind of hipsters and art school kids who way back in the '70s wouldn't have been big fans of Murray's. But there he was, standing reverently below Murray's gargantuan *Cracked Question* (1987), a piece that takes the shape of a massive fragmented black question mark over 16 feet tall. We stood together, looking up at this phenomenal, dark thing looming high above us on the wall. To look at this protean object is like beholding a whole brooding, crouching constellation of its own. I said to the guy, "You like this work?" and he said, "Are you kidding? This is awesome." And I said, "Oh, really?? I thought guys like you didn't really GET Elizabeth Murray, or don't really like her work." And he said, "Oh no. We're just SCARED of her." I thought, DAMN! That's cool! ♦

3. *Elizabeth Murray. Painting in the '80s*, presented at Pace Gallery, New York, November 2, 2017–January 13, 2018. [Editors' note]

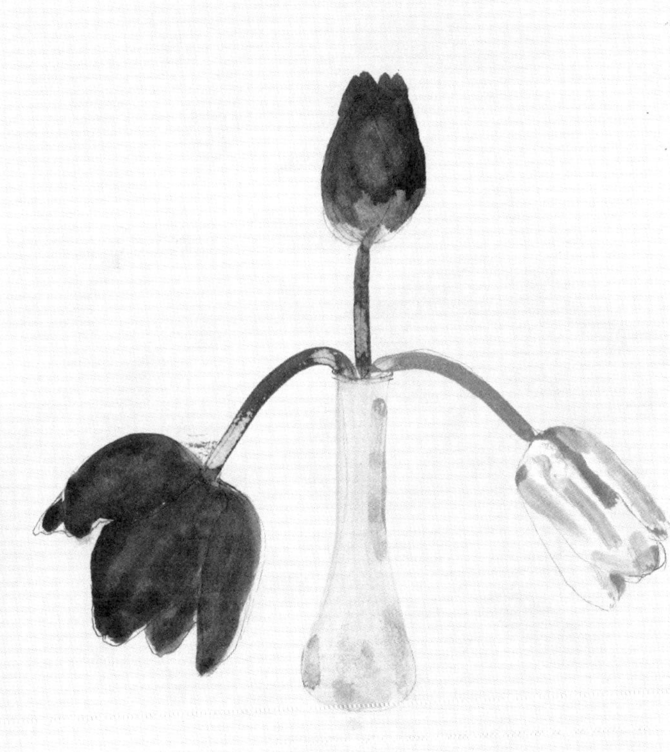

This text was originally published in Artforum *60, no. 3 (November 2021) as an homage to Louise Fishman, who had passed away in July 2021.*

Louise Fishman: Unstraight Lines

> "It is unstraight lines, or many straight and curved lines together, that are eloquent to the touch. They appear and disappear, are now deep, now shallow, now broken off or lengthened or swelling. They rise and sink beneath my fingers, they are full of sudden starts and pauses, and their variety is inexhaustible and wonderful." . . . The author is a blind woman, Helen Keller. Her sensitiveness shames us whose open eyes fail to grasp these qualities of form.
> —MEYER SCHAPIRO, "ON THE HUMANITY OF ABSTRACT PAINTING," 1960[1]

There was an email in my inbox on July 26 from Louise Fishman's wife, Ingrid Nyeboe, with the brief, startling headline "Louise died." Inside, I was cc'd on a sad notification: Louise had passed away the night before from complications of an illness. And with that, Louise was no more and, as the Jews say, may her memory be for a blessing.

What now stood in her place was the corpus of her work, a body of enormous heft. Louise's very presence had always been like a force of nature to me anyway. I'd known her since the 1970s, though not that well. She was never a hangout buddy but an elder stateswoman, a serious-ass painter, a living link to the New York School stretching back to painting giants like Mitchell, Guston, and De Kooning and forward to all us

1. Meyer Schapiro, "On the Humanity of Abstract Painting" (1960), in Schapiro, *Modern Art. 19th and 20th Centuries* (New York: George Braziller, 1978), 230.

wannabe-serious painters who were still in the grip of that kind of work. Sometimes I would see her in Chelsea walking around in utilitarian pants and sporty wraparound shades—and Louise was *literally* sporty. As a girl, she had wanted to be a professional ballplayer, and several writers since have made the connection between sports fields and Louise's canvases, both of which are delineated rectangles of activity in which coded sets of gestures are pitched, whether baseball pitches or paint strokes.[2] Anyway, when I saw her, I would not interrupt her because she was deep in thought—about what, who knows—but as De Kooning once said of someone, she had an abstract look on her face.[3]

Samuel Beckett said the artist's task is to find form to accommodate the mess.[4] Louise found a form that is both the mess and its accommodation: the rectangle. Her paintings are fundamentally blocklike constructions, hand-built like ancient walls; they are gridded, girded, gritty, and grouted, carved into with scrapers and knives. But they also manage to convey a surprising airiness via the gaps and reveals in their construction, through which you can see all the way back to the canvas behind. They're like front porches—rectangular thresholds

2. Amy Sillman herself "commented" a series of works by Louise Fishman as if they were innings in a baseball game, in a text published to accompany an online exhibition of works by Fishman organized by Karma, New York, in 2020. See "Nine Innings: Notes of a Color Commentator. On Nine Works by Louise Fishman", available online at https://karmakarma.org/texts/louise-fishman-amy-sillman-9-innings (last accessed June 5, 2022). [Editors' note]

3. That was with such a description of a man he used to know in Hoboken, that Willem de Kooning concluded his 1951 lecture at MoMA, "What Abstract Art Means to Me," first published in *The Museum of Modern Art Bulletin XVIII*, no. 3 (Spring 1951); available online at https://www.dekooning.org/documentation/words/what-abstract-art-means-to-me (last accessed June 5, 2022). [Editors' note]

4. See Tom F. Driver's interview, "Beckett by the Madeleine," *Columbia University Forum* 4 (Summer 1961), 21–25. [Editors' note]

with stuff stacked off-kilter on them, decked with strokes both taut and drooping or tangling, the jagged parts potchkied together, scrubbed and stained to various degrees of finish or unfinish. Louise's saturated palette is mitigated by tones of ash, mud, sludge, low-hanging clouds. Her painting spaces afford you enough room to go shallowly back and forth, in and out—a dynamic that is classically termed "push-pull" but that in Louise's hands feels more like "shove-drag," an athletic move, like wrestlers in a hold grappling with each other yet appearing to be standing still.[5] This inner tension in Louise's work contains the barometric pressure of moods that move through the paintings like weather fronts. You feel her atmospheres in her gestures and choices of tool, from the speed of the colored loops to the decorative way she dots, dashes, and scores rectangular planes to the clotted mash-ups of line, the mournful swipes of gray-blue, and the letters that spell out anger, the anger of women. Louise made her *Angry Women* paintings in 1973[6]; in them, the uninitiated can immediately perceive her purpose, which is definitely not the grid as a neutral space, or formalism per se, or anything universal, or about flatness. Instead, she makes gestural paintings that act like protest signs—waging a fight, lodging a complaint, naming a constituency, and reclaiming space.

As a self-described lesbian feminist Jewish abstract painter, Louise navigated this unstraight territory all her life. Having

5. "Push-pull" is the term at the heart of Hans Hofmann's conception of abstract painting—but it is indeed related to exercise as well. See also "On Color," page 52. [Editors' note]

6. All the paintings in this series bear the word "ANGRY," appended to female first names evoking feminist figures, famous women artists, as well as close relatives or friends to the artist. [Editors' note]

hyphenated identities meant that she had multiple allegiances and had to buck orthodoxy on many fronts. Maybe the classic diasporic Jewish attitude equips you for the long game: you feel like an outsider all the time, including at home, and come from that tradition of Torah wrestling (going back to Jacob, who, in the Book of Genesis, wrestled with an angel all night long and was blessed). Louise's blessing was her failure to assimilate neatly into an identity niche. She grew up in the '40s and '50s in an observant Jewish household, but she didn't understand Hebrew and later claimed that something always upset her about that language.[7] In the '60s, as a young painter in downtown New York, she realized quickly that, as a lesbian, she wasn't going to be sleeping her way to the top with the Cedar Tavern set.[8] In the '70s, she conscientiously tried to eliminate all straight-white-male influence from her work and to work with women's crafts, though later, in 2012, she noted sardonically that the project was "impossible, of course," and that she hated woman-craft.[9] She also started naming paintings after various Jewish ritual objects and holidays. In the '80s, she visited the concentration camps at Auschwitz and Terezín and collected ashes and pebbles that she mixed into the surfaces and solvents of subsequent paintings. In 2020, she published advice for young lesbian painters: "Don't stop looking at El Greco because he's not Jewish, or Chardin because he's not an abstract

7. See "Zero at the Bone: Louise Fishman Speaks with Carrie Moyer," *Art Journal* 71, no. 4 (Winter 2012), 43.

8. See "Always Wild At Heart – an Interview with Louise Fishman," *YEAST – Art of Sharing* (2017), available online at http://www.yeast-art-of-sharing.de/kunst/always-wild-at-heart-an-interview-with-louise-fishman (last accessed June 6, 2022). On the Cedar Tavern, see "AbEx and Disco Balls", note 4, page 131. [Editors' note]

9. "Zero at the Bone," *art. cit.*, 39.

painter, or Matisse because he's not a lesbian. By all means look at Agnes Martin and Georgia O'Keeffe and Eva Hesse. But don't forget Cézanne, Manet, and Giotto. If good painting is what you want to do, then good painting is what you must look at. Take what you want and leave the dreck."[10]

That was her kind of politics and her kind of love: start with your own struggle, look to the surrounding world to figure out your community, work out your relational lifelines by means of what you love, maintain an attitude of remembrance but noncompliance.

In her assertion of complex being, you can track Louise's work amid a wide swath of vitally materialist painters and sculptors who have also embraced abstraction's opacity, its complexity, difficulty, and hybridity, and whose work operates purposefully with an insiderly/outsiderly know-how. I'm thinking, for example, of the eloquent silence of Beverly Buchanan's rock piles, the iridescent shimmer of Ed Clark's swept fields, the compression and expansion of Jack Whitten's mosaicked cosmologies, and of many other fellow travelers, from Rochelle Feinstein to Stanley Whitney to Rodney McMillian to Torkwase Dyson to Tomashi Jackson to Rindon Johnson and beyond. All of them have dipped back into art history, taken what they needed to move forward, and made matter speak. Louise's work is a thick slab of painting history and an object lesson in both taking it and leaving it. She reclaimed some of the very qualities that high modernism tried valiantly to shed or tamp down: the personal, the sentimental, the anecdotal, the narrative. She made work about angry women, and work with an

10. Louise Fishman, "How I Do It: Cautionary Advice from a Lesbian Painter," in *Louise Fishman* (New York: Karma, 2020), 80.

attachment to studio labor. I'd call Louise an iconic anti-dandy for asserting negation and criticality not through indifference or absence, but rather through presence, attachment, and stubborn confrontation. It can be ugly/beautiful, this hard-won, thick-skinned kind of work. When I think of Louise's paintings, I think of Adrienne Rich's words: "The thing I came for: the wrecks and not the story of the wreck, the thing itself and not the myth."[11] Painting, the thing itself, was what was liberatory to Louise, and the painting's rectangle was no mythic picture plane but a literal life raft, a little rectangular zone you make by hand that you hang on to in the turbulent sea. Painting was the way you send out your signal, plot your course through precarious waters, navigate toward other vessels, other shorelines, other people. You steer that little square, and its unstraight lines, as it rises and sinks, and that's how you try to save your own life. ♦

11. Adrienne Rich, "Diving into the Wreck," in *Diving into the Wreck: Poems 1971–1972* (New York: W. W. Norton & Company, 1973), 23.

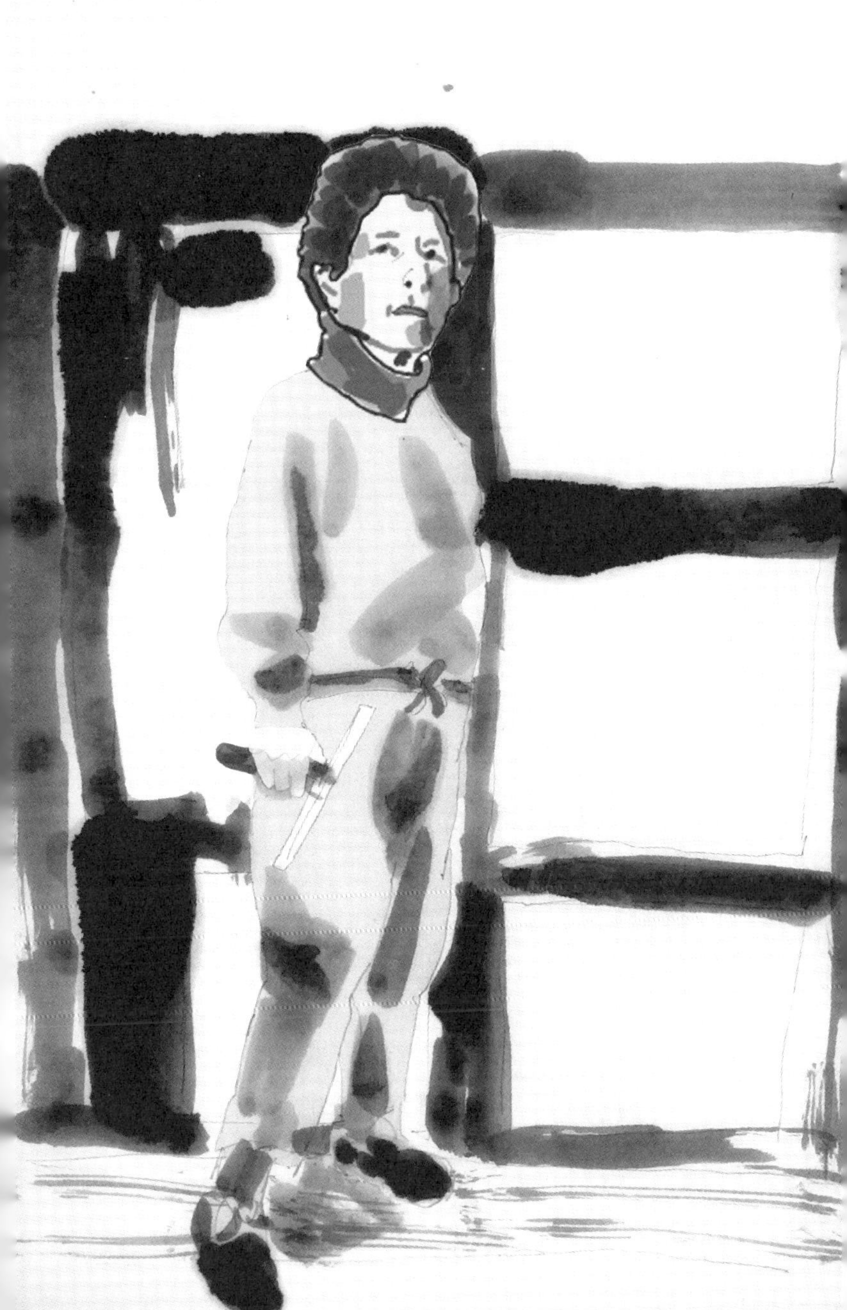

This review of the exhibition Cézanne Drawing, *curated by Jodi Hauptman and Samantha Friedman at the Museum of Modern Art, New York, June 6–September 25, 2021, was originally published in the "Best Shows of 2021" section of* Artforum *60, no. 4 (December 2021).*

The Drawings of Cézanne

As soon as I got back to New York from my COVID-period cave, I marched up to the Museum of Modern Art to see *Cézanne Drawing*, because, I mean, if you're a painter, you're supposed to somehow know how and why Paul Cézanne was a genius. But what's a genius anymore, and what does that even mean? Here was this introverted guy who lived in a vacuum, who ruffled up the picture plane like he was running his hands through its hair, unpinning it. I had seen an amazing portrait show a few years ago in Paris,[1] and I knew that the likes of Elizabeth Murray and Carolee Schneemann were big fans, but I hadn't really been in a relationship with the guy for a while, and I wanted to see if I could still feel something between us. So I went up to MoMA and dove in. At first, I was just going along with it, past heads, pears, statuettes, and jugs, but a few galleries later, in a room labeled "Time and Contemplation," the drug I call C started to take hold; the world literally went pear-shaped. I found myself in front of a picture of a rumpled dish towel on a rack, agog, saying out loud to no one in particular, *Oh, fuck*, because the dish towel had nimbly unhinged itself from reality and taken

1. *Portraits de Cézanne*, presented at the Musée d'Orsay, Paris, June 13–September 24, 2017. [Editors' note]

me with it. It was no longer a towel but an ontological condition, a permeable vibration, a singularity. Then there was a coat crumpled up on a chair, somehow transmitting most of being and nothingness to me from its folds. *What?* From then on, I realized I had been dosed; I was on the other side of the looking glass. I kept gasping out loud at stuff—peering through C's kaleidoscope at a world brimming with indeterminacy, at aqueous layers of diamond-shaped tesserae, the entanglement of a world overflowing with things and folds, branches and limbs seething with abundance yet containing audacious brevity and silence, air pumped into things and places where it wasn't before, like trees rendered as flat parallel lines and whole mountains pocked with holes and voids, lacunae in the flow of time. The idea of "ratio" is not usually a heart-stopper for me, but here it was mesmerizing—the ratio of space between trees and of trees to one another was hallucinatory; the simple outline of a putto's bare leg next to a patterned background could suggest a full-on psychic rearrangement as you simply moved your eyes from left to right across the paper.

C famously declared that there was no such thing as a line,[2] but his world is made of lines—stubby, insistent lines that keep breaking off and then starting up again, like the switches on the circuit board of a nervous system blinking on and off. The most astonishing thing of all was that C had envisioned this situation of abstraction from inside his body, in his fingertips, when there was no such thing yet. This was just about being *out there*, recording what he was looking at so hard that he saw through and past things to a world of chaosmotic change, where all that

2. See "Some Notes on Drawing," page 88. [Editors' note]

was solid really did melt into air. But this revolution was signaled by these notational lines in pencil on everyday paper. Abstraction was, or in C's hands could be, a situation of sheer potential, in which things are endlessly changing. Cézanne, who read Latin and Greek, knew the writings of philosophers like Lucretius and Anaximander, the latter of whom described matter as "things transformed one into another according to necessity . . . according to the order of time."[3]

Once I got it, I was inside. It was exactly like tripping, or mountain climbing, or going to outer space, or having a vision. C's effect was to lend me that kind of psychic scale shift you can have when on a plane, for example, where you might start crying at any moment because you realize that we are situated among fields, rocks, atoms, stars, matter, sensations, rays of light, the passage of time, and the organization of units, and also that we are strapped in there fully packed with ambiguity, doubt, and terror.

I came out of MoMA a few hours later in an altered state, and I couldn't get over it for weeks; it ruined the experience of other art shows, because the here and now just seemed so strategic, gravity-bound, self-conscious, art-worldly, while Cézanne (or C, the drug that he is) reminded me of an out-there, an elsewhere, probably enhanced by the year of COVID-19 isolation I'd just come from. It was exhilarating to feel such permissive and ambivalent sensations at a "drawing show"—if that's what I had just been at—being on this earth but *not*, in space and time but *not*, having a body but *not*. I forgot momentarily about art as money, as product, as hierarchy, as regulation, as country

3. See Carlo Rovelli, *The First Scientist: Anaximander and his Legacy*, trans. Marion Lignana Rosenberg (Yardley, PA: Westholme Publishing, 2011).

club, as something I'm cynical about. And I just thought that art was a way of being wrenched out of daily life and subsequently delivered back again in a more subtle form. There are other great art shows where I've felt this: at a Jack Whitten show, for example, and a Goya show, and a Nancy Spero show, and a Meret Oppenheim show. They don't call these people "geniuses" for nothing. We go in to see some art objects, and we come out full of some kind of radical amazement. So if that's what is meant by genius, then I'm down with it. It has something to do with soul. ♦

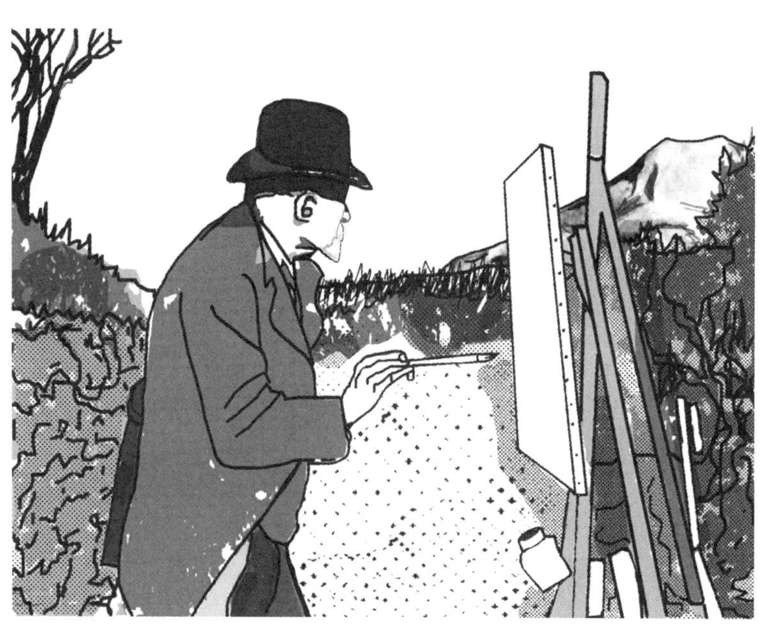

INDEX OF DRAWINGS

DRAWINGS BY AMY SILLMAN

COVER. *Untitled*, 2019. Ink on paper, 11 × 14 in / 27,94 × 35,56 cm.

4. *Untitled*, 2020. Ink on paper, 10 × 14 in / 25,40 × 35,56 cm.

5. *Untitled*, 2020. Ink on paper, 10 × 14 in / 25,40 × 35,56 cm

6–7. Sections of *Frieze for Venice*, 2022; each drawing, 2021. Ink on handmade Tibetan paper, 11 × 14 ½ in / 27,94 × 36,83 cm.

9. *Untitled*, 2021. Ink on handmade Tibetan paper, 11 × 14 ½ in / 27,94 × 36,83 cm.

12–13. *Quarantine Moods*, 2020. Digital drawing.

14–15. *Becoming Pleistocene*, 2020. Ink on paper, digitally altered, 10 × 12 in / 25,40 × 30,48 cm.

27. *Untitled*, 2020. Ink on paper, 18 × 12 in / 45,72 × 30,48 cm.

29. *Untitled*, 2020. Ink on paper, 18 × 12 in / 45,72 × 30,48 cm.

46. *Artist Gives Talk*, 2009. Ink on paper, 8¼ × 6 in / 20,96 × 15,24 cm.

47. *Audience*, 2009. Ink on paper, digitally altered, 8¼ × 6 in / 20,96 × 15,24 cm.

48–49. *Helen Frankenthaler (after a 1969 photograph by Ernst Haas)*, 2020. Ink on paper, 11 × 15 in / 27,94 × 38,1 cm.

53. *Lynda Benglis (after a 1969 photograph by Henry Groskinsky)*, 2019. Ink on paper, 11 × 14 in / 27,94 × 35,56 cm.

55. *Pearl Paint, NYC*, 2019. Ink on paper, digitally altered, 14 × 11 in / 35,56 × 27,94 cm.

56. *Hands*, 2018. Ink on paper, 8 × 11 in / 20,32 × 27,94 cm.

64–65. *Foxconn Workers*, 2019. Ink on paper, 11 ¼ × 15 ⅛ in / 28,58 × 38,42 cm.

67. *Isaac Newton*, 2018. Ink on paper, digitally altered, 6 × 8 in / 15,24 × 20,32 cm.

70. *Andy Warhol (after a 1964 photograph by Bob Adelman)*, 2019. Ink on paper, 7 ⅝ × 11 in / 19,37 × 27,94 cm.

72. *Jennifer Packer*, 2020. Digital drawing.

78. *Untitled*, 2019. Ink on paper, 14 × 11 in / 35,56 × 27,94 cm.

79. *Untitled*, 2019. Ink on paper, 14 × 11 in / 35,56 × 27,94 cm.

91. *Me and Ugly Mountain Update (for William Simmons)*, 2021. Ink and gouache on paper, 11 × 15 in / 27,94 × 38,10 cm.

101. *Frank Bowling (after a 2019 photograph by Mathilde Agius)*, 2020. Ink on paper, 13 × 13 in / 33,02 × 33,02 cm.

106. *Untitled*, 2020. Ink on paper, 18 × 12 in / 45,72 × 30,48 cm.

111. Six drawings, each *Untitled*, 2016. Charcoal on paper, 22 ½ × 30 in / 57,15 × 76,2 cm.

112–13. *Meaning of Symbols*, 2009. Ink on paper, 8 ¼ × 11 in / 10,95 × 27,94 cm.

114–15. *More Meaning of My Symbols*, 2009. Ink on paper, 8 ¼ × 11 in / 10,95 × 27,94 cm.

121. *Untitled*, 2019. Ink on rice paper mounted on board, 14 × 11 in / 35,56 × 27,94 cm.

122. *Untitled*, 2019. Ink on rice paper mounted on board, 14 × 11 in / 35,56 × 27,94 cm.

123. *Untitled*, 2019. Ink on rice paper mounted on board, 14 × 11 in / 35,56 × 27,94 cm.

INDEX OF DRAWINGS

124. *Untitled*, 2019. Ink on rice paper mounted on board, 14 × 11 in / 35,56 × 27,94 cm.
125. *Untitled*, 2019. Ink on rice paper mounted on board, 14 × 11 in / 35,56 × 27,94 cm.
126. *Untitled*, 2019. Ink on rice paper mounted on board, 14 × 11 in / 35,56 × 27,94 cm.
127. *Untitled*, 2019. Ink on rice paper mounted on board, 14 × 11 in / 35,56 × 27,94 cm.
130. *Jackson Pollock and Lee Krasner (after a 1950 photograph by Hans Namuth)*, 2020. Ink on paper, 11 × 14 in / 27,94 × 35,56 cm.
133. *Donna Summer (after the artwork of a 1976 EP)*, 2020. Digital drawing.
138. *Leidy Churchman's Painting Treatments (after a video still)*, 2020. Digital drawing.
141. *Joan Mitchell in her studio (after a 1957 photograph by Rudy Burckhardt)*, 2020. Ink on paper, 14 × 11 in / 35,56 × 27,94 cm.
155. *Untitled Seating Chart*, 2022. Pencil on paper, 8 × 9 in / 20,32 × 22,86 cm.
156. *Untitled Seating Chart*, ca. 2010. Ink on paper, 8 ⅞ × 11 ⅞ in / 22,54 × 30,16 cm.
157. *Untitled Seating Chart*, ca. 2010. Ink on paper, 8 ⅞ × 12 in / 22,54 × 30,48 cm.
158. *Untitled Seating Chart*, ca. 2010. Ink on paper, 9 × 12 in / 22,86 × 30,48 cm.
159. *Untitled Seating Chart*, ca. 2010. Ink on paper, 9 × 12 in / 22,86 × 30,48 cm.
160. *Untitled Seating Chart*, 2009. Ink on paper, 11 ⅜ × 11 in / 28,89 × 27,94 cm.
173. *Untitled*, 2018. Digital drawing.

177–83. *Train of Thought*, 2010. Ink on paper, each spread: 8 ¼ × 11 in / 10,95 × 27,94 cm.

237. *Maria Lassnig*, 2020. Ink on paper, digitally altered, 17 × 11 in / 43,18 × 27,94 cm.
243. *Carolee Schneemann Reading from the Interior Scroll (after a 1975 photograph by Anthony McCall)*, 2022. Digital drawing.
269. *Delacroix at the orgy*, 2019. iPhone drawing.
281. *Untitled*, 2020. Acrylic and pencil on paper, 22 ⅜ × 15 in / 56,8 × 38,1 cm.
289. *Louise Fishman*, 2022. Digital drawing.
295. *Cézanne Painting the Montagne Sainte-Victoire*, 2022. Digital drawing.

298–99. *Untitled*, 2020. Ink on rice paper, 18 × 12 in / 45,72 × 30,48 cm.

300. *Some Problems with Philosophy*, 2010/2022. Ink on paper, digitally altered.

DRAWINGS BY MICHAEL SMITH

196. *Couch*, 2020. Colored pencils and watercolor on paper, 9 × 12 in / 22,86 × 30,48 cm.
206. *John Chamberlain with The Supremes*, 2020. Colored pencils and watercolor on paper, 12 × 9 in / 30,48 × 22,86 cm.
209. *Collage*, 2020. Colored pencils and watercolor on paper, 9 × 12 in / 22,86 × 30,48 cm.
216. *Wadding*, 2020. Colored pencils and watercolor on paper, 12 × 9 in / 30,48 × 22,86 cm.

EDITORS' ACKNOWLEDGEMENTS

The project of this book started in 2017, as the two Paris-based organizations we are part of—the experimental school collective The Cheapest University, and the bookshop and publisher After 8 Books—had invited Amy Sillman to give a lecture in Paris. Amy came from Germany with her students from the Städelschule; her lecture, "On Color," was followed by a discussion with researcher Darla Migan, about the collisions between color theory, ethics, and cultural difference. Making this book was a way to continue the exchanges that had started in this self-initiated pedagogical context: we wanted to make Amy's writings and drawings available as a whole, and show the coherence of her "train of thought." We finalized the book in 2020, working from the distance; there was something urgent in making this book as we were all isolated because of the pandemic. The way Amy deals in her texts with "struggle" and engagement in art, highlighting the political dimension of work, shapes, attitudes, and emotions, feels even more crucial and meaningful today.

The book was first released in Fall 2020; a French edition followed in 2022. This revised, "expanded edition" comprises new essays that Amy has written or edited over the past years. The 2021 text, "Louise Fishman: Unstraight Lines," takes the place of the 2020 piece, "Nine Innings: Notes of a Color Commentator. On Nine Works by Louise Fishman." The order of the writings has been slightly modified to include the new ones.

We would like to thank, again and again, Amy for her energy, for all the ideas and passion she put in her writing, and for trusting us on this publication. We love you Amy!

Warm thanks to Michael Smith and Lynne Tillman for their contributions to the book.

Thanks also to Simone Battisti, Gil Presti, Emanuela Campoli; Janine Armin, Ailsa Cavers, Sabrina Robleh, Nate Heiges, and Lou Ellingson; Hilton Als, Rindon Johnson, and Jutta Koether.

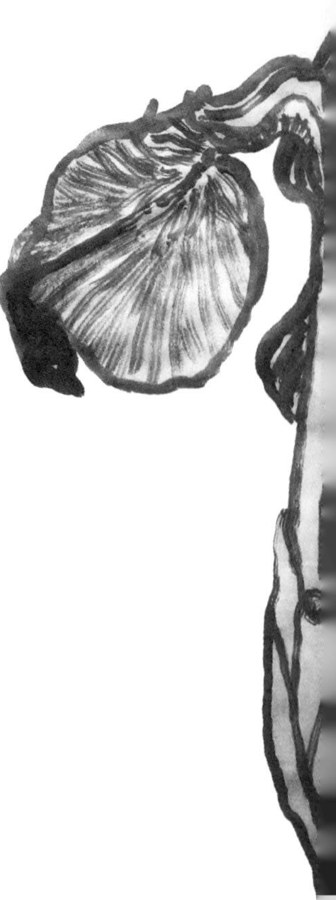

AUTHOR'S ACKNOWLEDGEMENTS

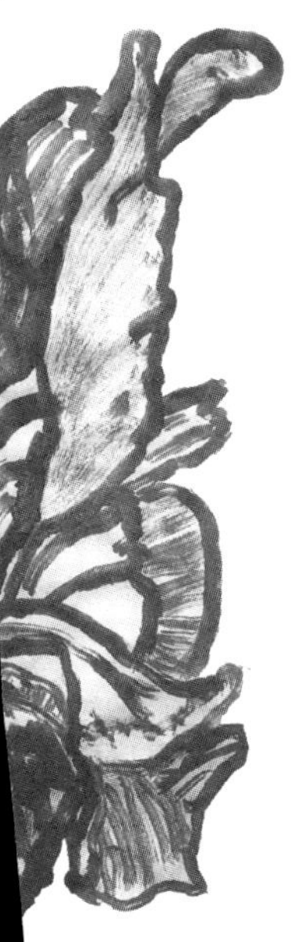

I can't believe I am lucky enough to have a book published by After 8 Books, that is now in its fourth printing! The footnotes alone are as exciting as anything I've ever written. This book is one of the joys of my life, and I am happy to express my ongoing gratitude and great affection for all the people who made it possible: Benjamin Thorel, who worked endlessly on those amazing footnotes, Antonia Carrara, Charlotte Houette, François Lancien-Guilberteau, and Marco Caroti, all of whose great contributions were essential, and who were a total joy to work with. Thanks also to Lynne Tillman, for contributing her brilliant foreword, and to Mike Smith, for his hilarious drawings for the Chamberlain essay. I am deeply indebted to all of you, and grateful from the bottom of my heart.

Thanks to all the people who invited me to write the essays that appear here, and then prodded them along to become better. Michelle Kuo, Pablo Larios, Isabelle Graw, Ewa Lajer-Burcharth, Jackie Saccoccio, David Velasco, Margaret Sundell, Siniša Mačković, Lloyd Wise, Chris Bayley, and Lotte Johnson are some of these people—there are many others who helped along the way, and I thank all of you. Enormous thanks always to everyone at my galleries—at Gladstone Gallery, Thomas Dane, and Capitain Petzel—you always have my back, and have contributed greatly to this publication. I dedicate this fourth edition of *Faux Pas* to the memory of Barbara Gladstone, an irreplaceable force of nature in my life.

I write about art in order to try to describe what's happening inside a process that's not really linguistic and not really explainable. I want to find words for something that happens inside, behind and underneath everyday life, inside the combustion of the body and the imagination. This book is dedicated to all the radical thinkers and makers and workers who are engaged in such a process—whether in art, writing, politics, or just everyday life—everyone who wants to see change happen and describe it more clearly.

SOME PROBLEMS IN PHILOSOPHY

	GREAT	NOT SO GREAT
DESCARTES:	THE COGITO	THE MIND-BODY SPLIT
SPINOZA:	GOD IS NATURE	NATURE IS GOD
LEIBNIZ:	MONADS	MONADS DON'T EXIST
HUME:	EXPERIENCE	IS THAT ALL THERE IS?
KANT:	THE ENLIGHTENMENT	KIND OF A KNOW-IT-ALL, DON'T YOU THINK? AND WHAT THE HELL IS A TRANSCENDENTAL EGO, ANYWAY?
HEGEL:	DIALECTICS, HISTORY	TOO RATIONAL — HISTORY IS BORING
KIERKEGAARD:	DOUBT	A NERVOUS WRECK
PEIRCE:	AMERICA'S GREATEST PHILOSOPHER! PRAGMATISM, SEMIOTICS	RIGHT PLACE AT THE WRONG TIME — AMERICA NOT IMPORTANT BACK THEN.
NIETZSCHE:	GOD IS DEAD & OTHER REVOLUTIONARY & CREATIVE IDEAS	ÜBERMENSCH SOUNDS GOOD TO NAZIS and is USED FOR EVIL PURPOSES
HUSSERL:	THE PHENOMENOLOGICAL REDUCTION	EVERYTHING INTERESTING BRACKETED AWAY
HEIDEGGER:	DASEIN — SUCH A BEAUTIFUL, COMPLEX THING TO THINK ABOUT	NATIONALISM, ANTI-SEMITISM, AND WEIRDO-SPIRITUALISM REALLY FUCK THE WHOLE THING UP.
WITTGENSTEIN:	LOGIC, LANGUAGE, THE MIND, & COLOR!	"PHILOSOPHY OF MIND" BY A GUY WHO IS PERPETUALLY IN A REALLY BAD MOOD
ADORNO:	CRITICAL THEORY — & A MUSIC LOVER!	SO NEGATIVE — A DOWNER — & HE REALLY MISSED THE BOAT WITH JAZZ!
SARTRE:	EXISTENTIALISM — RADICAL FREEDOM	CONCEITED + DISDAINFUL — HE HATES US!
MERLEAU-PONTY:	SENSATIONS	DROPPED DEAD BEFORE HE GOT PAST THE SENSATIONS
FOUCAULT:	STUDIES SEXY STUFF — & HE'S GAY!	PARANOID & PHALLOCENTRIC
DELEUZE:	THE PLANE OF IMMANENCE — + ARTISTS' FAVORITE PHILOSOPHER!	MANIC FRENCH STUFF THAT SERIOUS-MINDED GERMANS CANT TAKE SERIOUSLY
DERRIDA:	DIFFÉRANCE	WOULD IT REALLY UNDERMINE THE WHOLE PROJECT IF HE JUST WROTE A LITTLE MORE CLEARLY, FOR CRISSAKE?

ARENDT, WEIL, DE BEAUVOIR, TRUTH, HOOKS, LANGER, DAVIS, SPILLERS, KRISTEVA, IRIGARAY, BUTLER, CIXOUS, PIPER, ALLEN, BRAIDOTTI, ETC — WOMEN — WHO CARES WHAT THEY THINK?? DON'T EVEN BOTHER — PROBABLY MINOR STUFF —